From "The Shadow of the Vulture" by Robert E. Howard:

Oaths flowed in a steady stream from Sonya's red lips and she laughed wildly as her saber sang home and blood spurted along the edge. The last Turk on the battlement screamed and parried wildly as she pressed him; then dropping his scimitar, his clutching hands closed desperately on her dripping blade. With a groan, he swayed on the edge, blood gushing from his horribly cut fingers.

"Hell to you, dog-soul!" she laughed. "The devil can stir your broth for you!"

**Plus seven more
classic stories from
the golden age of
heroic fantasy!**

Other Tor Books by Karl Edward Wagner

Echoes of Valor (ed.)
Echoes of Valor II (ed.)
Why Not You and I?
Killer (with David Drake)

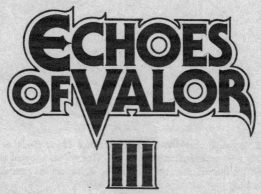

ECHOES OF VALOR

III

ROBERT E. HOWARD ✴ **JACK WILLIAMSON** ✴
MANLEY WADE WELLMAN ✴ *and others...*

EDITED BY
KARL
EDWARD
WAGNER

TOR
fantasy

A TOM DOHERTY ASSOCIATES BOOK
NEW YORK

This is a work of fiction. All the characters and events portrayed in this book are fictitious, and any resemblance to real people or events is purely coincidental.

ECHOES OF VALOR III

Copyright © 1991 by Karl Edward Wagner

Cover art by Sam Rakeland

A Tor Book
Published by Tom Doherty Associates, Inc.
49 West 24th Street
New York, N.Y. 10010

ISBN: 0-812-55758-1

First edition: September 1991

Printed in the United States of America

0 9 8 7 6 5 4 3 2 1

ACKNOWLEDGMENTS

*The editor also wishes to express
his thanks to Sam Moskowitz.*

To Jack Williamson—
who is not content to sit
with folded hands—

CONTENTS

I.

ROBERT E. HOWARD

INTRODUCTION

Robert E. Howard (1906–1936) was, as you almost certainly know, the creator of Conan of Cimmeria—the archetypal barbarian swordsman of heroic fantasy. In addition Howard created other series characters well known to fantasy fans: Kull, a savage warrior who became king of Atlantis; Bran Mak Morn, a Pictish king who battled the Romans in third-century Britain; Solomon Kane, a Puritan adventurer who sought out supernatural evil during the Age of Elizabeth. And, of course, Red Sonja, that curvaceous swords-and-sorcery heroine who leaps into the fray clad only in her skimpy mail bikini.

Wrong!

This Red Sonja was never created by Robert E. Howard. On the contrary, Red Sonja is a character created by Marvel Comics, and one whose popularity generated a series of novels by other authors and eventually sparked the 1985 film, *Red Sonja*, with the awesome Brigitte Nielsen in the title role. But Robert E. Howard never wrote a word about Red *Sonja*.

So why . . . ?

Robert E. Howard *did* create a character named Red *Sonya*, more formally known as Sonya of Rogatino, a sixteenth-century adventuress who was no one to get fresh with. Howard placed her in only one story, "The Shadow of the Vulture," which is presented here. That single appearance was powerful enough to inspire her modern-day transformation into the barbarian swordswoman, Red Sonja.

In 1930 *Weird Tales* launched a companion magazine entitled *Oriental Stories* in an attempt to enter the far more profitable market of adventure pulps. Contents ranged from historical to contemporary action-adventure, and authors and artists were mostly from the *Weird Tales* stable. While nowhere near the class of *Adventure* or *Blue Book*, the top of the adventure field, *Oriental Stories* was a pulp of consistently high quality. Nonetheless, it sold even worse than *Weird Tales*. With the January 1933 issue, its title was changed to *The Magic Carpet Magazine* in an effort to expand its audience. At 25¢ a copy, Depression readers weren't buying, and the magazine died with its January 1934 issue—coincidentally, the issue in which "The Shadow of the Vulture" appeared.

One wonders. Howard was selling regularly to this magazine, sometimes appearing twice in an issue, and Howard keenly enjoyed writing historical adventure. Had *Magic Carpet* survived, perhaps we might have read more of Red Sonya.

Another conjecture. Red Sonya was a contemporary of Solomon Kane. What would this dour Puritan adventurer have made of Red Sonya had their paths crossed? It would have been quite a story, and only Howard could have told it.

But at least Red Sonya had a more practical wardrobe than her successor, Red Sonja. Ever try romping about in a skimpy mail bikini?

THE SHADOW
OF THE VULTURE

by Robert E. Howard

1

"**A**re the dogs dressed and gorged?"

"Aye, Protector of the Faithful."

"Then let them crawl into the Presence."

So they brought the envoys, pallid from months of imprisonment, before the canopied throne of Suleyman the Magnificent, Sultan of Turkey, and the mightiest monarch in an age of mighty monarchs. Under the great purple dome of the royal chamber gleamed the throne before which the world trembled—gold-panelled, pearl-inlaid. An emperor's wealth in gems was sewn into the silken canopy from which depended a shimmering string of pearls ending a frieze of emeralds which hung like a halo of glory above Suleyman's head. Yet the splendor of the throne was paled by the glitter of the figure upon it, bedecked in jewels, the aigret feather rising above the diamonded white turban. About the throne stood his nine viziers, in attitudes of humility, and warriors of the imperial bodyguard ranged the dais—Solaks in armor, black and white and scarlet plumes nodding above the gilded helmets.

The envoys from Austria were properly impressed—the more so as they had had nine weary months for reflection in the grim Castle of the Seven Towers that overlooks the Sea of Marmora. The head of the embassy choked down his choler and cloaked his resentment in a semblance of submission—a strange cloak on the shoulders of Habordansky, general of Ferdinand, Archduke of Austria. His rugged head bristled incongruously from the flaming silk robes presented him by the contemptuous Sultan, as he was brought before the throne, his arms gripped fast by stalwart Janizaries. Thus were foreign envoys presented to the sultans, ever since that red day by Kossova when Milosh Kabilovitch, knight of slaughtered Serbia, had slain the conqueror Murad with a hidden dagger.

The Grand Turk regarded Habordansky with scant favor. Suleyman was a tall slender man, with a thin down-curving nose and a thin straight mouth, the resolution of which his drooping mustachios did not soften. His narrow outward-curving chin was shaven. The only suggestion of weakness was in the slender, remarkably long neck, but that suggestion was belied by the hard lines of the slender figure, the glitter of the dark eyes. There was more than a suggestion of the Tatar about him—rightly so, since he was no more the son of Selim the Grim than of Hafsza Khatun, princess of Crimea. Born to the purple, heir to the mightiest military power in the world, he was crested with authority and cloaked in pride that recognized no peer beneath the gods.

Under his eagle gaze old Habordansky bent his head to hide the sullen rage in his eyes. Nine months before, the general had come to Stamboul representing his master, the Archduke, with proposals for truce and the disposition of the iron crown of Hungary, torn from the dead king Louis' head on the bloody field of Mohacz, where the Grand Turk's armies opened the road to Europe. There had been another emissary before him—Jerome Lasczky, the Polish count palatine. Ha-

bordansky, with the bluntness of his breed, had claimed the
Hungarian crown for his master, rousing Suleyman's ire. Lasczky had, like a suppliant, asked on his bended knees that
crown for his countrymen at Mohacz.

To Lasczky had been given honor, gold and promises of
patronage, for which he had paid with pledges abhorrent even
to his avaricious soul—selling his ally's subjects into slavery,
and opening the road through the subject territory to the very
heart of Christendom.

All this was made known to Habordansky, frothing with
fury in the prison to which the arrogant resentment of the
Sultan had assigned him. Now Suleyman looked contemptuously at the staunch old general, and dispensed with the usual
formality of speaking through the mouthpiece of the Grand
Vizier. A royal Turk would not deign to admit knowledge of
any Frankish tongue, but Habordansky understood Turki. The
Sultan's remarks were brief and without preamble.

"Say to your master that I now make ready to visit him in
his own lands, and that if he fails to meet me at Mohacz or
at Pesth, I will meet him beneath the walls of Vienna."

Habordansky bowed, not trusting himself to speak. At a
scornful wave of the imperial hand, an officer of the court
came forward and bestowed upon the general a small gilded
bag containing two hundred ducats. Each member of his ret-
inue, waiting patiently at the other end of the chamber, under
the spears of the Janizaries, was likewise so guerdoned. Habordansky mumbled thanks, his knotty hands clenched about
the gift with unnecessary vigor. The Sultan grinned thinly,
well aware that the ambassador would have hurled the coins
into his face, had he dared. He half lifted his hand, in token
of dismissal, then paused, his eyes resting on the group of
men who composed the general's suite—or rather, on one of
these men. This man was the tallest in the room, strongly
built, wearing his Turkish gift-garments clumsily. At a gesture from the Sultan he was brought forward in the grasp of
the soldiers.

Suleyman stared at him narrowly. The Turkish vest and
voluminous khalat could not conceal the lines of massive

strength. His tawny hair was close-cropped, his sweeping yellow mustaches drooping below a stubborn chin. His blue eyes seemed strangely clouded; it was as if the man slept on his feet, with his eyes open.

"Do you speak Turki?" the Sultan did the fellow the stupendous honor of addressing him directly. Through all the pomp of the Ottoman court there remained in the Sultan some of the simplicity of Tatar ancestors.

"Yes, your majesty," answered the Frank.

"Who are you?"

"Men name me Gottfried von Kalmbach."

Suleyman scowled and unconsciously his fingers wandered to his shoulder, where, under his silken robes, he could feel the outlines of an old scar.

"I do not forget faces. Somewhere I have seen yours—under circumstances that etched it into the back of my mind. But I am unable to recall those circumstances."

"I was at Rhodes," offered the German.

"Many men were at Rhodes," snapped Suleyman.

"Aye," agreed von Kalmbach tranquilly. "De l'Isle Adam was there."

Suleyman stiffened and his eyes glittered at the name of the Grand Master of the Knights of Saint John, whose desperate defense of Rhodes had cost the Turk sixty thousand men. He decided, however, that the Frank was not clever enough for the remark to carry any subtle thrust, and dismissed the embassy with a wave. The envoys were backed out of the Presence and the incident was closed. The Franks would be escorted out of Stamboul, and to the nearest boundaries of the empire. The Turk's warning would be carried post-haste to the Archduke, and soon on the heels of that warning would come the armies of the Sublime Porte. Suleyman's officers knew that the Grand Turk had more in mind than merely establishing his puppet Zapolya on the conquered Hungarian throne. Suleyman's ambitions embraced all Europe—that stubborn Frankistan which had for centuries sporadically poured forth hordes chanting and pillaging into the East, whose illogical and wayward peoples had again and again seemed ripe for Moslem conquest, yet who had always emerged, if not victorious, at least unconquered.

It was the evening of the morning on which the Austrian emissaries departed, that Suleyman, brooding on his throne, raised his lean head and beckoned his Grand Vizier Ibrahim, who approached with confidence. The Grand Vizier was always sure of his master's approbation; was he not cup-companion and boyhood comrade of the Sultan? Ibrahim had but one rival in his master's favor—the red-haired Russian girl, Khurrem the Joyous, whom Europe knew as Roxelana, whom slavers had dragged from her father's house in Rogatino to be the Sultan's *harim* favorite.

"I remember the infidel at last," said Suleyman. "Do you recall the first charge of the knights at Mohacz?"

Ibrahim winced slightly at the allusion.

"Oh, Protector of the Pitiful, is it likely that I should forget an occasion on which the divine blood of my master was spilt by an unbeliever?"

"Then you remember that thirty-two knights, the paladins of the Nazarenes, drove headlong into our array, each having pledged his life to cut down our person. By Allah, they rode like men riding to a wedding, their great horses and long lances overthrowing all who opposed them, and their plate-armor turned the finest steel. Yet they fell as the firelocks spoke until only three were left in the saddle—the knight Marczali and two companions. These paladins cut down my Solaks like ripe grain, bur Marczali and one of his companions fell—almost at my feet.

"Yet one knight remained, though his visored helmet had been torn from his head and blood started from every joint in his armor. He rode full at me, swinging his great two-handed sword, and I swear by the beard of the Prophet, death was so nigh me that I felt the burning breath of Azrael on my neck!

"His sword flashed like lightning in the sky, and glancing from my casque, whereby I was half stunned so that blood gushed from my nose, rent the mail on my shoulder and gave me this wound, which irks me yet when the rains come. The Janizaries who swarmed around him cut the hocks of his horse, which brought him to earth as it went down, and the remnants of my Solaks bore me back out of the mêlée. Then the Hungarian host came on, and I saw not what became of the knight. But today I saw him again.''

Ibrahim started with an exclamation of incredulity.

''Nay, I could not mistake those blue eyes. How it is I know not, but the knight that wounded me at Mohacz was this German, Gottfried von Kalmbach.''

''But, Defender of the Faith,'' protested Ibrahim, ''the heads of those dog-knights were heaped before thy royal pavilion——''

''And I counted them and said nothing at the time, lest men think I held thee in blame,'' answered Suleyman. ''There were but thirty-one. Most were so mutilated I could tell little of the features. But somehow the infidel escaped, who gave me this blow. I love brave men, but our blood is not so common that an unbeliever may with impunity spill it on the ground for the dogs to lap up. See ye to it.''

Ibrahim salaamed deeply and withdrew. He made his way through broad corridors to a blue-tiled chamber whose gold-arched windows looked out on broad galleries, shaded by cypress and plane-trees, and cooled by the spray of silvery fountains. There at his summons came one Yaruk Khan, a Crim Tatar, a slant-eyed impassive figure in harness of lacquered leather and burnished bronze.

''Dog-brother,'' said the Vizier, ''did thy koumiss-clouded gaze mark the tall German lord who served the emir Habordansky—the lord whose hair is tawny as a lion's mane?''

''Aye, *noyon*, he who is called Gombuk.''

''The same. Take a *chambul* of thy dog-brothers and go after the Franks. Bring back this man and thou shalt be rewarded. The persons of envoys are sacred, but this matter is not official,'' he added cynically.

''To hear is to obey!'' With a salaam as profound as that accorded to the Sultan himself, Yaruk Khan backed out of the presence of the second man of the empire.

* * *

He returned some days later, dusty, travel-stained, and without his prey. On him Ibrahim bent an eye full of menace, and the Tatar prostrated himself before the silken cushions on which the Grand Vizier sat, in the blue chamber with the gold-arched windows.

"Great khan, let not thine anger consume thy slave. The fault was not mine, by the beard of the Prophet."

"Squat on thy mangy haunches and bay out the tale," ordered Ibrahim considerately.

"Thus it was, my lord," began Yaruk Khan. "I rode swiftly, and though the Franks and their escort had a long start, and pushed on through the night without halting, I came up with them the next midday. But lo, Gombuk was not among them, and when I inquired after him, the paladin Habordansky replied only with many great oaths, like to the roaring of a cannon. So I spoke with various of the escort who understood the speech of these infidels, and learned what had come to pass. Yet I would have my lord remember that I only repeat the words of the Spahis of the escort, who are men without honor and lie like——"

"Like a Tatar," said Ibrahim.

Yaruk Khan acknowledged the compliment with a wide dog-like grin, and continued, "This they told me. At dawn Gombuk drew horse away from the rest, and the emir Habordansky demanded of him the reason. Then Gombuk laughed in the manner of the Franks—huh! huh! huh!—so. And Gombuk said, 'The devil of good your service has done me, so I cool my heels for nine months in a Turkish prison. Suleyman has given us safe conduct over the border and I am not compelled to ride with you.' 'You dog,' said the emir, 'there is war in the wind and the Archduke has need of your sword.' 'Devil eat the Archduke,' answered Gombuk; 'Zapolya is a dog because he stood aside at Mohacz, and let us, his comrades, be cut to pieces, but Ferdinand is a dog too. When I am penniless I sell him my sword. Now I have two hundred ducats and these robes which I can sell to any Jew for a handful of silver, and may the devil bite me if I draw sword for any man while I have a penny left. I'm for the nearest Christian tavern, and you and the Archduke may go to the devil.' Then the emir cursed him with many great curses, and Gombuk rode away laughing, huh! huh! huh!, and singing a song about a cockroach named——''

"Enough!" Ibrahim's features were dark with rage. He plucked savagely at his beard, reflecting that in the allusion to Mohacz, von Kalmbach had practically clinched Suleyman's suspicion. That matter of thirty-one heads when there should have been thirty-two was something no Turkish sultan would be likely to overlook. Officials had lost positions and their own heads over more trivial matters. The manner in which Suleyman had acted showed his almost incredible fondness and consideration for his Grand Vizier, but Ibrahim, vain though he was, was shrewd and wished no slightest shadow to come between him and his sovereign.

"Could you not have tracked him down, dog?" he demanded.

"By Allah," swore the uneasy Tatar, "he must have ridden on the wind. He crossed the border hours ahead of me, and I followed him as far as I dared——''

"Enough of excuses," interrupted Ibrahim. "Send Mikhal Oglu to me."

The Tatar departed thankfully. Ibrahim was not tolerant of failure in any man.

The Grand Vizier brooded on his silken cushions until the shadow of a pair of vulture wings fell across the marble-tiled floor, and the lean figure he had summoned bowed before him. The man whose very name was a shuddering watchword of horror to all western Asia was soft-spoken and moved with the mincing ease of a cat, but the stark evil of his soul showed in his dark countenance, gleamed in his narrow slit eyes. He was chief of the Akinji, those wild riders whose raids spread fear and desolation throughout all lands beyond the Grand Turk's borders. He stood in full armor, a jeweled helmet on his narrow head, the wide vulture wings made fast to the shoulders of his gilded chain-mail hauberk. Those wings spread wide in the wind when he rode, and under their pinions lay the shadows of death and destruction. It was Suleyman's scimitar-tip, the most noted slayer of a nation of slayers, who stood before the Grand Vizier.

"Soon you will precede the hosts of our master into the lands of the infidel," said Ibrahim. "It will be your order, as always, to strike and spare not. You will waste the fields and the vineyards of the Caphars, you will burn their villages, you will strike down their men with arrows, and lead away their wenches captive. Lands beyond our line of march will cry out beneath your heel."

"That is good hearing, Favored of Allah," answered Mikhal Oglu in his soft courteous voice.

"Yet there is an order within the order," continued Ibrahim, fixing a piercing eye on the Akinji. "You know the German, von Kalmbach?"

"Aye—Gombuk as the Tatars call him."

"So. This is my command—whoever fights or flees, lives or dies—this man must not live. Search him out wherever he lies, though the hunt carry you to the very banks of the Rhine. When you bring me his head, your reward shall be thrice its weight in gold."

"To hear is to obey, my lord. Men say he is the vagabond son of a noble German family, whose ruin has been wine and women. They say he was once a Knight of Saint John, until cast forth for guzzling and——"

"Yet do not underrate him," answered Ibrahim grimly. "Sot he may be, but if he rode with Marczali, he is not to be despised. See thou to it!"

"There is no den where he can hide from me, O Favored of Allah," declared Mikhal Oglu, "no night dark enough to conceal him, no forest thick enough. If I bring you not his head, I give him leave to send you mine."

"Enough!" Ibrahim grinned and tugged at his beard, well pleased. "You have my leave to go."

The sinister vulture-winged figure went springily and silently from the blue chamber, nor could Ibrahim guess that he was taking the first steps in a feud which should spread over years and far lands, swirling in dark tides to draw in thrones and kingdoms and red-haired women more beautiful than the flames of hell.

2

In a small thatched hut in a village not far from the Danube, lusty snores resounded where a figure reclined in state on a ragged cloak thrown over a heap of straw. It was the paladin Gottfried von Kalmbach who slept the sleep of innocence and ale. The velvet vest, voluminous silken trousers, khalat and shagreen boots, gifts from a contemptuous sultan, were nowhere in evidence. The paladin was clad in worn leather and rusty mail. Hands tugged at him, breaking his sleep, and he swore drowsily.

"Wake up, my lord! Oh, wake, good knight—good pig—good dog-soul—will you wake, then?"

"Fill my flagon, host," mumbled the slumberer. "Who?—what? May the dogs bite you, Ivga! I've not another asper—not a penny. Go off like a good lass and let me sleep."

The girl renewed her tugging and shaking.

"Oh dolt! Rise! Gird on your spit! There are happenings forward!"

"Ivga," muttered Gottfried, pulling away from her attack, "take my burganet to the Jew. He'll give you enough for it, to get drunk again."

"Fool!" she cried in despair. "It isn't money I want! The whole east is aflame, and none knows the reason thereof!"

"Has the rain ceased?" asked von Kalmbach, taking some interest in the proceedings at last.

"The rain ceased hours ago. You can only hear the drip from the thatch. Put on your sword and come out into the street. The men of the village are all drunk on your last silver, and the women know not what to think or do. Ah!"

The exclamation was broken from her by the sudden

upleaping of a weird illumination which shone through the crevices of the hut. The German got unsteadily to his feet, quickly girt on the great two-handed sword and stuck his dented burganet on his cropped locks. Then he followed the girl into the straggling street. She was a slender young thing, barefooted, clad only in a short tunic-like garment, through the wide rents of which gleamed generous expanses of white flesh.

There seemed no life or movement in the village. Nowhere showed a light. Water dripped steadily from the eaves of the thatched roofs. Puddles in the muddy streets gleamed black. Wind sighed and moaned eerily through the black sodden branches of the trees which pressed in bulwarks of darkness about the little village, and in the southeast, towering higher into the leaden sky, rose the lurid crimson glow that set the dank clouds to smoldering. The girl Ivga cringed close to the tall German, whimpering.

"I'll tell you what it is, my girl," said he, scanning the glow. "It's Suleyman's devils. They've crossed the river and they're burning the villages. Aye, I've seen glares like that in the sky before. I've expected him before now, but these cursed rains we've had for weeks must have held him back. Aye, it's the Akinji, right enough, and they won't stop this side of Vienna. Look you, my girl, go quickly and quietly to the stable behind the hut and bring me my gray stallion. We'll slip out like mice from between the devil's fingers. The stallion will carry us both, easily."

"But the people of the village!" she sobbed, wringing her hands.

"Eh, well," he said, "God rest them; the men have drunk my ale valiantly and the women have been kind—but horns of Satan, girl, the gray nag won't carry a whole village!"

"Go you!" she returned. "I'll stay and die with my people!"

"The Turks won't kill you," he answered. "They'll sell you to a fat old Stamboul merchant who'll beat you. I won't stay to be cut open, and neither shall you——"

A terrible scream from the girl cut him short and he

wheeled at the awful terror in her flaring eyes. Even as he did so, a hut at the lower end of the village sprang into flames, the sodden material burning slowly. A medley of screams and maddened yells followed the cry of the girl. In the sluggish light figures danced and capered wildly. Gottfried, straining his eyes in the shadows, saw shapes swarming over the low mud wall which drunkenness and negligence had left unguarded.

"Damnation!" he muttered. "The accursed ones have ridden ahead of their fire. They've stolen on the village in the dark—come on, girl——"

But even as he caught her white wrist to drag her away, and she screamed and fought against him like a wild thing, mad with fear, the mud wall crashed at the point nearest them. It crumpled under the impact of a score of horses, and into the doomed village reined the riders, distinct in the growing light. Huts were flaring up on all hands, screams rising to the dripping clouds as the invaders dragged shrieking women and drunken men from their hovels and cut their throats. Gottfried saw the lean figures of the horsemen, the firelight gleaming on their burnished steel; he saw the vulture wings on the shoulders of the foremost. Even as he recognized Mikhal Oglu, he saw the chief stiffen and point.

"At him, dogs!" yelled the Akinji, his voice no longer soft, but strident as the rasp of a drawn saber. "It is Gombuk! Five hundred aspers to the man who brings me his head!"

With a curse von Kalmbach bounded for the shadows of the nearest hut, dragging the screaming girl with him. Even as he leaped, he heard the twang of bowstrings, and the girl sobbed and went limp in his grasp. She sank down at his feet, and in the lurid glare he saw the feathered end of an arrow quivering under her heart. With a low rumble he turned toward his assailants as a fierce bear turns at bay. An instant he stood, head outthrust truculently, sword gripped in both hands; then as a bear gives back from the onset of the hunters, he turned and fled about the hut, arrows whistling about him and glancing from the rings of his mail. There were no shots; the ride through that dripping forest had dampened the powder-flasks of the raiders.

Von Kalmbach quartered about the back of the hut, mindful of the fierce yells behind him, and gained the shed behind the hut he had occupied wherein he stabled his gray stallion. Even as he reached the door, someone snarled like a panther in the semi-dark and cut viciously at him. He parried the stroke with the lifted sword and struck back with all the power of his broad shoulders. The great blade glanced stunningly from the Akinji's polished helmet and rent through the mail links of his hauberk, tearing the arm from the shoulder. The Muhammadan sank down with a groan, and the German sprang over his prostrate form. The gray stallion, wild with fear and excitement, neighed shrilly and reared as his master sprang on his back. No time for saddle or bridle. Gottfried dug his heels into the quivering flanks and the great steed shot through the door like a thunderbolt, knocking men right and left like tenpins. Across the firelit open space between the burning huts he raced, clearing crumpled corpses in his stride, splashing his rider from heel to head as he thrashed through the puddles.

The Akinji made after the flying rider, loosing their shafts and giving tongue like hounds. Those mounted spurred after him, while those who had entered the village on foot ran through the broken wall for their horses.

Arrows flickered about Gottfried's head as he put his steed at the only point open to him—the unbroken western wall. It was touch and go, for the footing was tricky and treacherous and never had the gray stallion attempted such a leap. Gottfried held his breath as he felt the great body beneath him gathering and tensing in full flight for the desperate effort; then with a volcanic heave of mighty thews the stallion rose in the air and cleared the barrier with scarce an inch to spare. The pursuers yelled in amazement and fury, and reined back. Born horsemen though they were, they dared not attempt that break-neck leap. They lost time seeking gates and breaks in the wall, and when they finally emerged from the village, the

black, dank, whispering, dripping forest had swallowed up
their prey.

Mikhal Oglu swore like a fiend and leaving his lieutenant
Othman in charge with instructions to leave no living human
being in the village, he pressed on after the fugitive, following the trail, by torches, in the muddy mold, and swearing
to run him down, if the road led under the very walls of
Vienna.

3

Allah did not will it that
Mikhal Oglu should take Gottfried von Kalmbach's head in
the dark dripping forest. He knew the country better than
they, and in spite of their zeal, they lost his trail in the darkness. Dawn found Gottfried riding through terror-stricken
farmlands, with the flame of a burning world lighting the east
and south. The country was thronged with fugitives, staggering under pitiful loads of household goods, driving bellowing
cattle, like people fleeing the end of the world. The torrential
rains that had offered false promise of security had not long
stayed the march of the Grand Turk.

With a quarter-million followers he was ravaging the eastern marches of Christendom. While Gottfried had loitered in
the taverns of isolated villages, drinking up the Sultan's
bounty, Pesth and Buda had fallen, the German soldiers of
the latter having been slaughtered by the Janizaries, after
promises of safety sworn by Suleyman, whom men named
the Generous.

While Ferdinand and the nobles and bishops squabbled at
the Diet of Spires, the elements alone seemed to war for
Christendom. Rain fell in torrents, and through the floods
that changed plains and forest-bed to dank morasses, the
Turks struggled grimly. They drowned in raging rivers, and
lost great stores of ammunition, ordnance and supplies, when

boats capsized, bridges gave way and wagons mired. But on they came, driven by the implacable will of Suleyman, and now in September, 1529, over the ruins of Hungary, the Turks swept on Europe, with the Akinji—the Sackmen—ravaging the land like the drift ahead of a storm.

This in part Gottfried learned from the fugitives as he pushed his weary stallion toward the city which was the only sanctuary for the panting thousands. Behind him the skies flamed red and the screams of butchered victims came dimly down the wind to his ears. Sometimes he could even make out the swarming black masses of wild horsemen. The wings of the vulture beat horrifically over that butchered land and the shadows of those great wings fell across all Europe. Again the destroyer was riding out of the blue mysterious East as his brothers had ridden before him—Attila—Subotai—Bayazid —Muhammad the Conqueror. But never before had such a storm risen against the West.

Before the waving vulture wings the road thronged with wailing fugitives; behind them it ran red and silent, strewn with mangled shapes that cried no more. The killers were not a half-hour behind him when Gottfried von Kalmbach rode his reeling stallion through the gates of Vienna. The people on the walls had heard the wailing for hours, rising awfully on the wind, and now afar they saw the sun flicker on the points of lances as the horsemen rode in amongst the masses of fugitives toiling down from the hills into the plain which girdles the city. They saw the play of naked steel like sickles among ripe grain.

Von Kalmbach found the city in turmoil, the people swirling and screaming about Count Nikolas Salm, the seventy-year-old warhorse who commanded Vienna, and his aides, Roggendrof, Count Nikolas Zrinyi and Paul Bakics. Salm was working with frantic haste, levelling houses near the walls and using their material to brace the ramparts, which were old and unstable, nowhere more than six feet thick, and in many places crumbling and falling down. The outer palisade was so frail it bore the name of Stadtzaun—city hedge.

But under the lashing energy of Count Salm, a new wall

twenty feet high was thrown up from the Stuben to the Karnthner Gate. Ditches interior to the old moat were dug, and ramparts erected from the drawbridge to the Salz Gate. Roofs were stripped of shingles, to lessen the chances of fire, and paving was ripped up to soften the impact of cannon-balls.

The suburbs had been deserted, and now they were fired lest they give shelter to the besiegers. In the process, which was carried out in the very teeth of the oncoming Sackmen, conflagrations broke out in the city and added to the delirium. It was all hell and bedlam turned loose, and in the midst of it, five thousand wretched noncombatants, old men and women, and children, were ruthlessly driven from the gates to shift for themselves, and their screams, as the Akinjis swooped down, maddened the people within the walls. These hellions were arriving by thousands, topping the sky-lines and sweeping down on the city in irregular squadrons, like vultures gathering about a dying camel. Within an hour after the first swarm had appeared, no Christian remained alive outside the gates, except those bound by long ropes to the saddle-peaks of their captors and forced to run at full speed or be dragged to death. The wild riders swirled about the walls, yelling and loosing their shafts. Men on the towers recognized the dread Mikhal Oglu by the wings on his cuirass, and noted that he rode from one heap of dead to another, avidly scanning each corpse in turn, pausing to glare questioningly at the battlements.

Meanwhile, from the west, a band of German and Spanish troops cut their way through a cordon of Sackmen and marched into the streets to the accompaniment of frenzied cheers, Philip the Palgrave at their head.

Gottfried von Kalmbach leaned on his sword and watched them pass in their gleaming breastplates and plumed crested helmets, with long matchlocks on their shoulders and two-handed swords strapped to their steel-clad backs. He was a curious contrast in his rusty chain-mail, old-fashioned harness picked up here and there and slovenly pieced together—he seemed like a figure out of the past, rusty and tarnished, watching a newer, brighter generation go by. Yet Philip saluted him, with a glance of recognition, as the shining column swung past.

Von Kalmbach started toward the walls, where the gunners were firing frugally at the Akinji, who showed some disposition to climb upon the bastions on lariats thrown from their saddles. But on the way he heard that Salm was impressing nobles and soldiers in the task of digging moats and rearing new earthworks, and in great haste he took refuge in a tavern, where he bullied the host, a knock-kneed and apprehensive Wallachian, into giving him credit, and rapidly drank himself into a state where no one would have considered asking him to do work of any kind.

Shots, shouts and screams reached his ears, but he paid scant heed. He knew that the Akinji would strike and pass on, to ravage the country beyond. He learned from the tavern talk that Salm had 20,000 pikemen, 2,000 horsemen and 1,000 volunteer citizens to oppose Suleyman's hordes, together with seventy guns—cannons, demi-cannons and culverins. The news of the Turks' numbers numbed all hearts with dread—all but von Kalmbach's. He was a fatalist in his way. But he discovered a conscience in ale, and was presently brooding over the people the miserable Viennese had driven forth to perish. The more he drank the more melancholy he became, and maudlin tears dripped from the drooping ends of his mustaches.

At last he rose unsteadily and took up his great sword, muzzily intent on challenging Count Salm to a duel because of the matter. He bellowed down the timid importunities of the Wallachian and weaved out on the street. To his groggy sight the towers and spires cavorted crazily; people jostled him, knocking him aside as they ran about aimlessly. Philip the Palgrave strode by clanking in his armor, the keen dark faces of his Spaniards contrasting with the square florid countenances of the Lanzknechts.

"Shame on you, von Kalmbach!" said Philip sternly. "The Turk is upon us, and you keep your snout shoved in an ale-pot!"

"Whose snout is in what ale-pot?" demanded Gottfried, weaving in an erratic half-circle as he fumbled at his sword. "Devil bite you, Philip, I'll rap your pate for that——"

The Palgrave was already out of sight, and eventually Gottfried found himself on the Karnthner Tower, only vaguely aware of how he had got there. But what he saw sobered him suddenly. The Turk was indeed upon Vienna. The plain was covered with his tents, thirty thousand, some said, and swore that from the lofty spire of Saint Stephen's cathedral a man could not see their limits. Four hundred of his boats lay on the Danube, and Gottfried heard men cursing the Austrian fleet which lay helpless far upstream, because its sailors, long unpaid, refused to man the ships. He also heard that Salm had made no reply at all to Suleyman's demand to surrender.

Now, partly as a gesture, partly to awe the Caphar dogs, the Grand Turk's array was moving in orderly procession before the ancient walls before settling down to the business of the siege. The sight was enough to awe the stoutest. The low-swinging sun struck fire from polished helmet, jeweled saber-hilt and lance-point. It was as if a river of shining steel flowed leisurely and terribly past the walls of Vienna.

The Akinji, who ordinarily formed the vanguard of the host, had swept on, but in their place rode the Tatars of Crimea, crouching on their high-peaked, short-stirruped saddles, their gnome-like heads guarded by iron helmets, their stocky bodies with bronze breastplates and lacquered leather. Behind them came the Azabs, the irregular infantry, Kurds and Arabs for the most part, a wild motley horde. Then their brothers, the Delis, the Madcaps, wild men on tough ponies fantastically adorned with fur and feathers. The riders wore caps and mantles of leopard skin; their unshorn hair hung in tangled strands about their high shoulders, and over their matted beards their eyes glared the madness of fanaticism and bhang.

After them came the real body of the army. First the beys and emirs with their retainers—horsemen and footmen from the feudal fiefs of Asia Minor. Then the Spahis, the heavy cavalry, on splendid steeds. And last of all the real strength of the Turkish empire—the most terrible military organization in the world—the Janizaries. On the walls men spat in black fury, recognizing kindred blood. For the Janizaries were not Turks. With a few exceptions, where Turkish parents had smuggled their offspring into the ranks to save them from the grinding life of a peasant, they were sons of Christians— Greeks, Serbs, Hungarians—stolen in infancy and raised in the ranks of Islam, knowing but one master—the Sultan; but one occupation—slaughter.

Their beardless features contrasted with those of their Oriental masters. Many had blue eyes and yellow mustaches. But all their faces were stamped with the wolfish ferocity to which they had been reared. Under their dark blue cloaks glinted fine mail, and many wore steel skull-caps under their curious high-peaked hats, from which depended a white sleeve-like piece of cloth, and through which was thrust a copper spoon. Long bird-of-paradise plumes likewise adorned these strange head-pieces.

Beside scimitars, pistols and daggers, each Janizary bore a matchlock, and their officers carried pots of coals for the lighting of the matches. Up and down the ranks scurried the dervishes, clad only in kalpaks of camel-hair and green aprons fringed with ebony beads, exhorting the Faithful. Military bands, the invention of the Turk, marched with the columns, cymbals clashing, lutes twanging. Over the flowing sea the banners tossed and swayed—the crimson flag of the Spahis, the white banner of the Janizaries with its two-edged sword worked in gold, and the horse-tail standards of the rulers— seven tails for the Sultan, six for the Grand Vizier, three for the Agha of the Janizaries. So Suleyman paraded his power before despairing Caphar eyes.

But von Kalmbach's gaze was centered on the groups that labored to set up the ordnance of the Sultan. And he shook his head in bewilderment.

"Demi-culverins, sakers, and falconets!" he grunted. "Where the devil's all the heavy artillery Suleyman's so proud of?"

"At the bottom of the Danube!" a Hungarian pikeman

grinned fiercely and spat as he answered. "Wulf Hagen sank
that part of the Soldan's flotilla. The rest of his cannon and
cannon royal, they say, were mired because of the rains."

A slow grin bristled Gottfried's mustache.

"What was Suleyman's word to Salm?"

"That he'd eat breakfast in Vienna day after tomorrow—
the 29th."

Gottfried shook his head ponderously.

4

The siege commenced, with
the roaring of cannons, the whistling of arrows, and the blasting crash of matchlocks. The Janizaries took possession of
the ruined suburbs, where fragments of walls gave them shelter. Under a screen of irregulars and a volley of arrow-fire,
they advanced methodically just after dawn.

On a gun-turret on the threatened wall, leaning on his great
sword and meditatively twisting his mustache, Gottfried von
Kalmbach watched a Transylvanian gunner being carried off
the wall, his brains oozing from a hole in his head; a Turkish
matchlock had spoken too near the walls. The field-pieces of
the Sultan were barking like deep-toned dogs, knocking chips
off the battlements. The Janizaries were advancing, kneeling,
firing, reloading as they came on. Bullets glanced from the
crenelles and whined off venomously into space. One flattened against Gottfried's hauberk, bringing an outraged grunt
from him. Turning toward the abandoned gun, he saw a col-
orful incongruous figure bending over the massive breech.

It was a woman, dressed as von Kalmbach had not seen
even the dandies of France dressed. She was tall, splendidly
shaped, but lithe. From under a steel cap escaped rebellious
tresses that rippled red gold in the sun over her compact
shoulders. High boots of Cordovan leather came to her mid-
thighs, which were cased in baggy breeches. She wore a shirt

of fine Turkish mesh-mail tucked into her breeches. Her supple waist was confined by a flowing sash of green silk, into which were thrust a brace of pistols and a dagger, and from which depended a long Hungarian saber. Over all was carelessly thrown a scarlet cloak.

This surprising figure was bending over the cannon, sighting it in a manner betokening more than a passing familiarity, at a group of Turks who were wheeling a carriage-gun just within range.

"Eh, Red Sonya!" shouted a man-at-arms, waving his pike. "Give 'em hell, my lass!"

"Trust me, dog-brother," she retorted as she applied the glowing match to the vent. "But I wish my mark was Roxelana's——"

A terrific detonation drowned her words and a swirl of smoke blinded everyone on the turret, as the terrific recoil of the overcharged cannon knocked the firer flat on her back. She sprang up like a spring rebounding and rushed to the embrasure, peering eagerly through the smoke, which clearing, showed the ruin of the gun crew. The huge ball, bigger than a man's head, had smashed full into the group clustered about the saker, and now they lay on the torn ground, their skulls blasted by the impact, or their bodies mangled by the flying iron splinters from their shattered gun. A cheer went up from the towers, and the woman called Red Sonya yelled with sincere joy and did the steps of a Cossack dance.

Gottfried approached, eyeing in open admiration the splendid swell of her bosom beneath the pliant mail, the curves of her ample hips and rounded limbs. She stood as a man might stand, booted legs braced wide apart, thumbs hooked into her girdle, but she was all woman. She was laughing as she faced him, and he noted with fascination the dancing sparkling lights and changing colors of her eyes. She raked back her rebellious locks with a powder-stained hand and he wondered at the clear pinky whiteness of her firm flesh where it was unstained.

"Why did you wish for the Sultana Roxelana for a target, my girl?" he asked.

"Because she's my sister, the slut!" answered Sonya.

At that instant a great cry thundered over the walls and the girl started like a wild thing, ripping out her blade in a long flash of silver in the sun.

"I've heard that bellow!" she cried. "The Janizaries——"

Gottfried was already on his way to the embrasures. He too had heard before the terrible soul-shaking shout of the charging Janizaries. Suleyman meant to waste no time on the city that barred him from helpless Europe. He meant to crush its frail walls in one storm. The bashi-bazouki, the irregulars, died like flies to screen the main advance, and over heaps of their dead, the Janizaries thundered against Vienna. In the teeth of cannonade and musket volley they surged on, crossing the moats on scaling-ladders laid across, bridge-like. Whole ranks went down as the Austrian guns roared, but now the attackers were under the walls and the cumbrous balls whirred over their heads, to work havoc in the rear ranks.

The Spanish matchlock men, firing almost straight down, took ghastly toll, but now the ladders gripped the walls, and the chanting madmen surged upward. Arrows whistled, striking down the defenders. Behind them the Turkish field-pieces boomed, careless of injury to friend as well as foe. Gottfried, standing at an embrasure, was overthrown by a sudden terrific impact. A ball had smashed the merlon, braining half a dozen defenders.

Gottfried rose, half stunned, out of the debris of masonry and huddled corpses. He looked down into an uprushing waste of snarling impassioned faces, where eyes glared like mad dogs' and blades glittered like sunbeams on water. Bracing his feet wide, he heaved up his great sword and lashed down. His jaw jutted out, his mustache bristled. The five-foot blade caved in steel caps and skulls, lashing through uplifted bucklers and iron shoulder-pieces. Men fell from the ladders, their nerveless fingers slipping from the bloody rungs.

But they swarmed through the breach on either side of him. A terrible cry announced that the Turks had a foothold on the wall. But no man dared leave his post to go to the threatened point. To the dazed defenders it seemed that Vienna was ringed by a glittering tossing sea that roared higher and higher about the doomed walls.

Stepping back to avoid being hemmed in, Gottfried grunted and lashed right and left. His eyes were no longer cloudy; they blazed like blue bale-fire. Three Janizaries were down at his feet; his broadsword clanged in a forest of slashing scimitars. A blade splintered on his basinet, filling his eyes with fire-shot blackness. Staggering, he struck back and felt his great blade crunch home. Blood jetted over his hands and he tore his sword clear. Then with a yell and a rush someone was at his side and he heard the quick splintering of mail beneath the madly flailing strokes of a saber that flashed like silver lightning before his clearing sight.

It was Red Sonya who had come to his aid, and her onslaught was no less terrible than that of a she-panther. Her strokes followed each other too quickly for the eye to follow; her blade was a blur of white fire, and men went down like ripe grain before the reaper. With a deep roar Gottfried strode to her side, bloody and terrible, swinging his great blade. Forced irresistibly back, the Moslems wavered on the edge of the wall, then leaped for the ladders or fell screaming through empty space.

Oaths flowed in a steady stream from Sonya's red lips and she laughed wildly as her saber sang home and blood spurted along the edge. The last Turk on the battlement screamed and parried wildly as she pressed him; then dropping his scimitar, his clutching hands closed desperately on her dripping blade. With a groan he swayed on the edge, blood gushing from his horribly cut fingers.

"Hell to you, dog-soul!" she laughed. "The devil can stir your broth for you!"

With a twist and a wrench she tore away her saber, severing the wretch's fingers; with a moaning cry he pitched backward and fell headlong.

On all sides the Janizaries were falling back. The field-pieces, halted while the fighting went on upon the walls, were booming again, and the Spaniards, kneeling at the embrasures, were returning the fire with their long matchlocks.

Gottfried approached Red Sonya, who was cleansing her blade, swearing softly.

"By God, my girl," said he, extending a huge hand, "had you not come to my aid, I think I'd have supped in hell this night. I thank——"

"Thank the devil!" retorted Sonya rudely, slapping his hand aside. "The Turks were on the wall. Don't think I risked my hide to save yours, dog-brother!"

And with a scornful flirt of her wide coat-tails, she swaggered off down the battlements, giving back promptly and profanely the rude sallies of the soldiers. Gottfried scowled after her, and a Lanzknecht slapped him jovially on the shoulder.

"Eh, she's a devil, that one! She drinks the strongest head under the table and outswears a Spaniard. She's no man's light o' love. Cut—slash—death to you, dog-soul! There's her way."

"Who is she, in the devil's name?" growled von Kalmbach.

"Red Sonya from Rogatino—that's all we know. Marches and fights like a man—God knows why. Swears she's sister to Roxelana, the Soldan's favorite. If the Tatars who grabbed Roxelana that night had got Sonya, by Saint Piotr! Suleyman would have had a handful! Let her alone, sir brother; she's a wildcat. Come and have a tankard of ale."

The Janizaries, summoned before the Grand Vizier to explain why the attack failed after the wall had been scaled at one place, swore they had been confronted by a devil in the form of a red-headed woman, aided by a giant in rusty mail. Ibrahim discounted the woman, but the description of the man woke a half-forgotten memory in his mind. After dismissing the soldiers, he summoned the Tatar, Yaruk Khan, and dispatched him up-country to demand of Mikhal Oglu why he had not sent a certain head to the royal tent.

5

Suleyman did not eat his breakfast in Vienna on the morning of the 29th. He stood on the height of Semmering, before his rich pavilion with its gold-knobbed pinnacles and its guard of five hundred Solaks, and watched his light batteries pecking vainly away at the frail walls; he saw his irregulars wasting their lives like water, striving to fill the fosse, and he saw his sappers burrowing like moles, driving mines and counter-mines nearer and nearer the bastions.

Within the city there was little ease. Night and day the walls were manned. In their cellars the Viennese watched the faint vibrations of peas on drumheads that betrayed the sounds of digging in the earth that told of Turkish mines burrowing under the walls. They sank their counter-mines, accordingly, and men fought no less fiercely under the earth than above.

Vienna was the one Christian island in a sea of infidels. Night by night men watched the horizons burning where the Akinji yet scoured the agonized land. Occasionally word came from the outer world—slaves escaping from the camp and slipping into the city. Always their news was fresh horror. In Upper Austria less than a third of the inhabitants were left alive; Mikhal Oglu was outdoing himself. And the people said that it was evident the vulture-winged one was looking for someone in particular. His slayers brought men's heads and heaped them high before him; he avidly searched among the grisly relics, then, apparently in fiendish disappointment, drove his devils to new atrocities.

These tales, instead of paralyzing the Austrians with dread, fired them with the mad fury of desperation. Mines exploded, breaches were made and the Turks swarmed in, but always the desperate Christians were there before them, and in the choking, blind, wild-beast madness of hand-to-hand fighting they paid in part the red debt they owed.

* * *

September dwindled into October; the leaves turned brown and yellow on Wiener Wald, and the winds blew cold. The watchers shivered at night on the walls that whitened to the bite of the frost; but still the tents ringed the city; and still Suleyman sat in his magnificent pavilion and glared at the frail barrier that barred his imperial path. None but Ibrahim dared speak to him; his mood was black as the cold nights that crept down from the northern hills. The wind that moaned outside his tent seemed a dirge for his ambitions of conquest.

Ibrahim watched him narrowly, and after a vain onset that lasted from dawn till midday, he called off the Janizaries and bade them retire into the ruined suburbs and rest. And he sent a bowman to shoot a very certain shaft into a very certain part of the city, where certain persons were waiting for just such an event.

No more attacks were made that day. The field-pieces, which had been pounding at the Karnthner Gate for days, were shifted northward, to hammer at the Burg. As an assault on that part of the wall seemed imminent, the bulk of the soldiery was shifted there. But the onslaught did not come, though the batteries kept up a steady fire, hour after hour. Whatever the reason, the soldiers gave thanks for the respite; they were dizzy with fatigue, mad with raw wounds and lack of sleep.

That night the great square, the Am-Hof market, seethed with soldiers, while civilians looked on enviously. A great store of wine had been discovered hidden in the cellars of a rich Jewish merchant, who hoped to reap triple profit when all other liquor in the city was gone. In spite of their officers, the half-crazed men rolled the great hogsheads into the square and broached them. Salm gave up the attempt to control them. Better drunkenness, growled the old warhorse, than for the men to fall in their tracks from exhaustion. He paid the Jew from his own purse. In relays the soldiers came from the walls and drank deep.

In the glare of cressets and torches, to the accompaniment of drunken shouts and songs, to which the occasional rumble of a cannon played a sinister undertone, von Kalmbach dipped his basinet into a barrel and brought it out brimful and dripping. Sinking his mustache into the liquid, he paused as his clouded eyes, over the rim of the steel cap, rested on a strutting figure on the other side of the hogshead. Resentment touched his expression. Red Sonya had already visited more than one barrel. Her burganet was thrust sidewise on her rebellious locks, her swagger was wilder, her eyes more mocking.

"Ha!" she cried scornfully. "It's the Turk-killer, with his nose deep in the keg, as usual! Devil bite all topers!"

She consistently thrust a jeweled goblet into the crimson flood and emptied it at a gulp. Gottfried stiffened resentfully. He had had a tilt with Sonya already, and he still smarted.

"Why should I even look at you, in your ragged harness and empty purse," she had mocked, "when even Paul Bakics is mad for me? Go along, guzzler, beer-keg!"

"Be damned to you," he had retorted. "You needn't be so high, just because your sister is the Soldan's mistress——"

At that she had flown into an awful passion, and they had parted with mutual curses. Now, from the devil in her eyes, he saw that she intended making things further uncomfortable for him.

"Hussy!" he growled. "I'll drown you in this hogshead."

"Nay, you'll drown yourself first, boar-pig!" she shouted amid a roar of rough laughter. "A pity you aren't as valiant against the Turks as you are against the wine-butts!"

"Dogs bite you, slut!" he roared. "How can I break their heads when they stand off and pound us with cannon-balls? Shall I throw my dagger at them from the wall?"

"There are thousands just outside," she retorted, in the grip of madness induced by drink and her own wild nature, "if any had the guts to go to them."

"By God!" the maddened giant dragged out his great sword. "No baggage can call *me* coward, sot or not! I'll go out upon them, if never a man follow me!"

Bedlam followed his bellow; the drunken temper of the crowd was fit for such madness. The nearly empty hogsheads were deserted as men tipsily drew sword and reeled toward the outer gates. Wulf Hagen fought his way into the storm, buffeting men right and left, shouting fiercely, "Wait, you drunken fools! Don't surge out in this shape! Wait——" They brushed him aside, sweeping on in a blind senseless torrent.

Dawn was just beginning to tip the eastern hills. Somewhere in the strangely silent Turkish camp a drum began to throb. Turkish sentries stared wildly and loosed their matchlocks in the air to warn the camp, appalled at the sight of the Christian horde pouring over the narrow drawbridge, eight thousand strong, brandishing swords and ale tankards. As they foamed over the moat a terrific explosion rent the din, and a portion of the wall near the Karnthner Gate seemed to detach itself and rise into the air. A great shout rose from the Turkish camp, but the attackers did not pause.

They rushed headlong into the suburbs, and there they saw the Janizaries, not rousing from slumber, but fully clad and armed, being hurriedly drawn up in charging lines. Without pausing, they burst headlong into the half-formed ranks. Far outnumbered, their drunken fury and velocity was yet irresistible. Before the madly thrashing axes and lashing broadswords, the Janizaries reeled back dazed and disordered. The suburbs became a shambles where battling men, slashing and hewing at one another, stumbled on mangled bodies and severed limbs. Suleyman and Ibrahim, on the height of Semmering, saw the invincible Janizaries in full retreat, streaming out toward the hills.

In the city the rest of the defenders were working madly to repair the great breach the mysterious explosion had torn in the wall. Salm gave thanks for that drunken sortie. But for it, the Janizaries would have been pouring through the breach before the dust settled.

All was confusion in the Turkish camp. Suleyman ran to his horse and took charge in person, shouting at the Spahis. They formed ranks and swung down the slopes in orderly squadrons. The Christian warriors, still following their fleeing enemies, suddenly awakened to their danger. Before them the Janizaries were still falling back, but on either flank the horsemen of Asia were galloping to cut them off. Fear replaced drunken recklessness. They began to fall back, and the retreat quickly became a rout. Screaming in blind panic they threw away their weapons and fled for the drawbridge. The Turks rode them down to the water's edge, and tried to follow them across the bridge, into the gates which were opened for them. And there at the bridge Wulf Hagen and his retainers met the pursuers and held them hard. The flood of the fugitives flowed past him to safety; on him the Turkish tide broke like a red wave. He loomed, a steel-clad giant, in a waste of spears.

Gottfried von Kalmbach did not voluntarily quit the field, but the rush of his companions swept him along the tide of flight, blaspheming bitterly. Presently he lost his footing and his panic-stricken comrades stampeded across his prostrate frame. When the frantic heels ceased to drum on his mail, he raised his head and saw that he was near the fosse, and naught but Turks about him. Rising, he ran lumberingly toward the moat, into which he plunged unexpectedly, looking back over his shoulder at a pursuing Moslem.

He came up floundering and spluttering, and made for the opposite bank, splashing water like a buffalo. The blood-mad Muhammadan was close behind him—an Algerian corsair, as much at home in water as out. The stubborn German would not drop his great sword, and burdened by his mail, just managed to reach the other bank, where he clung, utterly exhausted and unable to lift a hand in defense as the Algerian swirled in, dagger gleaming above his naked shoulder. Then someone swore heartily on the bank hard by. A slim hand thrust a long pistol into the Algerian's face; he screamed as it exploded, making a ghastly ruin of his head. Another slim strong hand gripped the sinking German by the scruff of his mail.

"Grab the bank, fool!" gritted a voice, indicative of great effort. "I can't heave you up alone; you must weigh a ton. Pull, dolt, pull!"

Blowing, gasping and floundering, Gottfried half clam-

bered, was half lifted, out of the moat. He showed some
disposition to lie on his belly and retch, what of the dirty
water he had swallowed, but his rescuer urged him to his
feet.

"The Turks are crossing the bridge and the lads are closing
the gates against them—haste, before we're cut off."

Inside the gate Gottfried stared about, as if waking from a
dream.

"Where's Wulf Hagen? I saw him holding the bridge."

"Lying dead among twenty dead Turks," answered Red
Sonya.

Gottfried sat down on a piece of fallen wall, and because
he was shaken and exhausted, and still mazed with drink and
blood-lust, he sank his face in his huge hands and wept.
Sonya kicked him disgustedly.

"Name o' Satan, man, don't sit and blubber like a spanked
schoolgirl. You drunkards had to play the fool, but that can't
be mended. Come—let's go to the Walloon's tavern and drink
ale."

"Why did you pull me out of the moat?" he asked.

"Because a great oaf like you never can help himself. I
see you need a wise person like me to keep life in that hulk-
ing frame."

"But I thought you despised me!"

"Well, a woman can change her mind, can't she?" she
snapped.

Along the walls the pikemen were repelling the frothing
Moslems, thrusting them off the partly repaired breach. In the
royal pavilion Ibrahim was explaining to his master that the
devil had undoubtedly inspired that drunken sortie just at
the right moment to spoil the Grand Vizier's carefully laid
plans. Suleyman, wild with fury, spoke shortly to his friend
for the first time.

"Nay, thou hast failed. Have done with thine intrigues.
Where craft has failed, sheer force shall prevail. Send a rider
for the Akinji; they are needed here to replace the fallen. Bid
the hosts to the attack again."

6

The preceding onslaughts were naught to the storm that now burst on Vienna's reeling walls. Night and day the cannons flashed and thundered. Bombs burst on roofs and in the streets. When men died on the walls there was none to take their places. Fear of famine stalked the streets and the darker fear of treachery ran black-mantled through the alleys. Investigation showed that the blast that had rent the Karnthner wall had not been fired from without. In a mine tunnelled from an unsuspected cellar inside the city, a heavy charge of powder had been exploded beneath the wall. One or two men, working secretly, might have done it. It was now apparent that the bombardment of the Burg had been merely a gesture to draw attention away from the Karnthner wall, to give the traitors an opportunity to work undiscovered.

Count Salm and his aides did the work of giants. The aged commander, fired with superhuman energy, trod the walls, braced the faltering, aided the wounded, fought in the breaches side by side with the common soldiers, while death dealt his blows unsparingly.

But if death supped within the walls, he feasted full without. Suleyman drove his men as relentlessly as if he were their worst foe. Plague stalked among them, and the ravaged countryside yielded no food. The cold winds howled down from the Carpathians and the warriors shivered in their light Oriental garb. In the frosty nights the hands of the sentries froze to their matchlocks. The ground grew hard as flint and the sappers toiled feebly with blunted tools. Rain fell, mingled with sleet, extinguishing matches, wetting powder, turning the plain outside the city to a muddy wallow, where rotting corpses sickened the living.

Suleyman shuddered as with an ague, as he looked out over the camp. He saw his warriors, worn and haggard, toiling in the muddy plain like ghosts under the gloomy leaden skies. The stench of his slaughtered thousands was in his nostrils.

In that instant it seemed to the Sultan that he looked on a gray plain of the dead, where corpses dragged their lifeless bodies to an outworn task, animated only by the ruthless will of their master. For an instant the Tatar in his veins rose above the Turk and he shook with fear. Then his lean jaws set. The walls of Vienna staggered drunkenly, patched and repaired in a score of places. How could they stand?

"Sound for the onslaught. Thirty thousand aspers to the first man on the walls!"

The Grand Vizier spread his hands helplessly. "The spirit is gone out of the warriors. They cannot endure the miseries of this icy land."

"Drive them to the walls with whips," answered Suleyman, grimly. "This is the gate to Frankistan. It is through it we must ride the road to empire."

Drums thundered through the camp. The weary defenders of Christendom rose up and gripped their weapons, electrified by the instinctive knowledge that the death-grip had come.

In the teeth of roaring matchlocks and swinging broadswords, the officers of the Sultan drove the Moslem hosts. Whips cracked and men cried out blasphemously up and down the lines. Maddened, they hurled themselves at the reeling walls, riddled with great breaches, yet still barriers behind which desperate men could crouch. Charge after charge rolled on over the choked fosse, broke on the staggering walls, and rolled back, leaving its wash of dead. Night fell unheeded, and through the darkness, lighted by blaze of cannon and flare of torches, the battle raged. Driven by Suleyman's terrible will, the attackers fought throughout the night, heedless of all Moslem tradition.

Dawn rose as on Armageddon. Before the walls of Vienna lay a vast carpet of steel-clad dead. Their plumes waved in the wind. And across the corpses staggered the hollow-eyed attackers to grapple with the dazed defenders.

The steel tides rolled and broke, and rolled on again, till the very gods must have stood aghast at the giant capacity of men for suffering and enduring. It was the Armageddon of races—

Asia against Europe. About the walls raved a sea of Eastern faces—Turks, Tatars, Kurds, Arabs, Algerians, snarling, screaming, dying before the roaring matchlocks of the Spaniards, the thrust of Austrian pikes, the strokes of the German Lanzknechts, who swung their two-handed swords like reapers mowing ripe grain. Those within the walls were no more heroic than those without, stumbling among fields of their own dead.

To Gottfried von Kalmbach, life had faded to a single meaning—the swinging of his great sword. In the wide breach by the Karnthner Tower he fought until time lost all meaning. For long ages maddened faces rose snarling before him, the faces of devils, and scimitars flashed before his eyes everlastingly. He did not feel his wounds, nor the drain of weariness. Gasping in the choking dust, blind with sweat and blood, he dealt death like a harvest, dimly aware that at his side a slim pantherish figure swayed and smote—at first with laughter, curses and snatches of song, later in grim silence.

His identity as an individual was lost in that cataclysm of swords. He hardly knew it when Count Salm was death-stricken at his side by a bursting bomb. He was not aware when night crept over the hills, nor did he realize at last that the tide was slackening and ebbing. He was only dimly aware that Nikolas Zrinyi tore him away from the corpse-choked breach, saying, "God's name, man, go and sleep. We've beaten them off—for the time being, at least."

He found himself in a narrow winding street, all dark and forsaken. He had no idea of how he had got there, but seemed vaguely to remember a hand on his elbow, tugging, guiding. The weight of his mail pulled at his sagging shoulders. He could not tell if the sounds he heard were the cannon fitfully roaring, or a throbbing in his own head. It seemed there was someone he should look for—someone who meant a great deal to him. But all was vague. Somewhere, sometime, it seemed long, long ago, a sword-stroke had cleft his basinet. When he tried to think he seemed to feel again the impact of that terrible blow, and his brain swam. He tore off the dented head-piece and cast it into the street.

Again the hand was tugging at his arm. A voice urged, "Wine, my lord—drink!"

Dimly he saw a lean black-mailed figure extending a tankard. With a gasp he caught at it and thrust his muzzle into the stinging liquor, gulping like a man dying of thirst. Then something burst in his brain. The night filled with a million flashing sparks, as if a powder magazine had exploded in his head. After that, darkness and oblivion.

He came slowly to himself, aware of a raging thirst, an aching head, and an intense weariness that seemed to paralyze his limbs. He was bound hand and foot, and gagged. Twisting his head, he saw that he was in a small bare dusty room, from which a winding stone stair led up. He deduced that he was in the lower part of the tower.

Over a guttering candle on a crude table stooped two men. They were both lean and hook-nosed, clad in plain black garments—Asiatics, past doubt. Gottfried listened to their low-toned conversation. He had picked up many languages in his wanderings. He recognized them—Tshoruk and his son Rhupen, Armenian merchants. He remembered that he had seen Tshoruk often in the last week or so, ever since the domed helmets of the Akinji had appeared in Suleyman's camp. Evidently the merchant had been shadowing him, for some reason. Tshoruk was reading what he had written on a bit of parchment.

"My lord, though I blew up the Karnthner wall in vain, yet I have news to make my lord's heart glad. My son and I have taken the German, von Kalmbach. As he left the wall, dazed with fighting, we followed, guiding him subtly to the ruined tower whereof you know, and giving him drugged wine, bound him fast. Let my lord send the emir Mikhal Oglu to the wall by the tower, and we will give him into thy hands. We will bind him on the old mangonel and cast him over the wall like a tree trunk."

The Armenian took up an arrow and began to bind the parchment about the shaft with light silver wire.

"Take this to the roof, and shoot it toward the mantlet, as

usual," he began, when Rhupen exclaimed, "Hark!" and
both froze, their eyes glittering like those of trapped vermin—
fearful yet vindictive.

Gottfried gnawed at the gag; it slipped. Outside he heard
a familiar voice. "Gottfried! Where the devil are you?"

His breath burst from him in a stentorian roar. "Hey,
Sonya! Name of the devil! Be careful, girl——"

Tshoruk snarled like a wolf and struck him savagely on the
head with a scimitar hilt. Almost instantly, it seemed, the
door crashed inward. As in a dream Gottfried saw Red Sonya
framed in the doorway, pistol in hand. Her face was drawn
and haggard; her eyes burned like coals. Her basinet was
gone, and her scarlet cloak. Her mail was hacked and red-
clotted, her boots slashed, her silken breeches splashed and
spotted with blood.

With a croaking cry Tshoruk ran at her, scimitar lifted.
Before he could strike, she crashed down the barrel of the
empty pistol on his head, felling him like a ox. From the
other side Rhupen slashed at her with a curved Turkish dagger. Dropping the pistol, she closed with the young Oriental.
Moving like someone in a dream, she bore him irresistibly
backward, one hand gripping his wrist, the other his throat.
Throttling him slowly, she inexorably crashed his head again
and again against the stones of the wall, until his eyes rolled
up and set. Then she threw him from her like a sack of loose
salt.

"God!" she muttered thickly, reeling an instant in the center of the room, her hands to her head. Then she went to the
captive and sinking stiffly to her knees, cut his bonds with
fumbling strokes that sliced his flesh as well as the cords.

"How did you find me?" he asked stupidly, clambering
stiffly up.

She reeled to the table and sank down in a chair. A flagon
of wine stood at her elbow and she seized it avidly and drank.
Then she wiped her mouth on her sleeve and surveyed him
wearily but with renewed life.

"I saw you leave the wall and followed. I was so drunk
from the fighting I scarce knew what I did. I saw those dogs

take your arm and lead you into the alleys, and then I lost sight of you. But I found your burganet lying outside in the street, and began shouting for you. What the hell's the meaning of this?''

She picked up the arrow, and blinked at the parchment fastened to it. Evidently she could read the Turkish characters, but she scanned it half a dozen times before the meaning became apparent to her exhaustion-numbed brain. Then her eyes flickered dangerously to the men on the floor. Tshoruk sat up, dazedly feeling the gash in his scalp; Rhupen lay retching and gurgling on the floor.

"Tie them up, brother," she ordered, and Gottfried obeyed. The victims eyed the woman much more apprehensively than him.

"This missive is addressed to Ibrahim, the Wezir," she said abruptly. "Why does he want Gottfried's head?''

"Because of a wound he gave the Sultan at Mohacz,'' muttered Tshoruk uneasily.

"And you, you lower-than-a-dog,'' she smiled mirthlessly, "you fired the mine by the Karnthner! You and your spawn are the traitors among us.'' She drew and primed a pistol. "When Zrinyi learns of you,'' she said, "your end will be neither quick nor sweet. But first, you old swine, I'm going to give myself the pleasure of blowing out your cub's brains before your eyes——''

The older Armenian gave a choking cry. "God of my fathers, have mercy! Kill me—torture me—but spare my son!''

At that instant a new sound split the unnatural quiet—a great peal of bells shattered the air.

"What's this?'' roared Gottfried, groping wildly at his empty scabbard.

"The bells of Saint Stephen!'' cried Sonya. "They peal for victory!''

She sprang for the sagging stair and he followed her up the perilous way. They came out on a sagging shattered roof, on a firmer part of which stood an ancient stone-casting machine, relic of an earlier age, and evidently recently repaired. The tower overlooked an angle of the wall, at which there were no watchers. A section of the ancient glacis, and a ditch interior to the main moat, coupled with a steep natural pitch of the earth beyond, made the point practically invulnerable. The spies had been able to exchange messages here with little fear of discovery, and it was easy to guess the method used. Down the slope, just within long arrow-shot, stood up a huge mantlet of bullhide stretched on a wooden frame, as if abandoned there by chance. Gottfried knew that message-laden arrows were loosed from the tower roof into this mantlet. But just then he gave little thought to that. His attention was riveted on the Turkish camp. There a leaping glare paled the spreading dawn; above the mad clangor of the bells rose the crackle of flames, mingled with awful screams.

"The Janizaries are burning their prisoners," said Red Sonya.

"Judgment Day in the morning," muttered Gottfried, awed at the sight that met his eyes.

From their eyrie the companions could see almost all the plain. Under a cold gray leaden sky, tinged a somber crimson with dawn, it lay strewn with Turkish corpses as far as sight carried. And the hosts of the living were melting away. From Semmering the great pavilion had vanished. The other tents were coming down swiftly. Already the head of the long column was out of sight, moving into the hills through the cold dawn. Snow began falling in light swift flakes.

The Janizaries were glutting their mad disappointment on their helpless captives, hurling men, women and children living into the flames they had kindled under the somber eyes of their master, the monarch men called the Magnificent, the Merciful. All the time the bells of Vienna clanged and thundered as if their bronze throats would burst.

"They shot their bolt last night," said Red Sonya. "I saw their officers lashing them, and heard them cry out in fear beneath our swords. Flesh and blood could stand no more. Look!" she clutched her companion's arm. "The Akinji will form the rear-guard."

Even at that distance they made out a pair of vulture wings
moving among the dark masses; the sullen light glimmered
on a jeweled helmet. Sonya's powder-stained hands clenched
so that the pink, broken nails bit into the white palms, and
she spat out a Cossack curse that burned like vitriol.

"There he goes, the bastard, that made Austria a desert!
How easily the souls of the butchered folk ride on his cursed
winged shoulders! Anyway, old warhorse, he didn't get your
head."

"While he lives it'll ride loose on my shoulders," rumbled
the giant.

Red Sonya's keen eyes narrowed suddenly. Seizing Gottfried's arm, she hurried downstairs. They did not see Nikolas
Zrinyi and Paul Bakics ride out of the gates with their tattered
retainers, risking their lives in sorties to rescue prisoners.
Steel clashed along the line of march, and the Akinji retreated slowly, fighting a good rear-guard action, balking the
headlong courage of the attackers by their very numbers. Safe
in the depths of his horsemen, Mikhal Oglu grinned sardonically. But Suleyman, riding in the main column, did not
grin. His face was like a death-mask.

Back in the ruined tower, Red Sonya propped one booted
foot on a chair, and cupping her chin in her hand, stared into
the fear-dulled eyes of Tshoruk.

"What will you give for your life?"

The Armenian made no reply.

"What will you give for the life of your whelp?"

The Armenian stared as if stung. "Spare my son, princess," he groaned. "Anything—I will pay—I will do anything."

She threw a shapely booted leg across the chair and sat
down.

"I want you to bear a message to a man."

"What man?"

"Mikhal Oglu."

He shuddered and moistened his lips with his tongue.

"Instruct me; I obey," he whispered.

"Good. We'll free you and give you a horse. Your son

shall remain here as hostage. If you fail us, I'll give the cub to the Viennese to play with——"

Again the old Armenian shuddered.

"But if you play squarely, we'll let you both go free, and my pal and I will forget about this treachery. I want you to ride after Mikhal Oglu and tell him——"

Through the slush and driving snow, the Turkish column plodded slowly. Horses bent their heads to the blast; up and down the straggling lines camels groaned and complained, and oxen bellowed pitifully. Men stumbled through the mud, leaning beneath the weight of their arms and equipment. Night was falling, but no command had been given to halt. All day the retreating host had been harried by the daring Austrian cuirassiers who darted down upon them like wasps, tearing captives from their very hands.

Grimly rode Suleyman among his Solaks. He wished to put as much distance as possible between himself and the scene of his first defeat, where the rotting bodies of thirty thousand Muhammadans reminded him of his crushed ambitions. Lord of western Asia he was; master of Europe he could never be. Those despised walls had saved the Western world from Moslem dominion, and Suleyman knew it. The rolling thunder of the Ottoman power re-echoed around the world, paling the glories of Persia and Mogul India. But in the West the yellow-haired Aryan barbarian stood unshaken. It was not written that the Turk should rule beyond the Danube.

Suleyman had seen this written in blood and fire, as he stood on Semmering and saw his warriors fall back from the ramparts, despite the flailing lashes of their officers. It had been to save his authority that he gave the order to break camp—it burned his tongue like gall, but already his soldiers were burning their tents and preparing to desert him. Now in darkly brooding silence he rode, not even speaking to Ibrahim.

In his own way Mikhal Oglu shared their savage despondency. It was with a ferocious reluctance that he turned his back on the land he had ruined, as a half-glutted panther might be driven from its prey. He recalled with satisfaction the blackened, corpse-littered wastes—the screams of tortured men—the cries of girls writhing in his iron arms; recalled with much the same sensations the death-shrieks of those same girls in the blood-fouled hands of his killers.

But he was stung with the disappointment of a task undone—for which the Grand Vizier had lashed him with stinging words. He was out of favor with Ibrahim. For a lesser man that might have meant a bowstring. For him it meant that he would have to perform some prodigious feat to reinstate himself. In this mood he was dangerous and reckless as a wounded panther.

Snow fell heavily, adding to the miseries of the retreat. Wounded men fell in the mire and lay still, covered by a growing white mantle. Mikhal Oglu rode among his rearmost ranks, straining his eyes into the darkness. No foe had been sighted for hours. The victorious Austrians had ridden back to their city.

The columns were moving slowly through a ruined village, whose charred beams and crumbling fire-seared walls stood blackly in the falling snow. Word came back down the lines that the Sultan would pass on through and camp in a valley which lay a few miles beyond.

The quick drum of hoofs back along the way they had come caused the Akinji to grip their lances and glare slit-eyed into the flickering darkness. They heard but a single horse, and a voice calling the name of Mikhal Oglu. With a word the chief stayed a dozen lifted bows, and shouted in return. A tall gray stallion loomed out of the flying snow, a black-mantled figure crouched grotesquely atop of it.

"Tshoruk! You Armenian dog! What in the name of Allah——"

The Armenian rode close to Mikhal Oglu and whispered urgently in his ear. The cold bit through the thickest garments. The Akinji noted that Tshoruk was trembling violently. His teeth chattered and he stammered in his speech. But the Turk's eyes blazed at the import of his message.

"Dog, do you lie?"

"May I rot in hell if I lie!" A strong shudder shook Tshoruk and he drew his kaftan close about him. "He fell from his horse, riding with the cuirassiers to attack the rear-guard, and lies with a broken leg in a deserted peasant's hut, some three miles back—alone except for his mistress Red Sonya, and three or four Lanzknechts, who are drunk on wine they found in the deserted camp."

Mikhal Oglu wheeled his horse with sudden intent.

"Twenty men to me!" he barked. "The rest ride on with the main column. I go after a head worth its weight in gold. I'll overtake you before you go into camp."

Othman caught his jeweled rein. "Are you mad, to ride back now? The whole country will be on our heels——"

He reeled in his saddle as Mikhal Oglu slashed him across the mouth with his riding-whip. The chief wheeled away, followed by the men he had designated. Like ghosts they vanished into the spectral darkness.

Othman sat his horse uncertainly, looking after them. The snow shafted down, the wind sobbed drearily among the bare branches. There was no sound except the receding noises of the trudging column. Presently these ceased. Then Othman started. Back along the way they had come, he heard a distant reverberation, a roar as of forty or fifty matchlocks speaking together. In the utter silence which followed, panic came upon Othman and his warriors. Whirling away they fled through the ruined village after the retreating horde.

7

None noticed when night fell on Constantinople, for the splendor of Suleyman made night no less glorious then day. Through gardens that were riots of blossoms and perfume, cressets twinkled like myriad fireflies. Fireworks turned the city into a realm of shimmering magic, above which the minarets of five hundred mosques rose like towers of fire in an ocean of golden foam. Tribesmen on Asian hills gaped and marvelled at the blaze that pulsed and glowed afar, paling the very stars. The streets of Stamboul were thronged with crowds in the attire of holiday and rejoicing. The million lights shone on jeweled turban and striped khalat—on dark eyes sparkling over filmy veils—on shining palanquins borne on the shoulders of huge ebony-skinned slaves.

All that splendor centered in the Hippodrome, where in lavish pageants the horsemen of Turkistan and Tatary competed in breath-taking races with the riders of Egypt and Arabia, where warriors in glittering mail spilled one another's blood on the sands, where swordsmen were matched against wild beasts, and lions were pitted against tigers from Bengal and boars from northern forests. One might have deemed the imperial pageantry of Rome revived in Eastern garb.

On a golden throne, set upon lapis lazuli pillars, Suleyman reclined, gazing on the splendors, as purple-togaed Caesars had gazed before him. About him bowed his viziers and officers, and the ambassadors from foreign courts—Venice, Persia, India, the khanates of Tatary. They came—including the Venetians—to congratulate him on his victory over the Austrians. For this grand fête was in celebration of that victory, as set forth in a manifesto under the Sultan's hand, which stated, in part, that the Austrians having made submission and sued for pardon on their knees, and the German realms being so distant from the Ottoman empire, "the Faithful would not trouble to clean out the fortress [Vienna], or purify, improve, and put it in repair." Therefore the Sultan had accepted the submission of the contemptible Germans, and left them in possession of their paltry "fortress"!

Suleyman was blinding the eyes of the world with the blaze of his wealth and glory, and striving to make himself believe that he had actually accomplished all he had intended. He had not been beaten on the field of open battle; he had set his puppet on the Hungarian throne; he had devastated Austria; the markets of Stamboul and Asia were full of Christian slaves. With this knowledge he soothed his vanity, ignoring the fact that thirty thousand of his subjects rotted before Vienna, and that his dreams of European conquest had been shattered.

Behind the throne shone the spoils of war—silken and velvet pavilions, wrested from the Persians, the Arabs, the Egyptian memluks; costly tapestries, heavy with gold embroidery. At his feet were heaped the gifts and tributes of subject and allied princes. There were vests of Venetian velvet, golden goblets crusted with jewels from the courts of the Grand Moghul, ermine-lined kaftans from Erzeroum, carven jade from Cathay, silver Persian helmets with horse-hair plumes, turban-cloths, cunningly sewn with gems, from Egypt, curved Damascus blades of watered steel, matchlocks from Kabul worked richly in chased silver, breastplates and shields of Indian steel, rare furs from Mongolia. The throne was flanked on either hand by a long rank of youthful slaves, made fast by golden collars to a single long silver chain. One file was composed of young Greek and Hungarian boys, the other of girls; all clad only in plumed head-pieces and jeweled ornaments intended to emphasize their nudity.

Eunuchs in flowing robes, their rotund bellies banded by cloth-of-gold sashes, knelt and offered the royal guests sherbets in gemmed goblets, cooled with snow from the mountains of Asia Minor. The torches danced and flickered to the roars of the multitudes. Around the courses swept the horses, foam flying from their bits; wooden castles reeled and went up in flames as the Janizaries clashed in mock warfare. Officers passed among the shouting people, tossing showers of copper and silver coins amongst them. None hungered or thirsted in Stamboul that night except the miserable Caphar captives. The minds of the foreign envoys were numbed by the bursting sea of splendor, the thunder of imperial magnificence. About the vast arena stalked trained elephants, almost covered with housings of gold-worked leather, and from the jeweled towers on their backs, fanfares of trumpets vied with the roar of the throngs and the bellowing of lions. The tiers of the Hippodrome were a sea of faces, all turning toward

the jeweled figure on the shining throne, while the thousands
of tongues wildly thundered his acclaim.

As he impressed the Venetian envoys, Suleyman knew he
impressed the world. In the blaze of his magnificence, men
would forget that a handful of desperate Caphars behind rotting walls had closed his road to empire. Suleyman accepted
a goblet of the forbidden wine, and spoke aside to the Grand
Vizier, who stepped forth and lifted his arms.

"Oh, guests of my master, the Padishah forgets not the
humblest in the hour of rejoicing. To the officers who led his
hosts against the infidels, he has made rare gifts. Now he
gives two hundred and forty thousand ducats to be distributed
among the common soldiers, and likewise to each Janizary,
he gives a thousand aspers."

In the midst of the roar that went up, a eunuch knelt before
the Grand Vizier, holding up a large round package, carefully
bound and sealed. A folded piece of parchment, held shut by
a red seal, accompanied it. The attention of the Sultan was
attracted.

"Oh, friend, what has thou there?"

Ibrahim salaamed. "The rider of the Adrianople post delivered it, O Lion of Islam. Apparently it is a gift of some
sort from the Austrian dogs. Infidel riders, I understand, gave
it into the hands of the border guard, with instructions to
send it straightway to Stamboul."

"Open it," directed Suleyman, his interest roused. The
eunuch salaamed to the floor, then began breaking the seals
of the package. A scholarly slave opened the accompanying
note and read the contents, written in a bold yet feminine
hand:

> To the Soldan Suleyman and his Wezir Ibrahim and
> to the hussy Roxelana we who sign our names below
> send a gift in token of our immeasurable fondness and
> kind affection.
>
> > Sonya of Rogatino, and
> > Gottfried von Kalmbach

Suleyman, who had started up at the name of his favorite, his features suddenly darkening with wrath, gave a choking cry, which was echoed by Ibrahim. The eunuch had torn the seals of the bale, disclosing what lay within. A pungent scent of herbs and preservative spices filled the air, and the object, slipping from the horrified eunuch's hands, tumbled among the heaps of presents at Suleyman's feet, offering a ghastly contrast to the gems, gold and velvet bales. The Sultan stared down at it and in that instant his shimmering pretense of triumph slipped from him; his glory turned to tinsel and dust. Ibrahim tore at his beard with a gurgling, strangling sound, purple with rage.

At the Sultan's feet, the features frozen in a death-mask of horror, lay the severed head of Mikhal Oglu, Vulture of the Grand Turk.

II.

HENRY KUTTNER

INTRODUCTION

Henry Kuttner (1915–1958) is another author whose work is in dire need of revival. Extremely prolific and astonishingly versatile, from his first publication in 1936 Kuttner turned out hundreds of stories for the pulps—many of them written under a formidable array of pseudonyms. He is said to have written virtually an entire issue of Red Circle's notorious *Marvel Science Stories* (a.k.a. *Marvel Tales*, a.k.a. *Marvel Stories*), a feat which led one of his fellow science fiction professionals to heckle him at a barroom gathering with the greeting (with gestures): "Here comes Hank Kuttner. Kill a monster, grab a tit. Kill a monster, grab a tit."

It was a hackwork reputation Kuttner was slow to live down, and it was only after fans and fellow writers began to praise the work of one Lewis Padgett that this was revealed as yet another of Kuttner's pseudonyms. In 1940 he married the gifted author C. L. Moore, and following that most of their writing, although usually under a single byline, was done in collaboration. Henry Kuttner, Kuttner and Moore, whatever the byline or pseudonym, established himself/themselves in the front ranks of the science fiction/fantasy writers during the 1940s and 1950s. Heart failure cut short Kuttner's vigorous career in 1958, and his wife virtually disappeared from the field. And this is another of those instances where readers can only wonder what might have been.

Another tragedy, Robert E. Howard's suicide in 1936, likewise cut short a brilliant career and left pulp readers clamoring for more heroic fantasy tales. A number of authors charged unto the breach, and Kuttner was one of them. While not strictly in the Howard mold—Kuttner's stories more closely call to mind Michael Moorcock's Elric series of the present day—he was the best of those who sought to fill the gap left by Howard's death. (I'm not counting Fritz Leiber's Gray Mouser and Fafhrd stories, as the series was begun before Howard's death, although not published until well afterward.)

Henry Kuttner created two new heroic fantasy series. The first concerned Elak of Atlantis and his sidekick Lycon. Four stories (one a two-part serial) were published in *Weird Tales*, three in 1938 and the last in 1941, and one wonders whether the series was axed when Dorothy McIlwraith replaced Farnsworth Wright as editor in 1940, or whether Kuttner simply had better-paying markets to write for by then. Elak was your basic lithe adventurer, Lycon your basic roguish companion, and the stories are competently written and remain quite a good read—and far superior to much that has been written in this genre since.

Kuttner's other heroic fantasy series consisted of only two stories, "Cursed Be the City" and "The Citadel of Darkness," both published in *Strange Stories* in 1939. The characters are Prince Raynor and his sidekick Eblik, but the stories are rather moodier and grimmer than his Elak adventures, and are comparable to Moorcock's stories of Elric and Moonglum, written a quarter of a century later. But then, Kuttner was often well ahead of his time.

Strange Stories was another serious rival of *Weird Tales*. Introduced in February 1939, the pulp was a stuck-together but enthusiastic effort put out bimonthly by Better Publications, successful publishers of the new *Startling Stories*, the venerable *Thrilling Wonder Stories*, and a host of other "Thrilling Publications." While the money wasn't any better than *Weird Tales*, *Strange Stories* paid on time and drew in several of the *Weird Tales* crowd—often buying, according to Manly Wade Wellman and E. Hoffmann Price, stories previously bounced by *Weird Tales*. Considering *Strange Stories* to be a salvage market, often writers appeared there under pseudonyms—sometimes personal ones, sometimes house names. Covers were generally lurid and atrocious—some of them reworked from other Thrilling Publications. *Strange Stories* folded in February 1941 with its thirteenth issue, while its companion science fiction pulps lasted until the 1950s. Perhaps with a bit more to spend, *Strange Stories* would have hung around long enough to tell us more about Prince Raynor and Eblik. Instead, we'll have to be content with the only two stories in the series, presented together here.

CURSED BE THE CITY

by Henry Kuttner

This is the tale they tell, O King: that ere the royal banners were lifted upon the tall towers of Chaldean Ur, before the Winged Pharaohs reigned in secret Aegyptus, there were mighty empires far to the east. There in that vast desert known as the Cradle of Mankind— aye, even in the heart of the measureless Gobi—great wars were fought and high palaces thrust their minarets up to the purple Asian sky. But this, O King, was long ago, beyond the memory of the oldest sage; the splendor of Imperial Gobi lives now only in the dreams of minstrels and poets. . . .

— *The Tale of Sakhmet the Damned*

CHAPTER I
The Gates of War

In the gray light of the false dawn the prophet had climbed to the outer wall of Sardopolis, his beard streaming in the chill wind. Before him, stretching across the broad plain, were the gay tents and pavilions of the besieging army, emblazoned with the scarlet symbol of the wyvern, the winged dragon beneath which King Cyaxares of the north waged his wars.

Already soldiers were grouped about the catapults and scaling-towers, and a knot of them gathered beneath the wall where the prophet stood. Mocking, rough taunts were voiced, but for a time the white-bearded oldster paid no heed to the gibes. His sunken eyes, beneath their snowy penthouse brows, dwelt on the far distance, where a forest swept up into the mountain slopes and faded into blue haze.

His voice came, thin piercing.

"Woe, woe unto Sardopolis! Fallen is Jewel of Gobi, fallen and lost forever, and all its glory gone! Desecration shall come to the altars, and the streets shall run red with blood. I see death for the king and shame for his people. . . ."

For a time the soldiers beneath the wall had been silent, but now, spears lifted, they interrupted with a torrent of half-amused mockery. A bearded giant roared:

"Come down to us, old goat! We'll welcome you indeed!"

The prophet's eyes dropped, and the shouting of the soldiers faded into stillness. Very softly the ancient spoke, yet each word was clear and distinct as a sword-blade.

"Ye shall ride through the streets of the city in triumph. And your king shall mount the silver throne. Yet from the forest shall come your doom; an old doom shall come down upon you, and none shall escape. He shall return—*He*—the mighty one who dwelt here once. . . ."

The prophet lifted his arms, staring straight into the red eye of the rising sun. *"Evohé! Evohé!"*

Then he stepped forward. Two steps and plunged. Straight

down, his beard and robe streaming up, till the upthrust spears caught him, and he died.

And that day the gates of Sardopolis were burst in by giant battering-rams, and like an unleashed flood the men of Cyaxares poured into the city, wolves who slew and plundered and tortured mercilessly. Terror walked that day, and a haze of battle hung upon the roofs. The defenders were hunted down and slaughtered in the streets without mercy. Women were outraged, their children impaled, and the glory of Sardopolis faded in a smoke of shame and horror. The last glow of the setting sun touched the scarlet wyvern of Cyaxares floating from the tallest tower of the king's palace.

Flambeaux were lighted in their sockets, till the great hall blazed with a red fire, reflected from the silver throne where the invader sat. His black beard was all bespattered with blood and grime, and slaves groomed him as he sat among his men, gnawing on a mutton-bone. Yet, despite the man's gashed and broken armor and the filth that besmeared him, there was something unmistakably regal about his bearing. A king's son was Cyaxares, the last of a line that had sprung from the dawn ages of Gobi when the feudal barons had reigned.

But his face was a tragic ruin.

Strength and power and nobility had once dwelt there, and traces of them still could be seen, as though in muddy water, through the mask of cruelty and vice that lay heavy upon Cyaxares. His gray eyes held a cold and passionless stare that vanished only in the crimson blaze of battle, and now those deadly eyes dwelt on the bound form of the conquered king of Sardopolis, Chalem.

In contrast with the huge figure of Cyaxares, Chalem seemed slight; yet, despite his wounds, he stood stiffly upright, no trace of expression on his pale face.

A strange contrast! The marbled, tapestried throne-room of the palace was more suitable to gay pageantry than this grim scene. The only man who did not seem incongruously out of place stood beside the throne, a slim, dark youth, clad in silks and velvets that had apparently not been marred by the battle. This was Necho, the king's confidant, and, some said, his familiar demon. Whence he had come no one knew but of his evil power over Cyaxares there was no doubt.

A little smile grew on the youth's handsome face. Smoothing his curled dark hair, he leaned close and whispered to the king. The latter nodded, waved away a maiden who was oiling his beard, and said shortly:

"Your power is broken, Chalem. Yet are we merciful. Render homage, and you may have your life."

For answer Chalem spat upon the marble flags at his feet.

A curious gleam came into Cyaxares' eyes. Half inaudibly he murmured, "A brave man. Too brave to die. . . ."

Some impulse seemed to pull his head around until he met Necho's gaze. A message passed in that silent staring. For Cyaxares took from his side a long, bloodstained sword; he rose, stepped down from his dais—and swung the brand.

Chalem made no move to evade the blow. The steel cut through bone and brain. As the dead man fell, Cyaxares stood looking down without a trace of expression. He wrenched his sword free.

"Fling this carrion to the vultures," he commanded.

From the group of prisoners near by came an angry oath. The king turned to face the man who had dared to speak. He gestured.

A pair of guards pushed forward a tall, well-muscled figure, yellow-haired, with a face strong despite its youth, now darkened with rage. The man wore no armor, and his torso was criss-crossed with wounds.

"Who are you?" Cyaxares asked with ominous restraint, the sword bare in his hand.

"King Chalem's son—Prince Raynor."

"You seek death?"

Raynor shrugged. "Death has come close to me today. Slay me if you will. I've butchered about a dozen of your wolves, anyway, and that's some satisfaction."

Behind Cyaxares came a rustle of silks as Necho moved slightly. The king's lips twitched beneath the shaggy beard. His face was suddenly hard and cruel again.

"So! Well, you will crawl to my feet before the next sun

sets." He gestured. "No doubt there are torture vaults beneath the palace. Sudrach!"

A brawny, leather-clad man stepped forward and saluted. "You have heard my will. See to it."

"If I crawl to your feet," Raynor said quietly, "it'll be to hamstring you, bloated toad."

The king drew in his breath with an angry sound. Without another word he nodded to Sudrach, and the torturer followed Raynor as he was conducted out. Then Cyaxares went back to his throne and mused for a time, till a slave brought him wine in a gilded chalice.

But the liquor had no power to break his dark mood. At last he rose and went to the dead king's apartments, which the invaders had not dared to plunder for fear of Cyaxares' wrath. Above the silken couch a gleaming image hung from its standard—the scarlet wyvern, wings spread, barbed tail stiffly upright. Cyaxares stood silently staring at it for a space.

He did not turn when he heard Necho's soft voice. The youth said, "The wyvern has conquered once again."

"Aye," Cyaxares said dully. "Once again, through vileness and black shame. It was an evil day when we met, Necho."

Low laughter came. "Yet you summoned me, as I remember. I was content enough in my own place, till you sent your summons."

Involuntarily the king shuddered. "I would Ishtar had sent down her lightnings upon me that night."

"Ishtar? You worship another god now."

Cyaxares swung about, snarling. "Necho, do not push me too far! I have still some power—"

"You have all power," the low voice said. "As you wished."

For a dozen heart-beats the king made no answer. Then he whispered, "I am the first to bring shame upon our royal blood. When I was crowned I swore many a vow on the tombs of my fathers—and for a time I kept those vows. I ruled with truth and chivalry—"

"And you sought wisdom."

"Aye. I was not content. I sought to make my name great, and to that end I talked with sorcerers—with Bleys of the Dark Pool."

"Bleys," Necho murmured. "He was learned, in his way. Yet—he died."

The king's breathing was unsteady. "I know. I slew him—at your command. And you showed me what happened thereafter."

"Bleys is not happy now," Necho said softly. "He served the same master as you. Wherefore—" The quiet voice grew imperious. "Wherefore live! For by our bargain I shall give you all power on earth, fair women and treasure beyond imagination. But when you die—you shall serve me!"

The other stood silent, while veins swelled on his swarthy forehead. Suddenly, with a bellowing, inarticulate oath, he snatched up his sword. Bright steel flamed through the air—and rebounded, clashing. Up the king's arm and through all his body raced a tingling shock, and simultaneously the regal apartment seemed to darken around him. The fires of the flambeaux darkened. The air was chill—and it whispered.

Steadily the room grew blacker. Now all was midnight black, save for a shining figure that stood immobile, blazing with weird and unearthly radiance. Little murmurs rustled through the deadly stillness. The body of Necho shone brighter, blindingly. And he stood without moving or speaking, till the king shrank with a shuddering cry, his blade clattering on the marble.

"No!" he half sobbed. "For *His* mercy—*no*!"

"*He* has no mercy," the low voice came, bleak and chill. "Therefore worship me, dog whom men call king. *Worship me!*"

And Cyaxares worshiped. . . .

CHAPTER II
Blood in the City

Prince Raynor was acutely uncomfortable. He was stretched upon a rack, staring up at the dripping stones of the vault's roof, and Sudrach, the torturer, was heating iron bars on the hearth. A great cup of wine stood nearby, and occasionally Sudrach, humming under his breath, would reach for it and gulp noisily. "A thousand pieces of gold if you help me escape," Raynor repeated without much hope.

"What good is gold to a flayed man?" Sudrach asked. "That would be my fate if you escaped. Also, where would you get a thousand golden pieces?"

"In my apartment," Raynor said. "Safely hidden."

"You may be lying. At any rate, you'll tell me where this hiding place is when I burn out your eyes. Thus I'll have the gold—if it exists—without danger to myself."

Raynor made no answer, but instead tugged at the cords that bound him. They did not give. Yet Raynor strained until blood throbbed in his temples, and was no closer to freedom when he relaxed at last.

"You'll but wear yourself out," Sudrach said over his shoulder. "Best save your strength. You'll need it for screaming." He took an iron bar from the fire. Its end glowed redly, and Raynor watched the implement with fascinated horror. An unpleasant way to die. . . .

But as the glowing bar approached Raynor's chest there came an interruption. The iron door was flung open, and a tall, huge-muscled black entered. Sudrach turned, involuntarily lifting the bar as a weapon. Then he relaxed, his eyes questioning.

"Who the devil are you?" he grunted.

"Eblik, the Nubian," said the black, bowing. "I bear a message from the king. I lost my way in this damned palace, and just now blundered to my goal. The king has two more prisoners for your hands."

"Good!" Sudrach rubbed his hands. "Where are they?"

"In the—" The other stepped closer. He fumbled in his belt.

Then, abruptly, a blood-reddened dagger flashed up and sheathed itself in flesh. Sudrach bellowed, thrust out clawing hands. He doubled up slowly, while his attacker leaped free, and then he collapsed upon the dank stones and lay silent, twitching a little.

"The gods be praised!" Raynor grunted. "Eblik, faithful servant, you come in time!"

Eblik's dark, gargoylish face was worried. "Let me—" He slashed the cords that bound the prisoner. "It wasn't easy. When we were separated in the battle, master, I knew Sardopolis would fall. I changed clothes with one of Cyaxares' men—whom I slew—and waited my chance to escape. It was by the merest luck that I heard you had offended the king and were to be tortured. So—" He shrugged.

Raynor, free at last, sprang up from the rack, stretching his stiffened muscles. "Will it be easy to escape?"

"Perhaps. Many are drunk or asleep. At any rate, we can't stay here."

The two slipped cautiously out into the corridor. A guard lay dead, weltering in his blood, not far away. They hurried past him, and silently threaded their way through the palace, more than once dodging into passages to evade detection.

"If I knew where Cyaxares slept, I'd take my chances on slitting his throat," Raynor said. "Wait! This way!"

At the end of a narrow hall was a door which, pushed open, showed a moonlit expanse of garden. Eblik said, "I remember—I entered this way. Here—" He dived into a bush and presently emerged with a sword and a heavy battle-ax; the latter he thrust in his girdle. "What now?"

"Over the wall," Raynor said, and led the way. The high rampart was not easy to scale, but a spreading tree grew close to it, and eventually the two had surmounted the barrier. As Raynor dropped lightly to the ground he heard a sudden cry, and, glancing around, saw a group of men, armor gleaming in the moonlight, racing toward him. He cursed softly.

Eblik was already fleeing, his long legs covering the yards with amazing speed. Raynor followed, though his first impulse was to wait and give battle. But in the stronghold of Cyaxares such an action would have been suicidal.

Behind the pair the pursuers bayed menace. Swords came out flashing. Raynor clutched his comrade's arm, dragged him into a side alley, and the two sped on, frantically searching for a hiding-place. It was Eblik who found sanctuary five minutes later. Passing the blood-smeared, corpse-littered courtyard of a temple, he gasped a hasty word, and in a moment both Raynor and Eblik were across the moonlit stretch and fleeing into the interior of the temple.

From a high roof hung a golden ball, dim in the gloom. This was the sacred house of the Sun, the dwelling place of the primal god Ahmon. Eblik had been here before, and knew the way. He guided Raynor past torn tapestries and overthrown censers, and then, halting before a golden curtain, he listened. There was no sound of pursuit.

"Good!" the Nubian warrior said. "I've heard of a secret way out of here, though where it is I don't know. Maybe we can find it."

He drew the curtain aside, and the two entered the sanctuary of the god. Involuntarily Raynor whispered a curse, and his brown fingers tightened on his rapier hilt.

A small chamber faced them, with walls and floor and ceiling blue as the summer sky. It was empty, save for a single huge sphere of gold in the center.

Broken upon the gleaming ball was a man.

From the wall a single flambeau cast a flickering radiance on the twisted, bloodstained body, on the white beard that was dappled with blood. The man lay stretched across the globe, his hands and feet impaled with iron spikes that had been driven deeply into the gold.

Froth bubbled on his lips. His hoary head rolled; eyes stared unseeingly. He gasped, "Water! For the love of Ahmon, a drop of water!"

Raynor's lips were a hard white line as he sprang forward. Eblik helped him as he pried the spikes free. The tortured priest moaned and bit at his mangled lips, but made no outcry. Presently he lay prostrate on the blue floor. With a muttered word, Eblik disappeared, and came back bearing a cup which he held to the dying man's mouth.

The priest drank deeply. He whispered, "Prince Raynor! Is the King safe?"

Swiftly Raynor answered. The other's white head rolled.

"Lift me up—swiftly!"

Raynor obeyed. The priest ran his hands over the golden sphere, and suddenly, beneath his probing fingers, it split in half like a cloven fruit, and in its center a gap widened. A steep staircase led down into hidden depths.

"The altar is open? I cannot see well. Take me down there. They cannot find us in the hidden chamber."

Raynor swung the priest to his shoulders and without hesitation started down the steps, Eblik behind him. There was a low grating as the altar swung back, a gleaming sphere that would halt and baffle pursuit. They were in utter darkness. The prince moved cautiously, testing each step before he shifted his weight. At last he felt the floor level beneath his feet.

Slowly, a dim light began to grow, like the first glow of dawn. It revealed a bare stone vault, roughly constructed of mortised stones, strangely at variance with the palatial city above. In one wall a dark hole showed. On the floor was a circular disk of metal, its center hollowed out into a cup. Within this cup lay a broken shard of some rock that resembled gold-shot marble, half as large as Raynor's hand. On the shard were carved certain symbols the prince did not recognize, and one that he did—the ancient looped cross, sacred to the sun-god.

He put the priest down gently, but nevertheless the man moaned in agony. The maimed hands clutched at air.

"Ahmon! Great Ahmon . . . give me more water!"

Eblik obeyed. Strengthened, the priest fumbled for and gripped Raynor's arm.

"You are strong. Good! Strength is needed for the mission you must undertake."

"Mission?"

The priest's fingers tightened. "Aye; Ahmon guided your steps hither. You must be the messenger of vengeance. Not I. I have not long to live. My strength ebbs. . . ."

He was silent for a time, and then resumed, "I have a tale to tell you. Do you know the legend of the founding of Sardopolis? How, long ago, a very terrible god had his altar in this spot, and was served by all the forest dwellers . . . till those who served Ahmon came? They fought and prisoned the forest god, drove him hence to the Valley of Silence, and he lies bound there by strong magic and the seal of Ahmon. Yet there was a prophecy that one day Ahmon would be overthrown, and the bound god would break his fetters and return to his first dwelling place, to the ruin of Sardopolis. The day of the prophecy is at hand!"

The priest pointed. "All is dark. Yet the seal should be there—is it not?"

Raynor said, "A bit of marble—"

"Aye—the talisman. Lift it up!" The voice was now peremptory. Raynor obeyed.

"I have it."

"Good. Guard it well. Lift the disk now."

Almost apprehensively the prince tugged the disk up, finding it curiously light. Beneath was nothing but a jagged stone, crudely carved with archaic figures and symbols. A stone—yet Raynor knew, somehow, that the thing was horribly old, that it had existed from the dawn ages of Gobi.

"The altar of the forest god," said the priest. "He will return to this spot when he is freed. You must go to the Reaver of the Rock, and give him the talisman. He will know its meaning. So shall Ahmon be avenged upon the tyrant. . . ."

Suddenly the priest surged upright, his arms lifted, tears streaming from the blind eyes. He cried, *"Ohé—ohé!* Fallen forever is the House of Ahmon! Fallen to the dust. . . ."

He fell, as a tree falls, crashing down upon the stones, his arms still extended as though in worship. So died the last priest of Ahmon in Gobi.

Raynor did not move for a while. Then he bent over the lax body. A hasty examination showed him that the man was dead, and shrugging, he thrust the marble shard into his belt.

"I suppose that's the way out," he said, pointing to the gap in the wall, "though I don't like the look of it. Well—come on."

He squeezed himself into the narrow hole, cursing softly, and Eblik followed.

CHAPTER III
The Reaver of the Rock

With slow steps Cyaxares paced his apartment, his shaggy brows drawn together in a frown. Once or twice his hand closed convulsively on his sword-hilt, and again the secret agony within him made him groan aloud. But not once did he glance at the scarlet symbol of the wyvern that hung above his couch.

Going to a window, he looked down over the city, and then his gaze went out to the plain and the distant, forested mountains. He sighed heavily.

A voice said, "You may well look there, Cyaxares. For there is your doom, unless you act swiftly."

"Is it you, Necho?" the king asked heavily. "What new shamefulness must I work now?"

"Two men go south to the Valley of Silence. They must be slain ere they reach it."

"Why? What aid can they get there?"

Necho did not answer at first. His voice was hesitant when he said, "The gods have their own secrets. There is something in the Valley of Silence that can send all your glory and power crashing down about your head. Nor can I aid you then. I can only advise you now and if you follow my advice—well. But act I cannot and must not, for a reason which you need not know. Send out your men therefore, with orders to overtake those two and slay them—swiftly!"

"As you will," the king said, and turned to summon a servitor.

"Soldiers follow us," Eblik said, shading his eyes with a callused hand. He was astride a rangy dun mare, and beside him Raynor rode on a great gray charger, red of nostril and fiery of eye. The latter turned in the saddle and looked back.

"By the gods!" he observed. "Cyaxares has sent half an army after us. It's lucky we managed to steal these mounts."

The two had reined their horses at the summit of a low rise in the forest. Back of them the ground sloped to the great plain and the gutted city of Sardopolis; before them jagged mountains rose, covered with oak and pine and fir. The Nubian licked dry lips, said thirstily, "The fires of all hells are in my belly. Let's get out of this wilderness, where there's nothing to drink but water."

"The Reaver may feed you wine—or blood," Raynor said, "Nevertheless, our best chance is to find this Reaver and seek his aid. A mercenary once told me of the road."

He clapped his heels against the charger's flanks, and the steed bounded forward. In a moment the ridge had hidden them from the men of Cyaxares. So the two penetrated deeper and deeper into the craggy, desolate wilderness, a place haunted by wolves and great bears and, men whispered, monstrous, snake-like cockadrills.

They went by snow-peaked mountains that lifted white cones to the blue sky, and they fled along the brink of deep gorges from which the low thunder of cataracts rose tumultuously. And always behind them rode the pursuers, a grim and warlike company, following slowly but relentlessly.

But Raynor used more than one stratagem. Thrice he guided his charger up streams along which the wise animal picked its way carefully; again he dislodged an avalanche to block the trail. So it came about that when the two rode down into a great, grassy basin, the men of Cyaxares were far behind.

On all sides the mountains rose. Ahead was a broad, meadow-like valley, strewn with thickets and green groves.

Far ahead the precipice rose in a tall rampart, split in one place into a narrow canyon.

To the right of the gorge lifted a great gray rock, mountain-huge, bare save for a winding trail that twisted up its surface to a castle upon the summit. Dwarfed by distance, the size of the huge structure could yet be appreciated—a castle of stone, incongruously bedecked with fluttering, bright banners and pennons.

Raynor pointed. "He dwells there. The Reaver of the Rock."

"And here comes danger," Eblik said, whipping out his battle-ax. "Look!"

From a grove of nearby trees burst a company of horsemen, glittering in the afternoon sunlight, spears lifted, casques and helms agleam. Shouting, they rode down upon the waiting pair. Raynor fingered his sword-hilt, hesitating.

"Put up your blade," he directed Eblik. "We come in friendship here."

The Nubian was doubtful. "But do *they* know that?"

Nevertheless he sheathed his sword and waited till the dozen riders reined in a few paces away. One spurred forward, a tall man astride a wiry black.

"Are you tired of life, that you seek the Reaver's stronghold?" he demanded. "Or do you mean to enter in his service?"

"We bear a message," Raynor countered. "A message from a priest of Ahmon."

"We know no gods here," the other grunted.

"Well, you know warfare, or I've misread the dents in your armor," Raynor snapped. "Sardopolis is fallen! Cyaxares has taken the city and slain the king, my father, Chalem of Sardopolis."

To his amazement a bellow of laughter burst from the troop. The spokesman said, "What has that to do with us? We own no king but the Reaver. Yet you shall come safely before him, if that is your will. It were shameful to battle a dozen to two, and the rags you wear aren't worth the taking."

Eblik started like a ruffled peacock. "By the gods, you have little courtesy here! For a coin I'd slit your weasand!"

The other rubbed his throat reflectively, grinning. "You may have a trial at that later, if you wish, my ragged gargoyle. But come, now, for the Reaver is in hall, and tonight he rides forth on a raid."

With a nod Raynor spurred his horse forward, the Nubian at his side, and, surrounded by the men of the Reaver, they fled across the valley to the castle. Thence they mounted the steep, dangerous path up the craggy ramp, till at last they crossed a drawbridge and dismounted in a courtyard.

So they took Raynor before the Reaver of the Rock.

A great, shining, red-cheeked man he was, with grizzled gray beard and a crown set rakishly askew on tangled locks. He sat before a blazing fire in a high-roofed stone hall, an iron chest open at his feet. From this he was taking jewels and golden chains and ornaments that might have graced a king's treasury, examining them carefully, and making notes with a quill pen upon a parchment on his lap.

He looked up; merry eyes dwelt on Raynor's flushed face and tousled yellow hair.

"Well, Samar, what is it now?"

"Two strangers. They have a message for you—or so they say."

Suddenly the Reaver's face changed. He leaned forward, spilling treasure from his lap. "A message? Now there is only one message that can ever come to me . . . speak, you! Who sent you?"

Raynor stepped forward confidently. From his belt he drew the broken shard of marble, and extended it.

"A priest of Ahmon bade me give you this," he said. "Sardopolis is fallen."

For a heartbeat there was silence. Then the Reaver took the shard, examining it carefully. He murmured, "Aye. So my rule passes. For long and long my fathers held the Rock, waiting for the summons that never came. And now it has come."

He looked up. "Go, all of you, save you two. And you, Samar—wait, for you should know of this."

The others departed. The Reaver shouted after them, "Summon Delphia!"

He turned to stare into the fire. "So I, Kialeh, must fulfill the ancient pledge of my ancestors. And invaders are on my marches. Well—"

There came an interruption. A girl strode in, dark head proudly erect, slim figure corseted in dinted armor. She went to the Reaver, flung a blazing jewel in his lap.

"Is this my guerdon?" she snarled. "Faith o' the gods, I took Ossan's castle almost single-handed. And my share is less than the share of Samar here!"

"You are my daughter," the Reaver said quietly. "Shall I give you more honor, then, in our free brotherhood? Be silent. Listen."

Raynor was examining the girl's face with approval. There was beauty there, wild dark lawless beauty, and strength that showed in the firm set of the jaw and the latent fire of the jet eyes. Ebony hair, unbound, fell in ringlets about steel-corseleted shoulders.

The girl said, "Well? Have you had your fill of staring?"

"Let be," the Reaver grunted. "I have a tale for all of you . . . listen."

His deep voice grew stronger. "Ages on ages ago this was a barbarous land. The people worshipped a forest-god called"—his hand moved in a queer quick sign—"called Pan. Then from the north came two kings, brothers, bringing with them the power of the sun-god, Ahmon. There was battle in the land then, and blood and reddened steel. Yet Ahmon conquered.

"The forest-god was bound within the Valley of Silence, which lies beyond my castle. The two kings made an agreement. One was to rule Sardopolis, and the other, the younger, was to rear a great castle at the gateway of the Valley of Silence, and guard the fettered god. Until a certain word should come. . . ."

The Reaver weighed a glittering stone in his hand. "For

there was a prophecy that one day the rule of Ahmon should be broken. Then it was foretold that the forest-god should be freed, and should bring vengeance upon the destroyers of Sardopolis. For long and long my ancestors have guarded the Rock—and I, Kialeh, am the last. Ah," he sighed. "The great days are over indeed. Never again will the Reaver ride to rob and plunder and mock at gods. Never—what's this?"

A man-at-arms had burst into the hall, eyes alight, face fierce as a wolf's. "Kialeh! An army is in the valley!"

"By Shaitan!" Raynor cursed. "Cyaxares' men! They pursued us—"

The girl, Delphia, swung about. "Gather the men! I'll take command—"

Suddenly the Reaver let out a roaring shout. "No! By all the gods I've flouted—*no*! Would you grudge me my last battle, girl? Gather your men, Samar—but *I* command!"

Samar sprang to obey. Delphia gripped her father's arm. "I fight *with* you, then."

"I have another task for you. Guide these two through the Valley of Silence, to the place you know. Here—" He thrust the marble shard at the prince. "Take this. You'll know how to use it when the time comes."

Then he was gone, and curtains of black samite swayed into place behind him.

Raynor was curiously eyeing the girl. Her face was pale beneath its tan, and her eyes betrayed fear. Red battle she could face unflinchingly, but the thought of entering the Valley of Silence meant to her something far more terrible. Yet she said, "Come. We have little time."

Eblik followed Raynor and Delphia from the hall. They went through the harsh splendor of the castle, till at last the girl halted before a blank stone wall. She pressed a hidden spring. A section of the rock swung away, revealing the dim-lit depths of a passage.

Delphia paused on the threshold. Her dark eyes flickered over the two.

"Hold fast to your courage," she whispered—and her lips were trembling. "For now we go down into Hell. . . ."

CHAPTER IV
The Valley of Silence

Yet at first there seemed nothing terrible about the valley. They entered it from a cavern that opened on a thick forest, and, glancing around, Raynor saw tall mountainous ramparts that made the place a prison indeed. It was past sunset, yet already a full moon was rising over the eastern cliffs, outlining the Reaver's castle in black silhouette.

They entered the forest.

Moss underfoot deadened their footsteps. They walked in dim gloom, broken by moonlit traceries filtered through the leaves. And now Raynor noted the curious stillness that hung over all.

There was no sound. The noise of birds and beasts did not exist here, nor did the breath of wind rustle the silent trees. But, queerly, the prince thought, there *was* a sound whispering through the forest, a sound below the threshold of hearing, which nevertheless played on his taut nerves.

"I don't like this," Eblik said, his ugly face set and strained. His voice seemed to die away with uncanny swiftness.

"Pan is fettered here," Delphia whispered. "Yet is his power manifest. . . ."

Soundlessly they went through the soundless forest. And now Raynor realized that, slowly and imperceptibly, the shadowy whisper he had sensed was growing louder—or else his ears were becoming more attuned to it. A very dim murmur, faint and far away, which yet seemed to have within it a multitude of voices. . . .

The voices of the winds . . . the murmur of forests . . . the goblin laughter of shadowed brooks. . . .

It was louder now, and Raynor found himself thinking of all the innumerable sounds of the primeval wilderness. Bird-notes, and the call of beasts. . . .

And under all, a dim, powerful motif, beat a wordless

shrilling, a faint piping that set the prince's skin to crawling as he heard it.

"It is the tide of life," Delphia said softly. "The heart-beat of the first god. The pulse of earth."

For the first time Raynor felt something of the primal secrets of the world. Often he had walked alone in the forest, but never yet had the hidden heart of the wilderness reached fingers into his soul. He sensed a mighty and very terrible power stirring latent in the soil beneath him, a thing bound inextricably to the brain of man by the cords of the flesh which came up, by slow degrees, from the seething oceans which once rolled unchecked over a young planet. Unimaginable eons ago man had come from the earth, and the brand of his mother-world was burned deep within his soul.

Afraid, yet strangely happy, as men are sometimes happy in their dreams, the prince motioned for his companions to increase their pace.

The forest gave place to a wide clearing, with shattered white stones rearing to the sky. Broken plinths and peristyles gleamed in the moonlight. A temple had once existed here. Now all was overgrown with moss and the slow-creeping lichen.

"Here," the girl said in a low whisper. "Here. . . ."

In the center of a ring of fallen pillars they halted. Delphia pointed to a block of marble, on which a metal disk was inset. In a cuplike depression in the metal lay a broken bit of marble.

"The talisman," Delphia said. "Touch it to the other."

Silence . . . and the unearthly tide of hidden life swelling and ebbing all about them. Raynor took the amulet from his belt, stepped forward, fighting down his fear. He bent above the disk—touched marble shard to marble—

As iron to lodestone, the two fragments drew together. They coalesced into one. The jagged line of breakage faded and vanished.

Raynor held the talisman—complete, unbroken!

Now, quite suddenly, the vague murmurings mounted into a roar—gay, jubilant, triumphant! The metal disk shattered into fragments. Beneath it the prince glimpsed a small carved stone, the twin of the one beneath the temple of Ahmon.

Above the unceasing roar sounded a penetrating shrill piping.

Delphia clutched at Raynor's arm, pulled him back. Her face was chalk-white.

"The pipes!" she gasped. "Back—quickly! To see Pan is to die!"

Louder the roar mounted, and louder. In its bellow was a deep shout of alien laughter, a thunder of goblin merriment. The chuckle of the shadowed brooks was the crash of cataracts and waterfalls.

The forest stirred to a breath of gusty wind.

"Back!" the girl said urgently. "Back! We have freed Pan!"

Without conscious thought Raynor thrust the talisman into his belt, turned, and, with Delphia and Eblik beside him, fled into the moonlit shadows. Above him branches tossed in a mounting wind. The wild shrieking of the pipes grew louder.

Tide of earth life—rising to a mad paean of triumph!

The wind exulted:

"Free . . . free!"

And the unseen rivers shouted:

"Great Pan is free!"

Clattering of hoofs came from the distance. Bleating calls sounded from afar.

The girl stumbled, almost fell. Raynor gripped at her arm, pulling her upright, fighting the unreasoning terror mounting within him. The Nubian's grim face was glistening with sweat.

"Pan, Pan is free!"

"Evohé!"

The black mouth of a cavern loomed before them. At its threshold Raynor cast a glance behind him, saw all the great forest swaying and tossing. His breath coming unevenly, he turned, following his companions into the cave.

"Shaitan!" he whispered. "What demon have I loosed on the land?"

Then it was race, sprint, pound up the winding passage, up an unending flight of stone steps, through a wall that lifted at Delphia's touch—and into a castle shaking with battle. Raynor stopped short, whipping out his sword, staring at shadows flickering in the distance.

"Cyaxares' men," he said. "They've entered."

In the face of flesh-and-blood antagonists the prince was suddenly himself again. Delphia was already running down the corridor, blade out. Raynor and the Nubian followed.

They burst into the great hall. A ring of armed men surrounded a little group who were making their last stand before the hearth. Towering above the others Raynor saw the tangled locks and bristling beard of Kialeh, the Reaver, and beside him his lieutenant Samar. Corpses littered the floor.

"Ho!" roared the Reaver, as he caught sight of the newcomers. "You come in time! In time—to die with us!"

CHAPTER V
Cursed Be the City

Grim laughter touched Raynor's lips. He drove in, sheathing his sword in a brawny throat, whipped it out, steel singing. Nor were Eblik and Delphia far behind. Her blade and the Nubian's ax wreaked deadly havoc among Cyaxares' soldiers, who, not expecting attack from the rear, were confused.

The hall became filled with a milling, yelling throng, from which one soldier, a burly giant, emerged, shouting down the others.

"Cut them down! They're but three!"

Then all semblance of sanity was lost in a blaze of crimson battle, swinging brands, and huge maces that crashed down, splitting skulls and spattering gray brain-stuff. Delphia kept shoulder to shoulder with Raynor, seemingly heedless of dan-

ger, her blade flicking wasplike through the air. And the
prince guarded her as best he could, the sword weaving a
bright maze of deadly lightnings as it whirled.

The Reaver swung, and his sword crushed a helm and bit
deep into bone. He strained to tug it free—and a soldier thrust
up at his throat. Samar deflected the blade with his own
weapon, and that cost him his life. In that moment of inat-
tention a driven spear smashed through corselet and jerkin
and drank deep of the man's life-blood.

Silent, he fell.

The Reaver went beserk. Yelling, he sprang over his lieutenant's corpse and swung. For a few moments he held back
his enemies—and then someone flung a shield. Instinctively
Kialeh lifted his blade to parry.

The wolves leaped in to the kill.

Roaring, the Reaver went down, blood gushing through his
shaggy beard, staining its iron-gray with red. When Raynor
had time to look again, Kialeh lay a corpse on his own hearth,
his head amid bright jewels that had spilled from the over-
turned treasure-chest.

The three stood together now, the last of the defenders—
Raynor and Eblik and Delphia. The soldiers ringed them,
panting for their death, yet hesitating before the menace of
cold steel. None wished to be the first to die.

And, as they waited, a little silence fell. The prince heard
a sound he remembered.

Dim and far away, a low roaring drifted to his ears. And
the eerie shrilling of pipes. . . .

It grew louder. The soldiers heard it now. They glanced at
one another askance. There was something about that sound
that chilled the blood.

It swelled to a gleeful shouting, filling all the castle. A
breeze blew through the hall, tugging with elfin fingers at
sweat-moist skin. It rose to a gusty blast.

In its murmur voices whispered.

"Evohé! Evohé!"

They grew louder, mad and unchecked. They exulted.

"Pan, Pan is free!"

"Gods!" a soldier cursed. "What devil's work is this?" He swung about, sword ready.

The curtains of samite were ripped away by the shrieking wind. Deafeningly the voices exulted:

"Pan is free!"

The piping shrilled out. There came the clatter of ringing little hoofs. The castle rocked and shuddered.

Some vague, indefinable impulse made Raynor snatch at his belt, gripping the sun-god's talisman in bronzed fingers. From it a grateful warmth seemed to flow into his flesh—and the roaring faded.

He dragged Delphia and the Nubian behind him. "Close to me! Stay close!"

The room was darkening. No—it seemed as though a cloudy veil of mist dropped before the three, guarding them. Raynor lifted the seal of Ahmon.

The fog-veils swirled. Dimly through them Raynor could see the soldiers moving swiftly, frantically, like rats caught in a trap. He tightened one arm about Delphia's steel-armored waist.

Suddenly the hall was ice-cold. The castle shook as though gripped by Titan hands. The floor swayed beneath the prince's feet.

The mists darkened. Through rifts he saw half-guessed figures that leaped and bounded . . . heard elfin hoofs clicking. Horned and shaggy-furred beings that cried jubilantly as they danced to the pipes of Pan. . . .

Faun and dryad and satyr swung in a mad saraband beyond the shrouding mists. Faintly there came the screaming of men, half drowned in the loud shrilling.

"Evohé!" the demoniac rout thundered. *"Evohé! All hail, O Pan!"*

With a queer certainty Raynor knew that it was time to leave the castle—and swiftly. Already the great stone structure was shaking like a tree in a hurricane. With a word to his companions he stepped forward hesitantly, the talisman held high.

The walls of mist moved with him. Outside the fog-walls

the monstrous figures gamboled. But the soldiers of Cyaxares screamed no more.

Through a castle toppling into ruin the three sped, into the courtyard, across the drawbridge, and down the face of the Rock. Nor did they pause till they were safely in the broad plain of the valley.

"The castle!" Eblik barked, pointing. "See? It falls."

And it was true. Down it came thundering, while clouds of ruin spurted up. Then there was only a shattered wreck on the summit of the Rock. . . .

Delphia caught her breath in a little sob. She murmured, "The end of the Reavers for all time. I—I lived in the castle for more than twenty years. And now it's gone like a puff of dust before the wind."

The walls of fog had vanished. Raynor returned the talisman to his belt. Eblik, staring up at the Rock, swallowed uneasily.

"Well, what now?" he asked.

"Back along the way we came," the prince said. "It's the only way out of this wilderness that I know of."

The girl nodded. "Yes. Beyond the mountains lie deserts, save toward Sardopolis. But we have no mounts."

"Then we'll walk," Eblik observed, but Raynor caught his arm and pointed.

"There! Horses—probably stampeded from the castle. And—Shaitan! There's my gray charger. Good!"

So, presently, the three rode toward Sardopolis, conscious of a weird dim throbbing that seemed to pulse in the air all about them.

At dawn they topped a ridge and saw before them the plain. All three reined in their mounts, staring. Beneath them lay the city—but changed!

It was a ruin.

Doom had come to Sardopolis in the night. The mighty towers and battlements had fallen, and huge gaps were opened in the walls. Of the king's palace nothing was left but a single tower, from which, ironically, the wyvern banner flew. As they watched, that pinnacle, too, swayed and tottered and fell, and the scarlet wyvern drifted down into the dust of Sardopolis.

On fallen towers and peristyles distant figures moved, with odd, ungainly boundings. Quickly Raynor turned his eyes away. But he could not shut his ears to the distant crying of pipes, gay and pagan, yet with a faintly mournful undertone.

"Pan has returned to his first altar," Delphia said quietly. "We had best not loiter here."

"By all hell, I agree," the Nubian grunted, digging his heels into his steed's flanks. "Where now, Raynor?"

"Westward, I think, to the Sea of Shadows. There are cities on its shore, and galleys to take us to a haven. Unless—" He turned questioning eyes on Delphia.

She laughed, a little bitterly. "I cannot stay here. The land is sunk back into the pit. Pan rules. I go with you."

The three rode to the west. They skirted, but did not enter, a small grove where a man lay in agony. It was Cyaxares, a figure so dreadfully mangled that only sheer will kept him alive. His face was a bloody mask. The once-rich garments were tattered and filthy. He saw the three riders, and raised his voice in a weak cry which the wind drowned.

Beside the king a slim, youthful figure lounged, leaning idly against an oak-trunk. It was Necho.

"Call louder, Cyaxares," he said. "With a horse under you, you can reach the Sea of Shadows. And if you succeed in doing that, you will yet live for many years."

Again the king cried out. The wind took his voice and shredded it to impotent fragments.

Necho laughed softly. "Too late, now. They are gone."

Cyaxares let his battered head drop, his beard trailing in the dirt. Through shredded lips he muttered, "If I reach the Sea of Shadows . . . I live."

"True. But if you do not, you die. And then—" Low laughter shook the other.

Groaning, the king dragged himself forward. Necho followed.

"A good horse can reach the Sea of Shadows in three days.

If you walk swiftly, you may reach it in six. But you must hurry. Why do you not rise, my Cyaxares?''

The king spat out bitter oaths. In agony he pulled himself forward, leaving a trail of blood on the grass . . . blood that dripped unceasingly from the twin raw stumps just above his ankles.

''The stone that fell upon you was sharp, Cyaxares, was it not?'' Necho mocked. ''But hurry! You have little time. There are mountains to climb and rivers to cross. . . .''

So, in the trail of Raynor and Eblik and Delphia, crept the dying king, hearing fainter and ever fainter the triumphant pipes of Pan from Sardopolis. And presently, patient as the silent Necho, a vulture dipped against the blue and took up the pursuit, the beat of its wings distinctly audible in the heavy, stagnant silence. . . .

And Raynor and Delphia and Eblik rode onward toward the sea. . . .

The Citadel of Darkness

by Henry Kuttner

Hearken, O King, while I tell of high dooms and valorous men in the dim mists of long-passed aeons— aye, long and long ago, ere Nineveh and Tyre were born and ruled and crumbled to the dust. In the lusty youth of the world Imperial Gobi, Cradle of Mankind, was a land of beauty and of wonder and of black evil beyond imagination. And of Imperial Gobi, mistress of the Asian Seas, nothing now remains but a broken shard, a shattered stone that once crowned an obelisk— nothing is left but a thin high wailing in the wind, a crying that mourns for lost glories. Hearken again, O King, while I tell you of my vision and my dream. . . .
—The Tale of Sakhmet the Damned

CHAPTER I
The Sign of the Mirror

For six hours the archer had lain dying in the great oak's shadow. The attackers had not troubled to strip him of his battered armor—poor stuff compared to their own forged mail, glittering with brilliant gems. They had ridden off with their loot, leaving the wounded archer among the corpses of his companions. He had lost much blood, and now, staring into the afternoon dimness of the forest, he knew death was coming swiftly.

Parched lips gaped as the man gasped for breath. Once more he tried to crawl to where a goatskin canteen lay upon the glossy, motionless flank of a fallen war-horse. And again he failed. Sighing, he relaxed, his fevered cheek against the cool earth.

Faintly a sound came to the archer's ears—the drumming of hoofs. Were the raiders returning? One hand gripped the bow that lay beside him; weakly he strove to fit an arrow to the string.

Two horses cantered into view—a great gray charger and a dun mare. On the latter rode a tall, huge-muscled black man, his gargoylish face worried and anxious.

The gray's rider seemed small beside the Nubian, but his strong frame was unwearied by hours in the saddle. Under yellow, tousled hair was a hard young face, bronzed and eagle-eyed. He saw the shambles beneath the oak, reined in his steed.

"By Shaitan!" he snapped. "What devil's work is this?"

The dying man's fingers let the bow fall.

"Prince Raynor—water!" he gasped.

Raynor leaped to the ground, snatched a goatskin, and held it to the archer's lips.

"What's happened?" he asked presently. "Where's Delphia?"

"They—they took her."

"Who?"

"A band of warriors took us by surprise. We were ambushed. We fought, but—they were many. I saw them ride south with Delphia."

The archer of a sudden looked oddly astonished. His hand reached out and gripped the bow that lay beside him.

"Death comes," he whispered, and a shudder racked him. His jaw fell; he lay dead.

Raynor stood up, a hard, cold anger in his eyes. He glanced up at the Nubian, who had not dismounted.

"We also ride south," he said shortly. "It was a pity we fell behind, Eblik."

"I don't think so," Eblik observed. "It was an act of providence that your horse should go lame yesterday. Had we been trapped with the others, we'd have died also."

Raynor fingered his sword-hilt. "Perhaps not. At any rate, we'll have our chance to cross blades with these marauding dogs."

"So? I think—"

"Obey!" Raynor snapped, and vaulted to the saddle. He set spurs to the horse's flanks, galloped past the heap of bodies beneath the oak. "Here's a trail. And it leads south."

Grunting his disapproval, the Nubian followed.

"You may have been Prince of Sardopolis," he muttered, "but Sardopolis has fallen."

That was true. They were many days' journey from the kingdom where Raynor had been born, and which was no longer a home for him. Three people had fled from doomed Sardopolis—Raynor, his servant Eblik, and the girl Delphia—and in their flight they had been joined by a few other refugees.

And now the last of the latter had been slain, here in unknown country near the Sea of Shadows that lay like a shining sapphire in Imperial Gobi. When Raynor's horse had gone lame the day before, he and Eblik had fallen behind for an hour that stretched into a far longer period—and now the archers were slain and Delphia herself a captive.

The two rode swiftly; yet when night fell they were still within the great forest that had loomed above them for days. Raynor paused in a little clearing.

"We'll wait here till moonrise," he said. "It's black as the pit now."

Dismounting, the prince stretched weary muscles. Eblik followed his example. There was a brook nearby, and he found water for the horses. That done, he squatted on his haunches, a grim black figure in the darkness.

"The stars are out," he said at last, in a muffled tone.

Raynor, his back against a tree-trunk, glanced up. "So they are. But it's not moonrise yet."

The Nubian went on as though he had not heard. "These are strange stars. I've never seen them look thus before."

"Eh?" The young prince stared. Against the jet curtain of night the stars glittered frostily, infinitely far away. "They look the same as always, Eblik."

But—did they? A little chill crept down Raynor's spine. Something cold and indefinably horrible seemed to reach down from the vast abyss of the sky—a breath of the unknown that brooded over this primeval wilderness.

The same stars—yes! But why, in this strange land, were the stars dreadful?

"You're a fool, Eblik," Raynor said shortly. "See to the horses."

The Nubian shivered and stood up.

"I wish we had never come into this black land," he murmured, in an oddly subdued voice. "It is cold here—too cold for midsummer."

A low whisper came out of the dark.

"Aye, it is cold. The gaze of the Basilisk chills you."

"Who's that?" Raynor snarled. He whirled, his sword bare in his hand. Eblik crouched, great hands flexing.

Quiet laughter sounded. A shadow stepped from behind an oak trunk. A giant figure moved forward, indistinct in the gloom.

"A friend. Or at least, no enemy. Put up your blade, man. I have no quarrel with you."

"No?" Raynor growled. "Then why slink like a wolf in the dark?"

"I heard the noise of battle. I heard strange footsteps in the forest of Mirak. These called me forth."

A glimmer of wan, silvery light crept through the trees. The moon was rising. Its glow touched a great billow of white hair; shaggy, tufted eyebrows, a beard that rippled down upon the newcomer's breast. Little of the man's face could be seen. An aquiline beak of a nose jutted out, and somber dark eyes dwelt on Raynor. A coarse gray robe and sandals covered the frame of a giant.

"Who are you?"

"Ghiar, they call me."

"What talk is this of a—Basilisk?" Eblik asked softly.

"Few can read the stars," Ghiar said. "Yet those who can know the Dwellers in the Zodiac. Last night the sign of the Archer was eclipsed by the Fish of Ea. And this night the Basilisk is in the ascendancy." The deep voice grew deeper still; organ-powerful it rolled through the dark aisles of the forest. "Seven signs hath the Zodiac! The Sign of the Archer and the Sign of the Fish of Ea! The Sign of the Serpent and that of the Mirror! The Basilisk, and the Black Flower—and the Sign of Tammuz which may not be drawn. Seven signs— and the Basilisk rules tonight."

Meeting the brooding stare of those dark eyes, Raynor felt a nameless sense of unease.

"My business is not with the stars," half-angrily he said. "I seek men, not mirrors and serpents."

The tufted eyebrows lifted.

"Yet the stars may aid you, stranger, as they have aided me," Ghiar rumbled. "As they have told me, for example, of a captive maid in Malric's castle."

Raynor tensed. "Eh?"

"Baron Malric rules these marshes. His men captured your wench, and she is his prisoner now."

"How do you know this?" Raynor snapped.

"Does that matter? I have certain powers—powers which may aid you, if you wish."

"This is sorcery, Prince," Eblik muttered. "Best run your blade through his hairy gullet."

Raynor hesitated, as though almost minded to obey. Ghiar shrugged.

"Malric's castle is a strong one; his followers are many. You alone cannot save the girl. Let me aid you."

Raynor's laugh was hotly scornful. "You aid me, old man? How?"

"Old? Aye, I am older than you think. Yet these oaks, too, are ancient, and they are strong with age. Let me tell you a secret. Malric fears the stars. He was born under the Sign of the Fish of Ea, which serves the Sign of the Black Flower. I, too, was born under the Sign of the Fish of Ea, but to me has been given power to rule, not to serve. The baron knows my power, and in my name you may free the girl."

Eblik broke in. "What would you gain by this?"

For a moment Ghiar was silent. The cold wind ruffled his white beard and tugged at his gray robe.

"What would I gain? Perhaps vengeance. Perhaps Baron Malric is my enemy. What does that matter to you? If I give you my aid, that should be enough."

"True," Raynor said. "Though this smacks of sorcery to me. However"—he shrugged—"Shaitan knows we need help, if Malric be as strong as you say."

"Good!" Ghiar's somber eyes gleamed with satisfaction. He fumbled in his robe, brought out a small glittering object. "This amulet will be your weapon."

Raynor took the thing and scrutinized it with interest. The amulet was perhaps as large as his palm, a disc of silvery metal on which figures were graven clockwise.

Six signs the amulet bore.

An arrow and a fish; a serpent and a circle; a flower and a tiny dragon-like creature with a long tail and a row of spines on its back.

In the amulet's center was a jewel—cloudy black, with a gleaming star-point in its tenebrous heart.

"The Sign of Tammuz," whispered Ghiar. "Which may not be drawn! Yet by the star in the black opal ye may know him, Tammuz, Lord of the Zodiac!"

Raynor turned the object in his hand. On the amulet's back was a mirror-disc.

Ghiar said warningly, "Do not look too long in the steel. Through the Sign of the Mirror the power of the Basilisk is made manifest, and you may need that power. Show Malric the talisman. Order him, in my name, to free the girl. If he obeys, well. If he refuses"—the deep voice sank to an ominous whisper—"if he refuses, turn the amulet. Let him gaze into the Sign of the Mirror!"

Ghiar's hand lifted; he pointed south. "There is your road. The moon is up. Ride south!"

Raynor grunted, turned to his horse. Silently he vaulted to the saddle and turned the steed's head into the trail. Eblik was not far behind.

Once Raynor turned to look over his shoulder. Ghiar was still standing in the clearing, his shaggy head lifted, motionless as an image.

The warlock stared up at the stars.

CHAPTER II
The Sign of the Basilisk

So Eblik and Prince Raynor came to the outlaw's castle, a great gray pile of stone towering above the gloomy forest. They came out of the woods and stood silent for a time, looking across a broad grassy meadow, beyond which the castle brooded like a crouching beast. Red flame of lamps and flambeaux glittered from the mullioned windows. In the gateway light glistened on armor.

"Follow!" Raynor snapped, and spurred forward.

Across the sward they fled, and before the nodding guardsman had sprung to alertness, two muscular figures were almost upon him. Bearded lips opened in a shout that died unuttered. Gleaming steel thrust through a bare throat, slipped free, stained crimson. Choking on his own blood, the guard clawed at the gate and fell slowly, face down, to lie motionless in the moonlight.

"One guard," Raynor murmured. "Baron Malric fears few enemies, it seems. Well, that will make our task the easier. Come."

They went through the flagged courtyard and entered the castle itself. A bare sentry-room of stone, with a great oak door in the far wall—a room stacked with weapons, sword and mace and iron war-hook. Raynor hesitated, and then slipped quietly to the door. It was not barred. He pushed it gently open and peered through the crack. Eblik saw his master's figure go tense.

Raynor looked upon the castle's great hall. High-ceilinged it stretched up to oak rafters, blackened with smoke, that criss-crossed like a spider's web far above. The room itself was vast. Rich furs and rugs covered the floor; a long T-shaped table stretched almost from wall to wall. Around it, laughing and shouting in vinous mirth as they fed, were the men of Malric, his outlaw band.

Bearded men, wolf-fierce, gnawing on mutton-bones and swilling from great mugs of heady spiced liquor. At the head of the board, on an ornate throne, sat the baron himself—and he was truly a strange man to lord it over these lawless savages.

For Malric was slim and dark and smiling, with a gaily youthful face, and long hair that fell loosely about his slim shoulders. He wore a simple brown tunic, with loose, baggy sleeves, and his hands were busy twirling a gilded, filigreed chalice. He looked up as two burly outlaws entered, half dragging the slim form of a girl.

It was Delphia. She still wore her dinted armor, and her ebony hair, unbound, fell in ringlets about her pale face. There was beauty in that face, wild and lawless beauty, and fire and strength in the jet eyes. She straightened and glared at Malric.

"Well?" she snapped. "What new insult is this?"

"Insult?" the baron questioned, his voice calm and soft. "I intend none. Will you eat with us?" He motioned to a chair that stood vacant beside him.

"I'd sooner eat with wild dogs," Delphia declared.

And at her words a low, ominous growl rose from the outlaws. One man, a burly fellow with a cast in one eye and a white scar disfiguring his cheek, leaped up and hurried to the girl's side. There he turned to face Malric.

"Have I given you leave to rise, Gunther?" the baron asked gently.

For answer the other growled an oath. "By Shaitan!" he snarled. "You've kept me waiting long enough, Malric. This wench is my own. I captured her, and I'll have her. If she eats with us, she sits beside me!"

"So?" Malric's voice did not change. Ironic laughter gleamed in the dark eyes. "Perhaps you grow tired of my rule, Gunther. Perhaps you wish to sit in my throne, eh?"

The outlaws watched, waiting. A hush hung over the long table. Involuntarily Raynor's hand crept to his swordhilt. He sensed death in the air.

Perhaps Gunther sensed it too. The white scar on his cheek grew livid. He roared an inarticulate oath and whipped out a great blade. Bellowing, he sprang at Malric. The sword screamed through the air.

The baron scarcely seemed to move, so swift was his rising. Yet suddenly he stood facing Gunther, and his slim hand dipped into his loose sleeve and came out with the light glittering on bright metal.

Swift as a snake's striking was Malric's cast. And a lean knife shot through the air and found its mark unerringly. Through eye and thin shell of bone and into soft, living brain it sped. Gunther screamed hoarsely once and his sword missed its target, digging instead into the wood of the table.

The outlaw's body bent back like a drawn bow. Gunther clawed at his face, his nails ripping away skin and flesh in a death agony.

And he fell, his mail ringing and clashing, to lie silent at Malric's feet.

The baron seated himself, sighing. Once more his fingers toyed with the gilded chalice. Seemingly he ignored the shout of approbation that thundered up from the outlaws.

But after a moment he glanced up at Delphia. He gestured, and the two guards dragged her forward.

Watching at the door, Raynor decided that it was time to act. Madness, perhaps, walking into a den of armed enemies. But the prince had changed his opinion. He had developed a queer, inexplicable confidence in Ghiar's talisman. He found the disc in his belt, cupped it in his palm, and with a word to Eblik kicked open the door and stepped into the hall.

Ten steps he took before he was discovered. Ten steps, with the Nubian at his heels, great battle-ax ready.

Then the wolves saw him and sprang up, shouting.

Simultaneously Malric called an order. His voice penetrated knife-keen through the tumult, and silence fell. The baron sat motionless, a little frown between his eyes, watching the two interlopers.

"Well?" he demanded. "Who are you?" And he cast a swift glance at Delphia, whose slight start had been betraying.

"My name matters little," Raynor said. "I bring you a message from a certain Ghiar."

"Ghiar!"

A repressed whisper shuddered through the outlaws. There was fear in it, and bitter hatred.

"What is the message?" Malric demanded.

"That you free this girl."

The baron's youthful face was bland.

"Is that all?" he asked.

Raynor was conscious of a feeling of disappointment. He had expected some other reaction—what, he did not know. But Malric's calm passivity baffled him.

The baron waited. When no answer came, he made a quick gesture. And up from the board leaped armed men, shouting, blades bared. They poured down upon Raynor and on Eblik crouching behind him, gargoyle face twisted in battle lust.

So this was what came of warlocks' promises! Raynor grinned bitterly, whipped out his sword—and remembered the talisman. What had Ghiar said?

"If he refuses, turn the amulet. Let him gaze into the Sign of the Mirror!"

The foremost man was almost upon him as Raynor flung up his hand, the talisman cupped within it. From the mirror darted a ray of light—needle-thin, blindingly brilliant.

It struck full in the outlaw's face. It probed deep—deep!

Instantly a mask of stark, frightful horror replaced the look of savagery. The man halted, stood frozen and motionless as a statue, his eyes like those of a tortured animal.

Like a soundless whisper in Raynor's brain came the memory of the Ghiar's words:

"The gaze of the Basilisk chills you. . . ."

And now from the mirror in the talisman pale bright rays were streaming, cold as white fires, unearthly as the arrows of the fabled Moon-goddess. And like arrows, too, they flamed swiftly through the air, seeking and finding their marks; and one by one Malric's men stiffened and stood frozen.

The last was the baron himself. And then the fires of the talisman died and were gone.

"Delphia!" Raynor cried. The girl was already running toward him, down the length of the hall.

"This is sorcery, Prince," Eblik said. "And it is evil!"

"It aids us, at least," Raynor flung at him, and then turned to meet the girl.

And halted—staring.

A sudden, icy chill had dropped down upon the great hall. The lamps dimmed swiftly and faded into utter darkness.

Through the midnight black Raynor heard Delphia scream. He sprang forward, cursing.

His foot struck a prostrate body. He bent, and searching fingers found a man's bearded chin.

"Delphia!" he shouted.

"Raynor!" she called and her voice seemed to fade and dwindle as though from infinite distances. "Raynor! Help me!"

The prince's sword screamed through the dark. He stumbled forward blindly, seeking to penetrate the jet blackness, and quite suddenly one hand gripped hard, leathery flesh.

He heard an angry voice.

"Thou meddling fool! You dare to lift steel against the Lord of the Zodiac?"

The voice of—Ghiar! Ghiar, the warlock, come now to Malric's castle by some evil sorcery.

"Lift steel?" Raynor questioned furiously. "I'll give you a taste of it, skulking wizard!"

He thrust strongly just as Ghiar pulled free. A pain-filled screech rang out.

But Raynor had lost the wizard in the darkness, and he pushed forward hurriedly, before the oldster could escape.

"Thou fool!" Ghiar's voice whispered, cold with bitter menace. "Blind, rash fool!"

Raynor, groping in the dark, paused suddenly. A strange, greenish glow was beginning to pervade the hall. But its eerie light gave no illumination. Rather, it served only to reveal the source from which it sprang.

A gross and hideous bulk, scaled and shining, loomed above the man. It was shaped like a dragon, and Raynor suddenly remembered the symbol that he had seen on the talisman.

The Sign of the Basilisk!

Only instinct saved the prince then.

He knew, with a dreadful certainty, that to meet the dreadful gaze of the horror would mean death. And before he had time to catch but a flashing glimpse of the Basilisk, Raynor whirled, both hands lifted to his eyes. Through them, darting into the secret fortress of his mind, an icy chill had leaped suddenly—a cold beyond cold, a horror beyond life.

Four strides he took, blinded, his head throbbing with agony. Something soft and heavy caught his foot, and Raynor stumbled and crashed down upon the stones. The world went out in a blanket of merciful oblivion.

CHAPTER III
The Sign of the Black Flower

Raynor awoke suddenly. Sunlight was slanting down through the high oaks, and a gruff voice was cursing steadily in several outlandish dialects of Gobi. The prince realized that he was being carried on someone's back, and recognized the deep voice as Eblik's.

He wriggled free, dropped to the ground, and the Nubian turned swiftly, his ugly face twisted with delight.

"Shaitan!" he growled. "The gods be praised! So you're alive, eh?"

"Just about," Raynor said wryly. "What's happened?"

"How should I know? When the lights went out back in Malric's castle, I blundered out of the hall in the dark, and when I got back Delphia was gone and you were lying on your face with a bump as large as World-Mountain on your head. So I picked you up and headed east."

"Why east?" Raynor asked. "You have my thanks, but it might have been better to have remained in the castle. Delphia—"

"She's to the east," Eblik grunted. "At least, our best chance is to go in that direction. I picked up one of Malric's men and brought him with us. He woke up an hour ago, and I choked some information from the dog. Ghiar has a citadel in Mirak Forest, in that direction." He nodded toward the rising sun. "You were cursing the warlock in your sleep, so I guessed a little of what had happened. What now?"

"We go to Ghiar's citadel," Raynor decided. "You did well, Eblik." Swiftly he explained what had happened. "Where are our horses?"

"Shaitan knows. They took fright and ran off. It isn't far, however."

"So? Well, I'm beginning to understand now, Eblik. Ghiar used me as a cat's-paw. Though just how I still cannot understand."

Raynor pondered. No doubt Ghiar had abducted the girl,

but why had not the warlock stolen her by means of his magic, without seeking Raynor's aid? Could it be that the wizard had been unable to enter Malric's castle until someone had opened a gateway for him?

The prince had heard of such beings—creatures that could not enter a house unless they were lifted across the threshold, alien things that could never cross running water. Perhaps the amulet itself had given Ghiar power to materialize in the castle.

Reminded of the talisman, Raynor fumbled in his belt and found the disc there. He examined it with renewed curiosity. In the black jewel the star-point glowed with pale brilliance.

"Well, we go east, then," Raynor decided. "Come."

Without further words he set off at a steady, effortless lope that ate up the miles. The giant Nubian paced him easily, swinging his great ax as though in anticipation.

The oak forest stretched far and far, beyond their horizon. Overhead the sun grew hotter, pouring down its rays that would still be blasting upon Gobi when the empire would be not even a memory in the minds of men. But at last, hours later, the trees thinned and the two men found themselves at the top of a long slope that stretched down to the dark waters of a lake.

In the lake's center was an islet. And on the islet—Ghiar's citadel.

A citadel of darkness! Blacker than the nighted gulf of Abaddon was the great block of shining stone that towered up to the sky, a single, gigantic, polished oblong of jet, with neither tower nor window to break its grim monotony. No bridge spanned the lake.

The waters were steel-gray; frigid as polar seas they seemed.

On the islet, about the citadel, the ground was carpeted with darkness. The nature of this shadowy stain was a riddle; it was not stone, for now and again a long ripple would shudder across it as the wind sighed past.

The citadel lay in the shelter of a valley, and over all seemed to hang a slumbrous, eerie quiet. No sound stirred, save for the wind's occasional murmuring. And even that was oddly hushed.

Thus might sleep the fabled Elysian Fields, where the dead who have tasted Lethe wander to and fro, with a half-incurious yearning for lost delights, amid the eternal hush of the shadowland.

With a little shiver Raynor shook off the spell. He strode forward, the Nubian at his side. Eblik said nothing, but his keen barbaric senses guessed that sorcery dwelt in this valley. The black's eyes were distended; his nostrils twitched as though seeking to scent something that dwelt beyond the threshold of his realization.

As the two went down the slope a dim, unreal perfume seemed to rise and drift about them, an odor sensed rather than actually scented. And a drowsy languor made Raynor's eyes heavy.

Truly dark magic guarded Ghiar's citadel!

They reached the lake's shore. They circled swiftly, and discovered there was no means of crossing to the islet.

"Short of building a raft," Raynor observed, "which would take too long, I see nothing to it but a swim."

"Aye," Eblik assented, readily enough, but his somber eyes dwelt on the motionless gray waters. "Yet it would be well to have our blades ready, Prince."

A dagger hung at Raynor's side; he unsheathed this and gripped it between his teeth.

Without a word he dived into the lake, came up yards away, swimming strongly.

And the water was cold—cold! Frigid beyond anything Raynor had ever known.

The dreadful chill of it lanced deep into his bones, making them grind together with the sheer pain of the unearthly cold.

Looking down, he found that the water was opaque. A uniform dull grayness made it seem as though he was floating on clouds. What mystery might lurk in these hidden depths he could not guess; but at least nothing rose to halt his progress.

The lake was not wide; yet Raynor was curiously exhausted when at last he waded through shallows and on to dry land. Eblik was not far behind. Now, not far away, Ghiar's citadel rose blackly cryptic before them.

And at their feet were—the Black Flowers!

The ground could not be seen, so thickly they grew. A living carpet of velvety darkness, they covered the islet, weirdly beautiful, with stems and leaves and soft petals all of the same glossy black.

Ever and anon a soft wind whispered past, and waves rippled across the jet sea.

Save for the wind, it was utterly silent.

The two men moved forward. The flowers brushed against their ankles, and a soft cloud of disturbed pollen hung like smoke in their wake. And ever the insidious perfume crept into their nostrils—stronger now, vaguely repellent, and redolent of unknown and forbidden things.

His gaze riveted on the citadel, Raynor did not at first realize that he was making little progress. Then he glanced down quickly, or tried to. But his muscles seemed to respond with unwillingness, and it was with a genuine effort that he succeeded in looking down. The black flowers seemed to be swaying toward him; around his feet the smoky darkness hung.

The dim haze fingered up, questing!

Raynor tried to spring forward. His feet kicked up a great cloud of pollen, and it shrouded him like a pall.

He was unconscious of the fact that he had halted and was swaying to and fro, slowly.

Over his vision a dim curtain dropped.

He seemed to fall very slowly.

The black flowers leaned toward him hungrily. A velvet blossom brushed his cheek; another seemed to cup his mouth as though in dreadful simulacrum of a kiss. Raynor breathed the dark perfume of the flower's heart. . . .

Of a sudden veils were lifted, and he saw unimaginable things. A blaze of sound and light and color swirled into being. Trumpets shrilled in his ears, and he heard the thunder of high walls crumbling to ruin. Confused visions of the past came to Raynor, and he lived again, dimly as in a dream, things he remembered and things he had forgotten.

And always the strange, deadly perfume was strong in his nostrils; but he felt no urge to move. The soporific spell of the Lethean flowers held him bound in fetters of dark magic.

It was pleasant to lie here, to rest, and to remember.

Then a rough hand gripped Raynor's arm; he was lifted, and immediately fell again heavily. From an immense distance came a harsh, despairing cry.

The voice of Eblik!

The sound pierced through the mists that shrouded Prince Raynor's brain. The Nubian was in danger, had cried to his master for help. Realization of this gave the prince strength as he battled down the terrible urge to remain motionless, to sleep, and at last Raynor won. The effort left him sweating and exhausted, but abruptly the visions faded and were gone.

He looked upon Ghiar's citadel, and the haunted islet in the lake.

With a sobbing curse he staggered upright. At his feet lay the unconscious Nubian, and Raynor lifted the black to his shoulders. Then, holding his breath, he plunged forward across the dark sea, even at that moment of mad turmoil feeling an odd sense of sadness at the thought of the jet, velvety beauty he crushed underfoot.

A wind rippled the blooms; they seemed to sigh as in farewell.

The Sign of the Black Flower was conquered!

CHAPTER IV
The Sign of the Serpent

Now Ghiar's citadel loomed above them. Grimly enigmatic it towered there featureless, with no gate or window breaking the dull monotony of its gloomy structure. Sick and dizzy, Raynor plunged on. And, quite suddenly, he realized that he had been wrong. A portal gaped in the high wall just before him.

Had it previously escaped his searching gaze? Perhaps; it was more probable that a hidden door had slid silently aside to admit the interlopers. It was not a comforting thought, for it meant that eyes were invisibly watching Raynor—eyes of the warlock Ghiar.

Nevertheless, the prince sprang over the threshold. Instantly the portal shut behind him. With little hope Raynor turned and attempted to reopen the door, but he failed.

Even if he had succeeded, what then? His path lay into the heart of the citadel. And a dimly lighted passageway stretched slanting down before him. Smiling grimly, Raynor moved on, carrying the unconscious Eblik, who now, however, began to stir and twitch feebly.

In a moment the giant Nubian had regained his senses. With one cat-like movement he leaped free, the huge war-ax gripped in his hand. Then, seeing no enemy, he relaxed, grinning somewhat feebly at Raynor.

"We're in the citadel?" he asked. "Shaitan, there's magic in those damned flowers. Sorcery of the pit!"

"Keep your voice down," Raynor said. "Ghiar may have ways of hearing us, and watching us too. But we can't turn back now, and anyway I want to try my sword on Ghiar's ugly neck."

"I'm curious to see if necromancy will armor him against this," said Eblik, with a flash of white teeth, and the ax cleft the air in a deadly blow. The Nubian handled the heavy weapon as though it were light as a javelin.

Warily the two continued along the corridor. The dim light came from no discernible source; it seemed to gleam faintly from the air all about them. The walls and roof and floor were of the same dark stone.

The passage dipped, widened. The two men came out on a little ledge overhanging an abyss. At their feet was a gulf, dropping straight down to a milky, luminous shining far beneath. Nor was it water that lay at the pit's bottom, though it was certainly liquid. It glowed with a wan, eerie light that reflected palely upon the black room arching above.

Here the corridor broadened into a circular cavern. A bridge spanned the abyss. It arched from the ledge's lip, straight and unbroken as Bifrost Bridge that Norsemen say reaches to Valhalla's gate. It stretched to a black wall of rock and ended beneath an arched opening in the stone.

"Our path lies there," Raynor said grimly. "Pray to your Nubian gods, Eblik!"

The prince stepped forward upon the perilous bridge.

It was narrow, terribly so. Giddy vertigo clutched at the man's brain, impelling him to look down. He fought against the dangerous impulse, kept his eyes steadily upon his goal. He felt Eblik's hand grip his shoulder, heard the Nubian gasp:

"It draws me! Guide me, Prince—I dare not keep my eyes open."

"Hold fast," Raynor said between clenched teeth. Yet he looked down. He could not help it.

Nausea clutched him. Far below, in the milky slime, dark bodies moved slowly, writhing and squirming in the dimness. What they were Raynor could not tell, but the creatures had a sickeningly human aspect, despite their ambiguous outlines. A blind deformed face stared up; a shocking muzzle gaped; but no sound came.

The things squirmed and flopped their way through the pale liquid, and Raynor knew that his hasty glance down had been an error. He felt stronger than ever the weird compulsion that seemed to tug at him, drawing him, overbalancing him so that he swayed perilously on the giddy bridge.

With a grinding effort he looked again at the bridge's end. Through some secret reservoir of mind he drew strength and will. He stepped forward, slowly, carefully. But he could not banish the thought of the horrors that dwelt below.

Yet at last the two men reached their goal. Sweating and gasping, they stepped to solid footing. And before them the portal in the rock opened enigmatically.

"God!" Eblik groaned. "Must we cross that hell-bridge on our return? If we do return."

But Raynor had crossed the threshold, and was standing silent before the Snake.

He was in a small cave, high-roofed, dimly lit, and containing nothing but a crude throne of rock directly facing him. On the throne sat a thing that bore a vague resemblance to a man. Staring at it, Raynor was reminded of the creatures he had just seen in the abyss.

Black and hideous and deformed it towered there, a pulpy shapeless thing of darkness, less human than a crudely chiseled idol. The head was worst of all. It was flattened, snakelike, with bulging dull eyes that stared blindly. The lower part of the face was elongated into a muzzle, and the creature was entirely covered with scales.

It sat there motionless, and bound about its brow like a dreadful crown was a snake. Its flattened head was lifted as in the uraeus crown of the Pharaohs, and its wise, ancient gaze dwelt coldly upon Raynor.

He had never seen anything as lovely and as horrible as this serpent.

The scintillant colors in its body flickered, changed, fading as smoke fades from red to violet, emerald green, shining topaz, sun-yellow, all in an intricate design that also shifted and moved strangely. The blinding beauty of the snake struck through Raynor like a sword.

Its eyes held him.

Very horrible were those eyes, alien beyond all imagining. Their gaze was at first tender, almost caressing, like that of a well loved maiden. Strange magic reached out to grip the man.

The eyes of the snake probed into his soul. He felt nothing, heard nothing, saw nothing but the flood of alien sorcery pouring into his mind from the incredibly ancient eyes of the serpent.

He was unconscious of the fact that Eblik had halted behind him, motionless, paralyzed.

And those passionless bright eyes were not evil—no! They were older than evil; beyond it, above it, as a god is above human motives and ideals.

They spoke of a wisdom beyond earthly understanding.

They erased all else from Raynor's consciousness.

The cords that bound him to this earth, the human ties, slipped away slowly. He had not lost his memories of warm hearths, of laughing, fire-lit faces, of sword-play and of the mad high excitement of war. He remembered these things, with a distant, diamond-sharp clarity; but they had lost their significance.

They were unimportant.

They would pass, and be enveloped in the shadow of the ultimate night, and, in the end, they would not matter.

He remembered Eblik the Nubian, the pale proud face of Delphia rose up before him; but he felt no warmth of human kinship or understanding.

All these things were slipping away from him, in a clear, cold wisdom that came from beyond the stars. He envisioned man as a bit of animate clay moving for a little while upon a ball of mud and stone and water that drifted through the void, through the darkness that would finally engulf it.

So the Snake, that ancient one, gave to Raynor its vision. And the serpent uncoiled from the brow of the seated thing, and it slid down and glided across the stones to the prince, and it coiled about his body with a chill and merciless grip. The wise, flattened head lifted, till it was on a level with the man's face. The eyes of the serpent reached into Raynor's brain, into the secret fortress of his soul, and the prince stepped back one pace.

Then another. Slowly, like an automaton, he moved back toward the abyss that gaped behind him. He passed Eblik without seeing the black. For nothing existed but the dark, alien gaze of the serpent, brooding and old—old beyond earth-life!

The pit yawned behind him. Some stirring of human consciousness gave Raynor pause. He stopped, his sluggish thoughts feebly trying to rise free from the frigid ocean that held them motionless. Dimly he heard a cry from Eblik—muffled, faint, scarcely more than a despairing groan.

And that cry again saved him. Raynor could not have saved himself, but he knew that the Nubian called to his master for aid. And the thought of that was a faint, hot flame that rose and waxed brighter and slowly burned away the chill darkness that darkened his mind.

Slowly, slowly indeed, did the prince battle his way back to life. He swayed there upon the edge of the great gulf, while the serpent watched, and Eblik, after that one moan, was silent. And at last Raynor won.

Tide of life surged through his blood. He uttered a hoarse shout, gripped the cold, muscular body of the serpent, dragged it from his body. He flung the snake from him into the abyss.

A far sighing drifted up, unearthly, distant.

With that the spell lifted. Raynor came back to consciousness, no longer bound by the dark fetters of primeval magic; he swayed and leaped away from the edge of the pit.

He gave an inarticulate cry, somehow triumphant—exulting.

For the Sign of the Serpent was vanquished!

CHAPTER V
The Sign of the Fish of Ea

A movement caught Raynor's attention. The hideous image on the throne was moving slightly. Its misshapen black hand lifted; the muzzle gaped and shuddered. From the deformed mouth came a voice, deep as though it burst from the tongue of a corpse. Harsh, half-inarticulate, and muffled, it croaked:

"Mercy! In your mercy, slay me!"

The dull eyes looked upon Raynor. Shrinking a little in revulsion, the prince almost by instinct whipped out his sword. The monster slowly lifted its frightful head.

"Slay me! Slay me!"

"By all the gods," Raynor whispered through white lips, "what manner of being are you?"

"Once human, like you," the harsh voice groaned. "Once I ruled this citadel. Once I was a greater sorcerer than Ghiar."

A black paw beat the throne's side in agony. "Ghiar served me. I taught him the dark lore. And he turned to evil, and overthrew me, and prisoned me here. He set the Serpent to guard me. From my lips even now he learns wisdom. I serve him in ways I may not tell you. My soul roves between the stars to bring him knowledge."

Raynor forced himself to speak. "Know you aught of a girl, a captive of Ghiar's?"

"Aye! Aye! The warlock has need of a maiden once in a decade. Thus he renews his youth. Ghiar is old—death should have taken him centuries ago. But by the young blood of a maiden, and by her young soul, he drinks fresh vigor. He gains strength to work new evil. Follow this road, and you will find the girl."

Raynor made an impulsive gesture. But the horrible voice froze him in mid-stride.

"Hold! You have conquered the Snake. Yet I am still captive, still in agony you cannot imagine. Give me release, I pray you! Slay me!"

Raynor dared not look upon the hideous figure. "You seek death?"

"I should have died centuries ago. Free me now, and I shall aid you when you need aid most. Slay me!"

Raynor's lips tightened in resolution. He stepped forward, lifted his sword. As the blade swept down the monster croaked:

"Remember! The Sign of Tammuz is Lord of the Zodiac. It is the Master Sign."

Steel put a period to the words. The horror's head leaped from its shoulders; a foul-smelling ichor spurted a foot into the air. The creature toppled to lie motionless on the stones.

"Blood a' Shaitan!" Raynor muttered shakily. "I think we've walked into hell itself."

"Those be true words," said a low voice. "Once again you have saved us, master. But for what? Some worse doom, I think."

Eblik was rubbing his head, shivering. The prince gave a bark of laughter that held no mirth.

"Well, our road is open before us. And a brave man goes to meet his doom, instead of waiting for it to creep up on him. Hold fast to your ax, Eblik."

Raynor skirted the throne and entered a passage that gaped in the wall behind it. Once more the way led downward. It was a monotonous journey between dull walls of black stone.

What had the monster on the throne meant? "The Sign of Tammuz is Lord of the Zodiac." The Master Sign that could not be drawn—the sign of which the jet jewel in Ghiar's amulet was the symbol.

The passage turned and twisted, but always descended. They were far beneath ground level now, Raynor thought. His leg muscles were beginning to ache when at last the way was barred by a door of iron.

It was, however, unfastened, and moved aside at Raynor's cautious push.

He looked into a great circular room. Wan green light illuminated it dimly. The floor was of mosaic, figured in a bizarre design that centered in the Signs of the Zodiac. A golden Archer and a blue Fish; a scarlet Serpent and a black Flower; the Basilisk, all in shining green; and the disc of the Mirror in dull steel-gray.

In the exact center of the room was an immense jewel of jet set into the mosaic. A blindingly bright star-point glittered deep in the gem's heart.

It was frigidly cold. Looking up, Raynor realized why. The room was roofless. Its shaft probed up through the heart of the huge stone structure, a hollow tube that ended, far above, in a purple-black sky, shot with innumerable stars. The day had ended, and moonless night brooded over the warlock's citadel.

The stars looked down upon the Signs of the Zodiac.

The walls were hung with curtains of white samite. They parted now, and a slim figure entered. It was Delphia. She moved slowly, her gaze staring blindly before her, the coils of midnight hair clustering about the pale, keen face. Three paces she took, and halted.

"Delphia!" Raynor called, and stepped forward. The girl did not move.

She lifted her head, gazed up at the stars. There was a queer avidity in her face, a tenseness as though she waited eagerly for something. It was utterly silent—and cold, cold.

Raynor gripped Delphia's arm, shook her roughly.

"Wake up!" he said urgently. "Are you under a spell?"

"She has enchantment on her," Eblik grunted, peering into the girl's eyes. "Let me carry her, Prince. Once we're out of this evil place she may awaken."

Raynor hesitated. Before he could speak a new voice came, softly mocking.

"Nay, let me carry the wench! I shall be gentle."

With an oath Raynor whipped around, his sword bared. Eblik's war-ax was suddenly in his hand, quivering like a falcon straining to be released. There, filling the passage by which they had entered, were a dozen men, fierce-eyed, grinning with hate and triumph—the outlaws of Mirak Forest.

At their head stood Baron Malric. His youthful face wore a gay, reckless smile, despite the fact that he was in the heart of the wizard's stronghold.

"Hold!" he whispered. "Do not move! For if you do, I shall slay you." And one slim hand slipped toward the loose velvet sleeve and the sharp knife Malric wore strapped to his forearm.

"How the devil did you get here?" Raynor snarled.

"I followed the path you opened for me. I swam the lake and crossed the field of the Black Flowers. I tracked you here through the citadel. It was not an easily won victory—no! Of all my men, these few are all that remain. Some sleep amid the Black Flowers. Others died elsewhere. But it does not matter. Ghiar was too reckless when he hired you to steal the girl from my castle. Warlock he may be, but I rule Mirak!"

"Hired me?" Raynor said slowly. "You mistake. Ghiar is my enemy, as he is yours."

Malric laughed softly. "Well, it does not matter whether

you lie or tell truth. For you and this black shall both die here, and after I have found and slain Ghiar, I shall go back to my castle with the wench.''

''After you have slain Ghiar!''

The words whispered out; the samite curtains parted, and a man stepped through. It was the warlock. The dim green light touched the great billow of white beard, the shaggy eyebrows, of the giant. The dark, somber eyes held no emotion.

''You seek me, Malric? I am here. Slay me if you can.''

The baron, after a single start, stood motionless. His gaze locked in a silent, deadly duel with the cold stare of the wizard.

Abruptly, without warning, Malric moved. Too fast for eye to follow his hand dipped, came up flashing, brought death. Steel flickered through the air. The keen knife drove at Ghiar's throat—and fell blunted, ringing on the stones.

''Mortal fool,'' the warlock whispered. ''You seek to battle the stars in their courses. Malric, I am Lord of the Zodiac. I have power over the Signs that rule men's lives.''

The baron moistened his lips. His smile was crooked.

''Is this so? I know something of the Zodiac, Ghiar, and I know you do not rule all the Signs. You yourself once spoke to me of being born under the Sign of the Fish of Ea. As was I. How can you rule your ruler—or any other Sign? Nor are you Lord of the Stars. There is a certain Sign''—Malric glanced at the great black jewel in the mosaic's center—''Aye, there is Tammuz. He is Lord of the Master Sign.''

''Who can call on Tammuz?'' Ghiar said coldly. ''Once in a thousand years is a man born under his Sign. And only such a man may work the ultimate magic. Aye, I said to you I was born under the Sign of the Fish of Ea, but who are you that I should tell you full truth—as I do now?'' The warlock frowned at Raynor. ''As for you and your servant, you shall die with the others. Had you been wise, you would not have sought me here. This girl is mine; I need her life to give me renewed youth.''

"D'you think I fear a wizard?" Raynor snapped, and sprang. His sword sheared down, screaming through cleft air.

And rebounded, clashing. The weapon dropped from Raynor's nerveless hand, which was paralyzed as though by a strong electric shock. Snarling an oath, the prince tensed to leap, ready to close with the warlock with bare hands.

Ghiar's peremptory gesture halted him.

"Rash fools!" the wizard whispered, a chill and dreadful menace in the sibilant words. "You shall die as no man has died for a thousand years."

His arms lifted in a strange, archaic gesture. A gesture that reached up toward the stars far above, a gesture that summoned!

Bleak and ominous came the warlock's voice.

"Your doom comes. For now I call on the Sign of the Fish of Ea!"

CHAPTER VI
The Sign of Tammuz

The green light thickened and grew fainter. An eerie, cloudy emerald glow dropped down upon the roofless room. The figure of Ghiar was a dark shadow towering in the dimness. And the deep voice thundered out:

"Ea! Lord of Eridu and E-apsu! Dweller in the house of the watery deep! *Shar-apsi!* by the power of thy Sign I call on the Lord of that which is below, watcher of Aralu, home of the restless dead. Ea, troubler of the great waters, consort of Damkina, Damgal-nunna, rise now from the eternal abyss!"

The green darkness thickened. Raynor, straining his eyes, could see nothing. He made an effort to move, but found he could not. A weird paralysis held him helpless.

He heard a sound, faint and far away. The sound of waters. The tinkling of brooks, the rushing of mighty cataracts, the thunder of tides crashing on basalt cliffs. The noises of the great deep heralded the coming of Ea, Lord of the waters under the earth.

Nothing existed but the glowing emerald fogs. A deeper light began to grow above. The mists poured up toward it.

Thicker they grew, and thicker. They swirled into an inverted whirlpool, rushing up toward the bright green shining in the air, flooding into it, vanishing. Vanishing as though plunging into an abyss that had no bottom!

A figure swam slowly into view, stiff and rigid. One of Baron Malric's wolves. Raynor had a glimpse of a strained, agonized face, and then the man was caught up into the torrent and vanished into the emerald glow. A thin, high scream drifted faintly from afar.

There were others after that. One by one the outlaws were caught up by the tide of alien magic, drawn into the weird whirlpool, swirled into nothingness. All were gone at last save for Malric.

Now the baron came into view. His youthful face was expressionless, but in the wide eyes was a horror beyond life. The bright hair tossed as though the man floated through water.

No sound came from Malric. He drifted up—and vanished!

The tide gripped Raynor. He felt himself lifted weightless, felt himself circling, rising. The shining abyss loomed above him. Desperately he fought to escape from the necromantic spell.

Quite suddenly the green mists were blotted out. Raynor seemed to hang in a black, starless immensity. He was alone in the void of eternal night.

In the distance a white, chill light began to grow. It approached, meteor-like, and Raynor saw a round, oddly familiar object speeding toward him. Soon it hung in the void not far away, and the prince remembered the deformed monster that had sat on the throne above the abyss—the captive of the snake that he had slain. Here was the same misshapen, hideous head, with its glazed eyes and elongated muzzle, all covered with glittering scales.

The Thing spoke.

"My promise, Prince Raynor. You gave me release. And I promised aid when you should need it most. I bring that aid now."

"The amulet," said the monstrous disembodied head.

Abruptly Raynor remembered the talisman Ghiar had given him in Mirak forest, the disc that bore the Signs of the Zodiac on its surface. He did not seem to move, yet the amulet was in his hand, and lifted high. It had changed. The Signs were erased, all but the black jewel in its center. Within the gem the star-point pulsed and waned with supernal brilliance.

"Tammuz is Lord of the Zodiac," the hideous muzzle croaked. "His magic is above magic. He is master of truth. Through him you may cast away the fetters of glamour and sorcery. Once in a thousand years is a man born under this Sign, and only such a man may call on Tammuz. I am that man! I was born under the Master Sign! Ghiar lies—he boasts of that which he is not! And now, to keep my promise and to aid you, I summon the Lord of the Zodiac. I summon— *Tammuz*!"

Forthwith the black jewel blazed with an icy, incredible light, starkly pitiless and blindingly bright; and the fantastic vision snapped out and vanished. The talisman was snatched from Raynor's hand. He felt firm stone beneath his feet; a cold wind blew on his sweating face.

Once more he was in Ghiar's citadel. He stood in the roofless room of the Zodiac. But no longer was it filled with the green mists.

Delphia and Eblik stood motionless; near them towered the warlock. Of Malric and his wolves there was no trace.

Ghiar's beard fluttered in the frigid blast. His deep eyes were hate-filled. And, with a queer, strange certainty, Raynor knew that by the Sign and the power of the real Tammuz, all magic had been stripped from the wizard.

No longer master of dark sorcery, Ghiar was human, vulnerable!

Raynor's shout was madly exultant as he sprang. The armor of invulnerability had been torn from Ghiar. But inhuman strength still surged in the giant frame. Huge muscles rolled under the coarse robe.

Ghiar swept out his arm in a bone-crushing blow. The shock of it made Raynor reel. Shaking his head blindly, he reeled in and closed with the warlock.

The two men crashed down on the stones. Ghiar fell uppermost; his fingers stabbed down at Raynor's eyes. The prince rolled his head aside, and the warlock bellowed with pain as his hand smashed against rock. Abruptly Ghiar thrust himself away, and his mighty body dropped upon Raynor with an impact that drove the breath from the smaller man's lungs.

Weakly the prince drove a blow at the wizard's face. Blood spurted, staining the white beard. Roaring, Ghiar's hands fastened on Raynor's throat. They tightened remorselessly.

The prince rolled aside; he caught Ghiar's body between his legs, locking his feet together. Breath spewed from the warlock's lips in a foul gust; Ghiar bared his teeth in a murderous grin. And his fingers tightened—tightened.

A hot, throbbing agony was in Raynor's skull. He could not breathe. Knifelike pain thrust into his spine. A little more pressure, and his backbone would crack.

Sheer blind madness swept down on the prince then. Like a flood of red waters it poured through him, sweeping away all else but an insane lust to kill—and swiftly.

Raynor's thigh muscles bulged, holding Ghiar's body in a vise between them. The grinding strain of that frightful effort made sweat burst out on the prince's face; yet he knew that this was the crucial time. It was kill or be slain.

Bones cracked and gave sickeningly. There was a sudden softness in the wizard's body. Ghiar gave a frightful, howling shriek that seemed to burst up from the depths of his lungs. Blood spewed from the gaping mouth, frothed over the white beard, fell on Raynor.

The mighty hands released their grip on the prince's throat. Ghiar sprang up in one last convulsive effort. Dying, he thrust up his arms to the cold stars and screamed like a beast.

And he fell, as a tree falls, smashing down on the stones.

He lay inert. From him blood crept darkly across the mosaic, touching and then covering the Sign of the Fish of Ea, the Sign under which Ghiar had been born and had ruled.

The warlock was dead.

Consciousness left Raynor then. Merciful darkness blanketed him. Nor did he recover until he felt water poured between his lips, felt a cool, soft hand on his brow. He opened his eyes.

Above him sunlight slanted between the branches of an oak. The green, warm daylight of Mirak Forest was all about him. And Delphia knelt at his side, her eyes no longer blinded with sorcery, her face clouded with anxiety.

"Raynor," she said gratefully. "You're alive, thank the gods!"

"Alive?" growled Eblik, coming from behind an oak. "I'd not have carried him here if he hadn't been. How do you feel, Prince?"

"Well enough," Raynor said. "My legs ache like fire, but I'm unharmed, I think. You carried me out of the citadel, Eblik?"

"That he did," Delphia nodded. "And swam the lake with you. The Black Flowers were dead, Raynor, blasted as though by lightning."

"If you can walk, we'd best be moving," Eblik said impatiently.

Raynor stood up, wincing slightly. "True. We'll find horses and leave this accursed forest behind us."

Together he and Delphia set out along the winding path that led through Mirak. Eblik hesitated a moment before he followed. He looked up at the blue, cloudless sky.

"May the gods grant we get out of this wilderness before nightfall," he grunted. "Out of this black forest, and in another land—a land where the stars are less evil."

Gripping his war-ax, he hurried after Delphia and Raynor. And presently, the three of them were swallowed by the cool, dim aisles of the vast forest.

III.

MANLY WADE
WELLMAN

INTRODUCTION

Manly Wade Wellman (1903–
1986) is best known for his stories of the Southern mountains,
particularly those of a wandering folksinger named simply
"John." Two collections of these Southern fantasies have
been published since his death: *The Valley So Low* (Double-
day, 1987) and *John the Balladeer* (Baen, 1988). However,
Wellman was also author of two heroic fantasy series, both
begun during the 1930s and continued sporadically until his
death.

Wellman was always fascinated by the legends of Atlantis—as well as by stories of prehistoric mankind. He combined these interests into two separate fantasy series. One
concerned a roguish minstrel named Kardios, the sole survivor of Atlantis. Initially submitted to *Weird Tales*, the first
story, "The Straggler from Atlantis," was rejected by editor
Farnsworth Wright on the basis that he already had a guy
named Robert E. Howard who was writing that kind of stuff.
The Kardios series remained in limbo until the late 1970s,

when they began to appear in Andrew J. Offutt's *Swords Against Darkness* series at Zebra Books.

Wellman had greater success with his Hok series, with which readers of *Echoes of Valor II* will be familiar. Wellman had a pet theory that the hero Hercules, with his club and barbaric garb, was an anachronism within Greek mythology, and that Hercules was instead some mighty Stone Age warrior whose legend had been incorporated into later myth cycles. Thus, Hok is presented as the actual Hercules—mankind's first great hero, whose mighty exploits earned him a permanent place of honor within the history of the human race.

Like Kardios, Hok didn't fare too well at the start—at least with editors. The first Hok story, a crude effort called "The Love of Oloana," was bounced by *Spicy-Adventure Stories* in 1935. Just as well. A few years later, Wellman had refined both his prose and his creation, and the first published Hok story, "Battle in the Dawn," appeared in *Amazing Stories* for January 1939. This story, one of Wellman's personal favorites out of all his voluminous works, drew accolades from readers and launched four sequels in *Amazing Stories* and its companion magazine, *Fantastic Adventures*, between 1939 and 1942. Four decades later, Wellman had begun work on a new Hok story, when a crippling fall ended his career and eventually his life.

Hok was a very real character to Wellman, as evidenced by more than half a century of creative lifetime within the author's imagination. This sincerity of belief imparts a distinct personal enthusiasm to Hok that lifts the series above the level of pulp formula hackwork and carries the reader past the unsophisticated prose. Wellman studiously worked to enhance the genuineness of his creation by embellishing the stories with footnotes—after all, *Amazing Stories* was a science fiction magazine—just another example of the heartfelt seriousness of his approach to Hok. Wellman bitterly claimed that the 1940 film, *One Million B.C.*, had been stolen from the Hok stories, and, while this was simply not the case, there was never any convincing him. I think he identified with Hok much the same as Robert E. Howard did with Conan.

Four of the Hok stories were reprinted (without payment or permission) in *Fantastic* between 1967 and 1970. The remaining story, ''Hok Goes to Atlantis,'' escaped this fate and is reprinted here for the first time.

HOK GOES TO ATLANTIS
by Manly Wade Wellman

The Legendary Land of Atlantis

All peoples and continents have memories of it, so it must have existed—fair, lost Atlantis, the land that was the greatest in all the ancient world for strength and beauty, and was swallowed by the maw of ocean.

Where did that bright country once rise? An island in mid-Atlantic, of which only the mountain-tops show today as the Azores and the Canaries? In the heart of the Sahara, near the peaks called Atlas? In the Gulf of Mexico, touching Aztec and Maya to pronounce the mystic word Atl?

Or was it the vast rich valley between the continents, the warm, green country that glaciers never touched, that existed when our fathers, the first of the true men, were wresting Europe from the bestial paws of the monstrous Neanderthalers? That valley is filled with blue water today, and is called the Mediterranean—the midst

*of the Earth. Its forests and meadows are drowned; but
from them may have come the people who bore and
cradled culture in the nations around that inmost sea—
nations "like frogs around a puddle," as said Plato,
who also knew of Atlantis.*

*Tremendous as was the glory of that lost land, more
tremendous still was her doom. It beggars imagination,
the rush and triumph of ocean, breaking the barrier
and filling the sunken basin that was like an inverted
continent, drowning forests, cities, nations. How could
even one escape from the judgment? Yet some one did,
and told his children of what he had seen and escaped,
and they told those who came after them, down to the
present day. How else could we know?*

*Who was that survivor of Atlantis? He must have
been a mighty man. He may even have been the hero
we remember as Hercules.*

CHAPTER I
The Horsemen and the Valley

The wolves had been chasing Hok for three days.

Hok had become great, in body and in fame, since the
days when he, barely past his boyhood, entered the northern
game-lands and purged them of the inhuman Gnorrls.* Ma-
turity had made him taller than ever, and more bull-strong
and leopard-swift and lion-tawny. He wore a short, soft beard,
like the fiber which his wife, the lovely Oloana, beat from
autumn grasses and wove into baskets and pouches. He ruled
a fighting tribe of valiant hunters and handsome women, and

*Stone age men called the Neanderthal beast men *Gnorrls*. See "Battle
in the Dawn," *Amazing Stories*, January, 1939.—Ed.

also was respected and deferred to by the allied clans of his brother Zhik and his father-in-law Zorr. His hunting grounds yielded fat game, and there were still Gnorrls to fight if the time passed heavily. Yet Hok had not outgrown his enthusiasm for exploration; and so, telling Zhik to command for him, he had gone away on a spring jaunt to the south and west, into country he and his did not know.

And the wolves, a good forty of them, picked up his scent and hunted him through the forest for three foodless, sleepless days and nights.

Now they gave tongue exultantly, for they were driving him toward a great cliff, against which he must come to bay; but Hok, who ran like the deer and fought like the lion, also climbed like the ape. He scaled the rocky wall nimbly, laughing backward at the famished howls of the pack, and dragged himself to the brow of the cliff in the bright morning. Standing erect, he gazed afar into a valley.

But such a valley! It stretched down and down, gently but ceaselessly. He gazed into sloping meadows, with groves beneath them, and water-courses, and broken country, for the distance of many marches—falling down, down, down, gently but steadily. As for the valley's other side, it was lost in far blue mist as though it were hidden beyond a piece of the sky. Things were green and fresh, and Hok heard birds, saw the cautious motion of game in tall brush. It must be a good hunting land. If he had not cast away his two flint-headed javelins at the wolves—it was always that way when you had nothing to throw. Here came some horses toward him, around that thicket.

No, not horses—men! . . .

No, not men—but not horses, either!

Hok's bright beard stirred with excitement. He shaded his blue eyes with a wide, hard palm. Surely the things had hoofs—four each—and horsey tails. But why did the heads and shoulders of men thrust up from each? And then Hok saw, and wondered still more. The horses were normal, and so were the men—but the men were riding upon the horses, as baby monkeys ride on their mothers' backs.*

It was almost too much for the caveman's simple mind. To him, a horse was a toothsome creature that yielded much meat—no more. He had never thought of riding one. Yet, whatever his surprise, he did not fear. He moved forward to the rimrock that jutted above the valley, and gazed.

Hok was naked except for leopard-skin kilt and moccasins of tough bison hide. At his girdle hung a pouch and a sheath that carried a finely worked dagger of deer-horn. He bore, too, a stone-headed axe, chipped of blue flint, its keen edge a full span in width. His body was tanned and superbly muscled but, save for his hair and beard, it showed as smooth as a peach. Not even in those fierce days was one apt to see a bigger or better specimen of manhood.

The horsemen came close toward him, then halted their animals at a signal from their leader. There were as many of them as there had been hungry wolves below. Most of them seemed swarthy and bearded, and wore strange clothing, either pale or shining. If it was of leather or fur, Hok had never seen such beasts as yielded it.

The leader came forward by a horse's length—a trim, smooth-faced individual, in a close-fitting garment that seemed to be made of huge fish-scales.

"You on the rock!" came a clear challenge, in a tongue not too dissimilar to Hok's own. "Who are you?"

"Aye," growled a deeper voice from the party of riders, "and tell us your people, and the name of your master."

"I am Hok," shouted back the caveman. "My people are those who hunt to north and east, beating back the hairy Gnorrls. I have no master."

"The fellow flouts us, he is a madman," grumbled the deep voice, and its owner sidled his horse out to join the leader. This second speaker was squat and black-bearded,

---

*From some such introduction to mounted men must have come the first conception of the centaur.—Author.

and even at the distance Hok saw that he was fierce of face and sharp eyed.

"If I am mad," Hok threw at him, "I may come down and make you fear my bite."

With an oath, the bearded one lifted himself in his seat, whirled a spear backward, and launched it at the defiant Hok, who stood still to watch the course of the weapon. It was a sure cast, but not too strong, according to caveman standards. As it came at Hok, he swayed his big, lithe body sidewise, shot out his right hand like a snake, and seized the flying shaft by the middle. Whirling it end for end, he sped it back the way it had come, with all the strength and skill of his mighty muscles behind it. Forty throats whooped in startled anger as the black-beard spun off of his beast, transfixed by his own weapon. Hok's answering shout of laughter defied them. It had all happened in two breaths of time.

For more than two breaths thereafter, the company hesitated. To them it seemed that the spear had bounced back from Hok and punished its hurler—a feat of magic. None cared to attack magicians in those times. Again the leader spoke:

"I did not order my man to cast at you, and I do not take up his quarrel. Come down and make peace."

Hok did not stir.

"Come down," came the invitation a second time. "I swear by my honor, and by my god, the Many-Legged Ghirann, that you will find only profit."

Hok felt sincerity in that oath. He scrambled down the face of the inner bluff, and strode forward. The leader trotted out to meet him, and Hok grew sure of what he had been suspecting—that the leader was a woman, young and of a certain sturdy beauty. Her jaw was square and her nose straight, and her hair and eyes were dark. Around her throat was a collar-like string of sun-glowing lumps. Hok's own blue eyes met her dark ones, and he tossed back his lion's mane of hair.

"Hok, you call yourself?" said the horsewoman. "I am

Maie, a chieftainess of Tlanis. Now, by your act, we ride one short. Will you make our band whole again?''

"If I refuse?" he suggested, hand on her bridle-rein. "If I become your enemy?"

She smiled, without showing her teeth. Her tight lips could be hard, he saw.

"You cannot fling back all our spears, Hok. Be wise, take the horse and tackle of him you slew."

A man was leading the sturdy, shaggy brown beast forward. A gourd at its withers danced and gave forth liquid sounds. Hok, who feared not Maie or all her followers, was thirsty enough to let this item persuade him.

"I seek new sights and peoples," he consented. "I will ride with you." And he vaulted upon the proffered animal, confidently though a bit clumsily. "Where do we go, warrior woman, and on what errand?"

Like him, the mounted troop had been exploring. When she heard from him that beyond the rimrock was a great steep cliff, and only trackless forest beyond that, Maie gave a signal to turn. "We will ride back five days to our own place," she said, "and if you are indeed a stone-chipper and cave-dweller, we can promise you your fill of strange sights."

They rode away. When they made camp that night, at a grove of palm-like trees with a spring at the center, Hok had learned to manage his mount in a way that bespoke his great courage and aptitude. There were other wonders harder for him to fathom. The drink in the gourd—wine, Maie called it—was at once fiery and refreshing; the weapons of the man he had supplanted were of strange bright material, neither stone nor bone, but tougher and keener than either, and called bronze by his new companions. Their clothing, too, was partially of that material (Hok was a little scornful of the idea of armor) and partially of woven threads of plant fiber or animal fleece, a fabric like Oloana's grass baskets, but finer.

On the next day he rode beside Maie at the head of the party. The slope took them down and ever down, and as they descended the country grew richer and warmer. Hok, used to tough-grassed meadows, hardy bushes and cone-bearing trees, gaped with wonder upon feathery palms and shrubs with bright flowers a foot across, on clusters of red and yellow fruit, on broad-leafed, sky-aspiring groves, in which played gay-plumed birds and chattering monkeys. Yet his wonder was tinctured with a ghostly sense of familiarity, as though within him stirred the memory of his own dim ancestries, spent in such an environment.

He also learned about the people of Tlanis.

They lived, said Maie, in a stronghold near the ocean, and had neither to hunt nor to steal for sustenance. This great valley, many days' journey across, was full of subject tribes who provided food and other necessities for their rulers in Tlanis. Hok heard in half-comprehending wonder that other animals besides horses were kept captive, and fed fat for leisurely butchering; and that fields were planted with seeds, to bring forth vegetable stores that Tlanis gathered far more surely and easily than the women of Hok's people gathered fruits and nuts in the forest.

He was full of questions, that lasted even to the fifth and final morning of the ride. Maie answered them all.

"And now, great wielder of stone," she asked him at length, "are you not convinced that our way of living is better and softer than yours, among caves and wild beasts?"

"I think," he replied, "that soft living makes soft men."

"But is there not an advantage?"

"I cannot yet say that, Maie."

She smiled as she heard him speak her name. "You might say, at least, that you like me, Hok."

"I do not know yet if I like you," he replied. And no more he did, although he had loved and wanted Oloana within the first instant of seeing her. This woman, Maie, was beautiful and wise, and so far had treated him with more than fairness; but Hok reserved judgment upon her.

He looked again at the collar of gleaming yellow objects she wore. They were beads, curiously worked and engraved, and strung on a thread or wire of the same substance.

"What are those?" he asked Maie.

"They are gold."

"What is gold?"—And she sighed, as though she must give up trying to instruct him.

They rode in silence through a lush, sweet-smelling forest, and before noon came out in open country.

A height of rock and earth rose against the horizon. It extended to left and right, beyond reach of the eye, and beyond it shone, or seemed to shine, a bright blueness—water, more water than Hok had ever seen.

Directly ahead of the riders, lifting from the level of this barrier, appeared a broken peak. From its top floated a wispy plume of dark smoke, as of a great beacon fire.* And beneath the barrier, at the point where the peak crowned it, lay heaped and clustered strange mineral shapes, of various angles and sizes and plans, but somehow ordered in their relationships. Hok stared.

"What things lie there at the foot of the cliff?" he demanded.

"They are houses," said Maie. "Walls and palaces and streets. Did I not promise you wonders? Yonder is the city of Tlanis, which rules the world."

CHAPTER II
A Summons from Cos

To describe the city of Tlanis, words and comparisons are needed which were utterly strange to Hok as he rode with his new friends down the broad paved trail.

Built at the "end of the world"—that is, under the lee of a mighty barrier that held back the high-piled wastes of the

---

*The volcanic character of the rocks at Gibralter, and across the straits in Morocco, suggests that a great volcano once rose there, shutting back the ocean from the sunken valley which now holds the Mediterranean.—Author.

ocean—it was far below sea level, nestled against the steep slopes and lower ledges of the great natural dam of volcanic rock that kept the valley from being flooded. On the landward side, a great artificial wall of stone, cut and mortared, defended the place, with green meadows, orchards and grainfields close to its foot. Within mighty gates of hewn logs, each a cunning interlacement like a giant's mat-weaving, were squares and clumps of houses, one and two and three stories high. The passage-spaces between—Hok must learn to call them streets—were faced with flat slabs of stone, and thronged with men, horses, litters, wooden-wheeled carts. Maie pointed out to him the various classes of citizens, the laborers, merchants, soldiers, farmers, nobles, beggars.

The city rose on a succession of broad ledges or terraces. Each of these was strung with buildings, a lengthwise street or two, and occasional ramps to other levels. Passing upward, the company came to the market level, in which great arcades and small shops were filled with foodstuffs, fabrics, weapons, utensils, jewelry and other wonders, over which merchants and customers chaffered in yelling multitudes. Hok listened to Maie's explanation of commerce, but the idea of money—pieces of metal, sun-yellow or moon-white—he could not grasp. Maie's gold beads he understood. They were ornaments, such as women prized. Beyond that, gold was nothing—not good to eat, too soft for weapons.

"I think that some of these people work too hard, and others too little," he announced. "That man with the curly beard and the red cloak, whom you call a rich merchant, is too fat. So is that other, who comes and talks to him. They are short-breathed and flabby-muscled. I have a son at home, a little boy, who would live longer than they in the forest."

"This is not a forest," Maie reminded him. They mounted to a higher level, where only soldiers marched or lounged on the street, and dwelt in the sturdy barracks buildings of stone and timber. Here, Maie ordered her horse and Hok's to be led away.

"Come," she said to him. "I will show you places of delight in this city."

They went down a ramp on foot, passed through a howling market—the voices were too shrill to please Hok—and came to an open-fronted, palm-thatched shop with tables, benches, and the scent of food and wine. At Maie's motion, Hok entered, and they both sat down. A slender youth with curly hair brought them steaming portions of meat and vegetables on clay platters, also metal mugs of wine.

"Thank you," Hok said cordially to the waiter. "It is kind for you to give a stranger food and drink."

"Strangers must pay, like others," was the reply, and Maie took coins from her belt-pouch.

"Why is gold given for food?" demanded Hok when the waiter had gone. "It is a matter too deep for me."

"I am afraid you hate gold," smiled Maie.

"All except the beads you wear. They are beautiful."

"You like them?" And at once Maie undid the collar from her neck, and held it out. "They are yours."

Hok was about to refuse, with thanks, when it occurred to him that his wife, Oloana, would demand a present when he returned to the caves. And so he accepted the present, and fastened it around his corded wrist, where it hung like a bangle.

"I have many such beads," Maie told him. "I am rich, I have lands and servants and warriors."

"I never before saw a woman who led fighting men," said Hok.

"My father had no sons, and when he died I became a chief in his place. Is that strange? Will not your little son, of whom you spoke, be chief after you?"

"I hope he will," replied Hok, "but he must earn and prove his right to lead, when he is a man. No son stands on his dead father's legs with us."

The two ate and watched the passing market-crowd. Many a gaze answered theirs, admiring and appraising the stalwart tawniness of a cave chieftain. Hok listened as Maie continued her explanations of the government, the organization and lifeways of Tlanis.

"I still think it is bad," he said, when she had finished. "From what you say, many are poor—some even hungry— in this big sunken valley, which to my notion is the fullest and finest place in the world. There must be food enough for everybody, almost for the taking."

"But there can be no taking without paying," Maie assured him patiently. "All this belongs to our rulers—to Cos."

"Who is Cos?"

"The master of Tlanis, and of the great valley. Of all the world."

"He is not my master," replied Hok doggedly. "I never heard of him. But he must be tremendously big and hungry to eat all the good things I have seen."

"He is a great man, and his appetite is good," admitted Maie.

"But to feed this one man, many go hungry and wretched," argued Hok.

"He has soldiers to feed, and slaves, and more than fifty women," Maie elaborated.

"Fifty women!" cried Hok, and shook his head in refusal to believe. "One is enough for any man."

Maie was thoughtful. "Cos does not think so," she said. "He is always taking more. Just now he wants me, he has asked me to enter his palace. I will be his favorite if I will leave off adventuring and exploring, and give myself to him."

"You love him?" asked Hok.

"My family is great in Tlanis. Since my father died, I have become chieftainess of many men, horse and foot, with other property. Yet, if I accept Cos, I may be even greater."

"Why should you want to be greater?" demanded Hok, and Maie seemed unable to answer. "I do not know if I like Cos," Hok went on. "He takes food from others, and to starve is a bad death. He should go hungry himself, to learn how it feels."

As they finished their food and wine, a tall, lean man in a long robe came up to them. He had a face like a wise eagle, and a tag of beard on his chin. "Greetings, Maie," he said in a high, disagreeable voice. "Cos has heard that you are in Tlanis."

"The ears of Cos are long, priest," replied the young chieftainess.

"He wonders why you do not come to make report to him of your explorations, instead of sitting in a wine-shop with a great bull of a stranger."

"Call me bull, and I will gore you," said Hok, getting up and kicking back his bench.

The eagle-faced man turned pale and shrank away, while Maie hastily interposed. "Do him no harm, Hok; he is a priest, full of wisdom and authority."

"Does the authority allow him to insult strangers?" demanded Hok. He glared wrathfully, and the priest slunk away. Maie stared at her guest from the wilderness. Her dark eyes were full of light, half fearful, half admiring.

"Come," she said. "Cos has spies who have told him of us. He is jealous. We had better both go to see him. Are you afraid?"

Hok feared nothing, and said so. They left and climbed again, to the highest level of the city, a grand terrace overlooking the rising clumps of houses, the wall at the foot of the height, and the fertile valley beyond.

This terrace was carpeted with green grass, and tufted with trees and flowering bushes. Hok wondered still more when he learned that all this planting was by man's labor, as in the fields of grain and vegetables below. Among the shrubbery loomed a great cube of a building, white-pigmented with lime, which Maie called a palace; to one side was a wall, with a gate. The two came to this gate, were admitted by a sentry in armor, and entered.

They stood in a courtyard, paved with white gravel, and completely surrounded by spike-crowned walls, with the blue sky above. At the side where the great building abutted, was a canopy of striped fabric, raised on poles against the warm sun. Beneath the canopy was set a chair, of carved and gilded wood; and upon that chair, flanked on either side by a dozen sentries braced to attention, sat Cos, the master of Tlanis.

CHAPTER III
Defiance and Doom

Hok stared at Cos, and was deeply disappointed. This man, who ruled more land than one could cross in many days' journey, and more people than one could count in weeks, who could hold back supplies of food from the mouths of hungry tribes, he had already judged as unkind. Now that Cos was in view, Hok saw plainly that he was neither brave nor strong; and courage, strength and fairness were, to Hok, the criterions of chieftainship.

Cos was flabby and bunch-bellied, with sleek, soft calves and biceps. His beard, trained into black curls, cascaded down his bare, dark chest. In the midst of the gleaming thicket of hair showed a plump red mouth, like a spoiled fruit—the mouth of an idle sensualist. His eyes, set as close as a spider's, had shifty lights, detracting from the proud power of brow and nose. He wore bracelets, fillet, and girdle of hammered gold, and his kilt and sandals were embroidered with small glittering stones of red, blue and green.

Maie bowed before him with ceremonious respect. "Hail, Lord of Tlanis," she spoke. "I am come from my explorations, to give you news of unknown wild lands toward the north. Men live there, and other creatures. I have brought with me one such man, himself a master of peoples."

"With whom you prefer to loll and drink," Cos added poutingly. His spider-eyes wandered to Hok. "Give account of yourself, stranger."

Hok did so. Cos listened, with disdainful hostility at first, then with almost greedy interest. As Hok told about his enemies, the hairy, half-human Gnorrls, Cos exclaimed delightedly, and began to ask questions.

"I have heard a little about this race you call Gnorrls," he said at last. "You say they are very strong creatures? And cunning, though less wise than men? . . . Good. I will send soldiers to encounter them."

"To kill the Gnorrls?" suggested Hok.

"Hmmmmm . . . No. Not kill them. Capture them. They are strong beyond human strength, and wise enough to learn, but not to overthrow. I will have them brought here, for slaves." Cos licked his loose lips over the prospect of conquest, as a hungry man might relish the thought of good food. "And now, caveman," he went on, "tell of your own people."

Hok amplified his first remarks about his kinsmen and followers, living and hunting in the country they had wrested in fierce combat from overwhelming spawns of Gnorrls. Cos listened eagerly, as before, then shook his gold-circled head. "I do not think I will enslave your tribe," he said.

"It is well not to try," Hok assured him.

"They would make bad slaves, I am sure," continued Cos. "They are proud, wise, fierce-tempered." He mentioned those characteristics as though they were faults. "No, not for slaves. My men will kill them all, and take their country."

It was briefly and plainly said, even for that age of scant diplomacy and frank statements. Hok glared at this evil, greedy wielder of great numbers and wealth. He wished that he had not told of his people. Anger grew against himself and Cos. Into his throat rose a deep growl of challenge.

"I will go to prepare my people for war," he announced, and turned toward the gate. Cos made a finger-wagging motion. The line of sentries at his left deployed, spears at the ready, to cut off Hok's departure.

"Stay where you are, chief of the stone-chippers," commanded Cos. "My own soldiers will bear the news of war to your land. Be thankful if you yourself escape."

Hok's anger burst like a hurricane. "Unsay those words!" he roared. "Otherwise, you will not live to speak others!" And his big stone axe, stirring in his bulky fist, lifted its blue head like a threatening snake.

Cos grinned, and made another languid motion. The guardsman at his right elbow moved forward.

Hok swung to face this new challenger. The man was beard-tufted and lank, with not half of Hok's volume of muscle; but he threatened the cave-man with a strange device.

It looked like an apple or melon, a round smooth sphere of bronze. From a small hole in it protruded what looked like a twisted, blackened rag, hanging free as the soldier poised it in his ready right hand. The left hand lifted something else—a smouldering saucer of oily fool, like a lamp, not more than a hand's breadth from the dangling tip of the rag.

"Have a care, stone-chipper," chuckled Cos in his curly beard. "If you threaten me, I will sweep you away with the weapon of thunder and lightning."

"Thunder! Lightning!" echoed Hok, in unbelieving scorn. "Do not lie. Only Sky-Dwellers wield such things."

"Ah," said Cos, "and I am as great as the Sky-Dwellers. Ghirann the Many-Legged made their secret of destruction mine."

"It is true, Hok," muttered Maie fearfully, close to his ear. "The lightning-stuff is made by the slaves of Ghirann's priest—it has long been known and used in Tlanis."*

But Hok did not show the slightest fear or hesitation. He addressed the soldier: "I will take that fruit-thing from you, and your hand and arm along with it."

"Oh, show the fool," snapped Cos, and the soldier, dipping his fuse into the fiery saucer, lifted and flung the bomb.

Maie shrieked and sprang frantically away; but Hok, still holding his axe in his right hand, shot up his left, caught the flying missile as it came toward his face and hurled it instantly back, as he had hurled the spear a few days before.

There was a fearsome roar, a blinding flash, a cloud of soot-black smoke; and through it Hok could see that Cos had been knocked from his throne-chair, his beard half singed away, while four of the twelve men on his right hand sprawled, burnt and broken, in death.

"See!" yelled Hok. "I have given you back your evil magic!" And he charged at the overthrown Cos.

But the rest of the sentries rushed at him from either hand. They levelled bronze-tipped spears at his heart as they closed

---

*Ignatius Donelly, in his interesting work, *Atlantis*, offers an interesting collection of legends about explosives among Atlanteans.—Author.

in. Hok emitted a short, fierce spurt of laughter, and swept the blade of his axe horizontally in front of him. Its keen-flaked edge found and shore away the heads of three spears, and he sprang into the gap thus made. His swooping weapon bit through a helmet, and through the skull beneath it to the nose-bridge, and as he strove to wrench loose the wedged flint, the others were upon him.

"Take him alive!" roared Cos, starting to his feet; and a score and more of hands clutched at Hok's body and shoulders. He strove and cursed, kicking and buffeting. With one full-armed swing of his fist he smashed a bearded jaw, with a grasp and a wrench he dislocated a shoulder. But the soldiers were too many for him, and in the end he lay prone on the gravel, his wrists and ankles bound by the belts of the sentries.

Cos now dared grin and exult. "The hero of the forest lies at my feet," he sneered. "So will his people, when my soldiers march upon them. Take him away."

"Where, master?" panted a sentry.

"Where but to the sea-barrier above?" replied Cos. "Let him enter the dwelling of Ghirann our god, whose food is the blood of the wicked and proud—Ghirann the Many-Legged, the Terrible, who has waited over-long for sacrifice from Cos, his brother!"

"Not Ghirann!" ventured a shaky voice—Maie, who had stood apart and marvelled at the strength and fierceness of Hok. "Stop and think, Cos! Might not the courage of this prisoner merit a better death?"

"He would merit a worse one, if I could invent it," growled Cos. "Take him away, soldiers, and let me hear this night that Ghirann has feasted full upon his blood and body."

CHAPTER IV
The Cave of Ghirann

Up the face of the cliff above
the city ran a sloping way, cut slantwise, like a crossbelt on
a giant's chest; and up that way the detail of soldiers shoved
and dragged the bound chieftain. Hok could not tear loose
from his bonds, and so he stopped trying. Philosophically he
looked out across the scene below—the huddled city, the cultivated lands beyond, and the valley afar, all groves and plains
and slopes. Surely this was the land of fruits and dalliances,
a paradise where winter never came—and it was ruled by
Cos, the selfish and cowardly tyrant.

Hok's greatest regret at the time was that he had not fleshed
his stone axe in the scornful face of Cos. . . . Regretting, he
was borne to the top of the great barrier-cliff under which
Tlanis nestled.

Even though Maie had told him that the sea flowed higher
by far than the tallest roof in the city, it was a surprise to
come out upon a rocky shore, with the limitless blue waters
beating almost at one's feet. The top of the mountainous barrier now appeared as a vast extending causeway, losing itself
in foggy distances to either direction, with the sea close at
hand on one side, the valley far below on the other. The
slanting upward trail had taken Hok and his captors well beyond the position of Tlanis, so that the peak now appeared
at a distance. In the other direction they proceeded, toward
a square-built stone hutch or house.

Hok, as he hobbled along, gazed once to landward. He
realized, for the first time, how deep the valley truly was—a
sort of sky-pointing cavern. No wonder that things were always green and warm here, he mused.

And then the sentries were hailing someone who came from
the square stone house.

It was the tall, eagle-faced priest in long robes, with whom
Hok had come close to quarrelling in the wine-shop. He

grinned sardonically when he saw the prisoner and heard the report.

"I knew he was meat for Ghirann when first I saw him," he informed the guards, fingering his tag of beard. "Leave him in my charge." To Hok he said, "Come with me, you meat for the god."

Hok, his ankles hobbled with a leather thong, raged unavailingly as the priest shoved and chivvied him along the rocky shore to the stone building. From the doorway came another man to meet them—a filthy, tousle-haired creature in a red kilt, with vacant eyes and a twitching, slobbering mouth. Hok gazed with loathing; his own people were accustomed, for the sake of mercy and practicality, to kill the feeble-minded.* But this creature, apparently a favored companion of his new guard, danced and gibbered, gnashing long yellow fangs.

"Is this Ghirann, who is to eat me?" Hok demanded of the priest. "It is to be expected that the people of Tlanis would worship a crazy man."

The priest turned pale with anger at the slur, but then smiled harshly. "Ghirann has touched his mind, and made him holy,"** he explained. "There is always such a one, in the service of the god. But Ghirann himself, the Many-Legged Hungry One, will appear even more strange to you—for the little time you will see him."

With the scrawny hand of the priest urging him forward and the mad acolyte jigging and twittering, Hok came to the house, but was pushed around it instead of entering the curtained door. Then he saw that the stonework was only an augmentation of a rocky protuberance, apparently the mouth of a cave. A smaller opening, full of blackness and closed by a grating of wire-bound wood, faced away from the sea.

---

*The splendid physical proportions and large skull capacities of the Cro-Magnon skeletons have led scientists to conclude that the Stone Age Spartans, Hok's people, systematically destroyed the weak in body and mind, thereby improving the breed.—Author.

**This belief is common today, among many ancient peoples.—Author.

"You will go in there," said Hok's captor. "The cave runs far back, into the salt water. And Ghirann lives within, silent and hungry."

"Free me of these bonds," said Hok, "and I will face and fight Ghirann, or any other living thing."

"You would resist a god's hunger? I overlook the blasphemy," said the priest; and, to the madman, "Open."

The grating was drawn back, and Hok pushed in, so violently that he fell full-sprawl upon wet, smooth rock. To the imbecile's giggle was added the bitter, superior chuckling of the priest. Then the grating fell in place again, and was fastened with a heavy bronze hook.

Hok lay still, trying to pierce the gloom with his eyes. That the hole was closed up suggested that Tlanis did not care to have its god emerge—it might devour worshippers as well as sacrifices. When would it appear? Hok gritted his teeth and his beard stiffened. Would he, who had come safe out of the clutches of tiger, lion, bear, wolf and Gnorrl, be eaten at last by a monster called the "Many-Legged"? If only he were free, to fight for his life with his mighty hands. . . .

He could see now, a little, as his eyes grew accustomed to the darkness. The cave was large, extending downward rather than up, and the water of the sea filled its bottom so that the ledge on which he lay was none too spacious for his stalwart, helpless body. At some little distance a bluish glow of light showed. Apparently there was a seaward mouth to the cavern, just now under water.

Hok surged with all his strength against his bonds, until his muscles cracked; but the belts and thongs were of stout make, doubled and tripled. Horses could not have burst them apart. He tried to roll toward the water, hoping to soak the leather and so stretch it; but at the very lip of the ledge were wooden pegs, driven deep into the rock. Over them he could not hoist himself.

He turned his attention to the wooden pegs, as a possible cutter or ripper, and scowled. Many years of water-washing had smoothed them, rounded them. No escape there; he rolled back toward the better light under the grated doorway, and studied his bonds.

The soldiers had tied his wrists in front of him, and then had encircled his arms and body with other bands, so that he could not get his strong teeth to the fastenings. His ankles and thighs were similarly fastened together. Drawing up his knees, Hok studied the twisted belt that was drawn tight just above them. Then he grinned, and in inspiration.

Into that belt had been sewn a rough red garnet for ornament. Hok, by straining, extended his wrists a hand's-breadth from the bonds that held them to his body. He drew up his knees, closer and closer. The wrist-clamping leather rasped against the red stone. Again—again—

Hok had begun to pant by the time he had scraped through the cord on his wrists, but the other bonds were easy to unfasten then. He did not go to the grating at once, but lay at the rim of the ledge, thrusting his arms between the pegs to cool the chafed skin in the water.

And he could see well enough in the cavern's dimness to realize that he was not alone.

First a ripple of the water; then a blotting away of the blue patch of light, as though a bulk crowded in from the sea; and finally a churning of the surface, a great curved lump of darkness, a thrash of many cable-like limbs—and Ghirann came stalking through the shallows in search of his prey.

Hok, rising on his knee, saw the god of Tlanis plain.

Limbs as pliable as snakes and as strong as spear-shafts bore Ghirann wrigglingly forward. Above, and centrally, rode a puffy bladder of a body, as large around as Hok's arms might clasp, liver-dark and smooth. Intent, bright eyes seemed to probe Hok with animous hunger. Ghirann was of a ghastly, baleful dignity, that has impressed younger cultures than worshipping Tlanis.*

The god charged, with a churning splash, and Hok did not retreat.

*The octopus is represented in the votive art of ancient Crete, pre-Spanish Mexico, and Japan.—Author.

There was grim grappling on the ledge. Ghirann's legs became arms, embracing Hok's bare flanks and shoulders, clinging to his flesh with a multitude of round red mouths. In such an embrace had many a luckless victim perished; but Hok was free, and full of battle. His strength was perhaps as great as that of any adversary Ghirann had ever encountered. He wrenched himself free from two of the tentacles, and drove back Ghirann with fierce kicks against the flab by body. Ghirann splashed into the water again, but with two mouth-lined cables still clung to Hok's waist and thigh. Other tentacles made fast to some anchorage under water. Then Ghirann began to drag his prey from the ledge.

Hok cursed at the drawing pain of the suckers on his flesh, and braced himself against the row of wooden pegs. Ghirann's dragging arms drew tight across the wet surface of the rock, bent at the angle of his lip. It was a tug-of-war, and a stern one; Hok, with something of embarrassment, knew that Ghirann was stronger than he. When his braced limbs relaxed, he would be whipped into the water.

He clung to a projecting point of rock on the floor, with all his strength. It held for a moment, then started from its bed, as a loose tooth starts from a jaw. Again Hok cursed, but suddenly broke the curse—the yielding of that rock had provided him with a weapon.

The fragment was big, heavy, and had a rough edge. In his great hand he poised it, like the haftless axes of the Gnorrls. Sighting quickly, he struck at the nearest clutching arm of Ghirann, where it was drawn taut against the rock. He felt the tough tissue yield, and struck again, harder still. The tentacle parted like a chopped vine. Hok laughed fiercely in joy of battle, and struck with the edged stone at the other arm that held him. It, too, smashed in twain, and he was free.

Ghirann bled darkly in the water, but started erect upon the six limbs left him. He loomed above Hok like an immense spider above a stinging wasp. Crouched low on the ledge, his rock-weapon ready, Hok could see the under-center of Ghirann's body, in the midst of those writhing legs. In that center, like the heart of some nightmare flower, was Ghir-ann's mouth, a hooked, ravenous beak, opening and shutting viscidly.

Ghirann came on again, and Hok hurled his edged stone. It struck and obliterated one of those unwinking eyes, but the god of Tlanis barely faltered. Hok, too, rose erect, retreated a step, and found himself against a rough wall of stone. He tore fragments from it, with desperation of strength, and hurled them in a volley. That gave Ghirann pause, though his tentacle-tips still came gropingly after Hok.

The caveman laid both hands to a lump of stone, twice the size of his head, and fully half his weight. It would not come from the wall. Hok dragged and wrenched, and then Ghirann made another rush, enveloping him with tentacles.

The monster pulled strongly, and Hok held himself to the wall by the projection he had clutched. Another pull, that Hok thought would fetch his shoulders from their sockets—and then he was flat on the ledge, being dragged along by the gripping tentacles. But his hands were full of weight—the big rock had broken from its place, by Ghirann's strength as much as Hok's.

With a supreme flexing effort, Hok rose erect on the very brink of the ledge, all twined from ankle to armpit with the snakes that grew from Ghirann's body. But that body lay below him, against the stone floor. Straight at the remaining eye Hok brought down the great missle he had lifted, driving it with all his massed brawn.

And Ghirann, the Many-Legged Hungry One, diety of Tlanis, was smashed like a worm.*

When Hok, pushing away the slack tentacles of his dead enemy, turned toward the landward opening, he realized for the first time that he had an audience. The long-robed priest stood there, his eagle face vacant with awe that now turned to terror. Hok strode to the wire-bound grating, and smashed his way through as a bull smashes through a cane-brake. The

---

*See the myth of Hercules, and his conquest of Geyron, the six-legged man-monster, in a land far to the west of Greece.—Author.

priest who had thought to feed him to a sea-monster fell nervelessly on his knees, with bony hands lifted to plead for mercy.

CHAPTER V
The Wise Stone and the Thunder Secret

"**D**o not kill me," stammered the bony man. "I did not know your strength, great lord, or your courage! I crawl before you—"

"I do not kill, except in battle or for food," Hok interrupted contemptuously. "Yet I think you will die, without my help. This Tlanis affords strange ways for men to get their livings. Your living, I take it, was from those who worshipped the god Ghirann. Now that I have pounded him to death, you will go hungry."

"No, no," the priest made haste to say. "You have killed a god, you yourself are godlike. I will serve you, mighty one, as I served Ghirann. Give me your commands."

"First of all, get up." Under the blazing eyes of his erstwhile captive, the priest rose, trembling and fawning. "Now, then, there is one secret that I would learn."

"Anything," was the quavering reply, but the priest was stealthily plucking at something under his robe. Hok made a quick grab, drew back the folds, and possessed himself of a long bronze dagger, which he thrust into his own girdle. He went on speaking, as though there had been no interruption:

"What I would know is this thunder weapon which Cos, your ruler, says comes from Ghirann."

The priest rolled his eyes and shook his head. Hok showed his teeth, and offered to draw the dagger.

"But it is Ghirann's secret," protested the lean one.

"I have killed Ghirann, and his property becomes mine," replied Hok, stating a law that governed the cave folk.

"Thunder would blast us both," the priest wailed. "Come, the Wise Stone will advise us."

"The Wise Stone?" echoed Hok, once again mystified. "Now, how can a stone be wise?" And he allowed the priest to lead him into the house. The half-witted attendant scampered away before them, toward the path that led cityward.

Inside were couches, stools, and various great stone chests and jars. From one of the latter, the bony priest drew something like a stick with a lump at one end. That lump was huge and shiny. This he carried forth into the daylight.

Hok examined the object. At some time in the past, a stout stem or branch had been split, and a piece of stone inserted. Later, when the division had healed to clasp and hold the lump, the stick had been cut away well below, to make a handle the length of a man's arm. The stone itself was an angular ovoid, thrice the size of Hok's big fist, and of a semitransparent whiteness. It glowed and flashed, too, as though from fires within. Hok had never seen its like, but he failed to show the awe with which the priest hoped to inspire him.

"What is this stone's wisdom?" he demanded, and touched it with his forefinger. There was a tallowy feel to it, though it looked clean enough.

"It holds visions within itself, and tells the future," was the deep-toned reply.

Hok laughed. "Then it lies, and so do you. The future cannot be told, but is what men make it."

"I will show." The priest held the thing up by its wooden shaft, like a torch toward the sun, and stood thus for some time; then he carried it back into the hut, Hok following. With his free hand, the priest drew the curtain of heavy woolen fabric across the door, shutting them into darkness. "Look!" he bade.

The big stone now shone softly, as with diluted moonlight.*

"It casts light upon things to come," came the priest's hollow whisper. "Within it unfolds a picture. I see you blasted by fire, and all the world with you, because of your blasphemy and disbelief—"

---

*Diamonds are often phosphorescent in complete darkness.—Author.

Hok, staring over the other's shoulder, saw nothing but the moon-glow of the stone. "Stop that babbling!" he growled, and, putting out his hand in the dark, snatched away the Wise Stone by its haft. "I count this thing as no more to be feared than Ghirann. Like Ghirann, it shall be smashed."

Surprisingly, the priest laughed, with a scorn to match his own. "Try it," he dared Hok.

"I will," and Hok thrust aside the curtain and emerged into the light. He turned toward the stout rocky front of the house, swung the stone against it like a hammer. The priest laughed again; for the clear crystal lump remained unchipped, while a sizable niche showed where it had struck.

Hok studied the phenomenon with a scowl, then drew the bronze knife he had appropriated. With the stone firmly clenched in one fist, he pressed the metal point hard and fair against it. His muscles poured pressure upon the contact. He heard an audible clink, saw the point bend; but not so much as a scratch marred the Wise Stone.

"Well!" he said, and drew a breath. "It is very hard. I will keep it—for a club, since it cannot be chipped into an axe. Lead me to the thunder secret."

And the priest did so, because he must.

He conducted Hok along the barrier, between sea and sunken valley, toward the peak that gave off a veil of smoke. As they drew near, Hok saw caves in the lower slopes of the peak.

"Is the thunder made there?" demanded Hok.

"Yes—by slaves and prisoner," was the answer. "They must make much of the stuff, for Cos needs it to rule his people, and to conquer others."

At the entrance to the largest cave, they paused to look in. There, under two heavy-faced overseers, toiled many squatting men and women, all naked and miserable-looking. Some stirred messes of black-looking muck in pots of clay and stone. Others spread the muck carefully on the hearth of a fire that gave both heat and light to the operations. Still others were rubbing dried flakes of the material into meal, between pestle and mortar.

"Is this the thunder stuff?" Hok asked. "I still do not understand." He sniffed, and wrinkled his nose distastefully. "It smells like rotten eggs in there."

"That comes from one of the materials used," the priest told him. "Come, I will show you that also."

They skirted the peak, and looked into a smaller cave. It gave into a long tunnel, full of the sharp eggy smell Hok had noticed. The lower end held a little soft rose of light.

"That way leads to the heart of the smoking mountain," the priest said.

"Fire?" suggested Hok.

"Smoke, on which the deeper fire reflects. From those depths comes a part of the thunder weapon. See."

A skinny, wretched-looking slave came up, gasping from heat and foul vapors. He bore a shoulder-pole, with baskets slung to either end. Those baskets were full of yellow fragments, duller than gold. Hok, bending to examine, sneezed and stepped back. The priest found himself able to smile maliciously.

"That yellow cake from the mountain's entrails is mixed with black wood, which we make by roasting willow."

"You burn it?" Hok tried to elaborate, but the bony head shook.

"No, burnt wood has no life. We roast it black, in clay pots."

Hok stared after the slave. "Black willow wood, and that yellow dirt! Are thunder and lightning made from those?"

Again the head shook. "Not entirely. The yellow and the black, placed together in equal proportions, make up only a fourth part. There is another thing, which we add—little grains and crystals, coming from the heaps of seaweed that rot along this water's edge.* Three times as much of that as the yellow and black together—the whole stirred and melted

---

*Saltpeter can be produced in beds of dessicating kelp and other sea plants rich in nitrates. The priest's formula has not been too far improved upon—25 percent of charcoal and sulphur combined, with 75 percent of saltpeter, has made a powerful explosive for later ages than his.—Author.

in water, then dried and ground. It is the thunder, speaking loudly and killing many at the command of its master.''

''Yet I have seen it strike such a master,'' growled Hok, remembering how he threw back the bomb at Cos's guardsman. ''Well, the more I hear of the weapon, the less I like it. With it a woman can stand safe and slay a warrior, but not cleanly, as with a spear-throw. This,'' and he flourished his diamond-headed club, ''is more to my taste and understanding.''

''What is your will now?'' asked his companion as they turned from the mouth of the cave.

''To depart from this insane place,'' Hok was beginning to say, when his eye caught a figure, hurrying along the rocks toward them from the direction of the slanting runway and the priest's house.

It was the mad attendant. He skipped, gestured and grimaced, but the sounds he made were unintelligible. Both men questioned him—Hok roughly, the priest nervously. All he could do was point to the landward rim of the barrier, and they all three went to peer down upon the city of Tlanis.

Nearest to them, though still far below, was the green, flower-rimmed terrace that held Cos's white palace and courtyard. It appeared black and crawling with humanity, which bunched up suddenly, then split into little struggling groups. Hok had seen battles too often to mistake this one, even from a distance above it.

''Fighting,'' he said, and the priest gaped. ''Yes,'' went on Hok, ''someone has roused his friends and attacks that fat spider, Cos.''

''But who would dare?'' demanded the priest, of the unanswering sky. His imbecilic companion whimpered to attract attention, and put out a trembling finger to Hok's wrist. He plucked at the gold collar fastened there. The priest understood the gesture.

''Ehhh!'' he ejaculated. ''He has been down to the city— he has seen. It is the woman, Maie—she has power and popularity. For some reason she has rebelled against Cos.''

CHAPTER VI
War in Tlanis

Had the priest been as wise in human thought as he deemed himself, he would have known Maie's reason for rebellion.

It was simply that she had never welcomed the insistent love-profferings of her ruler. Had she been less handsome, Cos would have ignored her. Had she been less powerful, he would have taken her. Things being what they were, he had wooed her for many moons without ceasing and without making real progress.

Hok's defiance in the gravel-strewn courtyard, with his capture and departure for the sacrifice, had been the occasion rather than the reason for what happened. Maie, who had first begged for the cave chieftain's life and had been refused, turned and hurried from the courtyard. Cos had called commandingly for her to return, and, as she passed the sentry and vanished from his sight, he made up his mind that there should be no further flouting of him. He called for a messenger and issued orders.

Meanwhile, Maie reached her own dwelling, a sprawling stone house on the level below the palace. In the front room she sat alone, trembling with emotions she found hard to analyze. She kept envisioning the blond giant who had walked by her side to Cos's audience, and had departed in bonds. She thought of his engaging ignorances, his strange philosophy of life, his puzzling questions and his definite statements. He was the strongest man she had ever known, and the most honest, and the most handsome. And she loved him—at least she assured herself that she did. Perhaps she really did. Such things were so hard to know.

In the midst of this, a slave came to her inner sitting-room to say that an armored man was asking for her at the door. She went, inquiringly, to find that the visitor was the courier from Cos.

"You are to come with me to the palace," he announced. "Cos wants you. Today you become his chief woman."

Maie shook her dark head, her mouth too dry to speak. The long, frustrating consideration of whether she would yield to the master of Tlanis was now up for a decision; and she was deciding against it.

The courier frowned. "You cannot disobey your master."

"Cos is not my master," said Maie at once. She was quoting Hok, and it was treasonable. The courier put out a hand to seize her arm and drag her along.

Maie screamed. At the sound of her voice, a soldier of her own following dashed around the corner of the house. In his hand was a chopping-sword, like a very long-bladed bronze cleaver. He cut down the courier with one stout blow, and faced his mistress across the wilting, bloody body that lay on the outer threshold.

They were lost, they both knew—a representative of Cos had come on his master's errand, and had been resisted and killed. There was only one thing for Maie's retainer to say, and he said it immediately and sturdily: "Mistress, I shall not desert you." To this he added: "No, nor will the other men."

"But we are few against Cos," objected Maie. "Drag this body out of sight, and let us think."

Fate granted them scant time for thinking. The event had been seen by a lounger, who ran to report to others, and even as Maie and her servitor bent above the bloody form, the foremost of a curious throng came in view of the doorway.

Once again Maie screamed. Others of her household ran out, thinking to protect her from some danger. The mob, already numerous, but unarmed and not particularly vicious, was daunted. Maie took time to exhort them.

"Do not betray me, people of Tlanis," she begged. "Cos sent evil fellow to threaten me. My man came to my defense—there was nothing else to do. Am I to blame?"

"Not a whit!" shouted a citizen in the forefront of the gathering, a man with a loud voice and a secret grudge against the ruler of Tlanis. A murmur of agreement went up, and he was emboldened to speak further: "Would that Cos lay dead here instead of his slave!"

"Well said, friend!" responded one of Maie's armed men heartily. This soldier was an opportunist, and saw a chance of real resistance against the fate that would soon move against him and his comrades. "Who else is for us and against the tyrant?"

Had a philosopher been present, he might have spoken learnedly about the spirit which sways mobs, all unprepared, to one common fierce impulse. But there were no philosophers—only loiterers and poor laborers, most of them with valid grievances against the cruel, greedy man up yonder in the palace. They began to speak out, bravely, and to roar for blood and vengeance. Maie, more frightened than ever, tried to calm them—she had never quite thought of actual rebellion; but the affair had passed quite out of her hands.

Some of her soldiers, ready fellows without too much forethought or discipline, had plunged zealously through the press of people, and shouted for volunteers to storm the palace and do justice on Cos, the monster. The air was rent with the shouts of those who were anxious to comply—some for sympathy with Maie, who was neither unknown nor unrespected in the community; some for hate of Cos, who had been arbitrary and oppressive for years; and some for the chance of loot and excitement. They drew daggers, flourished sticks and cobblestones. Others, drawn by the commotion, ran in from byways and adjoining squares and streets, then joined the group without real realization of what the disturbance was about.

The mob, with Maie's soldiers at its head, tramped loudly along the main thoroughfare and came to a small party of Cos's guardsmen at an intersection. This detachment mistakenly called on the mob to stand. There was a brief, cruel clash, and the men of Cos were slashed and pounded to pieces without exception. Citizens, exultantly blooded, caught up the armor and arms of the slain. "On to the palace!" went up a concerted cry. Maie, the cause of the business, was already forgotten.

She ran, a lone and lithe figure, up a ramp and away toward the terraced height where Cos sat awaiting her, all unaware of the danger below. Pushing past the sentry at the gate, she came into the courtyard and faced Cos, who had summoned a barber to trim his singed beard. He looked at her with a sort of tigerish zest, that had very little of love in it.

"It is time you came here," he grumbled. "Hereafter there will be no misunderstanding between us. I am the master, and you—"

"No time for that," she panted. "Danger comes—men, armed and angry—are after your blood."

"Huh!" He stared stupidly at her, and pushed away the barber. "What are you talking about?"

"Listen!" she bade him.

He listened. There was a sullen mutter, growing to a roar, from the levels below.

"What trick is this?" snorted Cos, jumping up. His sentries also pressed forward, listening. The threatening note in the racket was unmistakable, and all pressed out into the open, Cos prudently coming last. They moved toward the edge of the terrace, to peer down, when the answer to Cos's question came on fagged but scurrying feet.

A soldier dashed up from the city below. He was a mass of sweat and blood, his armor cut and smashed, his spear lost. He almost fell at the feet of Cos.

"Master, master!" he gurgled. "They fight, they kill your servants, they cry out for your life!"

"Rouse the town!" thundered Cos; but it had already risen, and more of it against the tyrant than for him. The conflict was loud enough to convince any ear. Cos turned upon Maie.

"This is your doing," he accused and put out a hand as if to clutch her shoulder.

At that moment there was a multiple scamper of feet, a chorus of howls, and the first of the revolutionists mounted the terrace. They saw Maie in the grip of the tyrant, and their angry shouting made the air shake. A spear sped at Cos, to be narrowly deflected by a guardsman who struck it aside with his own weapon. Then, at Cos's shouts, the soldiers of the palace poured forth, and battle joined on the very lawn in front of the ruler's dwelling.

Again forgotten, Maie ran for the second time. There was only one avenue of possible escape—the slanting way up the barrier to the sea above. And she took it because she must.

But before she had mounted far, cries rose behind her. The soldiers of Cos had begun to turn back the rebels, and some could be spared to pursue the woman who was being blamed for it all.

The pursuers gained, for Maie was only a woman, and badly spent. She doubted if she could reach the top—yes, she was almost there—but her way was barred, by a fierce, towering figure. He lifted a missile, a great piece of stone, and hurled it.

It buzzed past her, and clashed on armor behind. A moment later the giant had run down, and seized her to help her along.

"Are you hurt, Maie?" asked a voice she knew.

"Hok!" she whimpered gladly. "Oh, Hok!—" And her weary arms sought to embrace him, the rest of the world forgotten; but he thrust her away and up to the head of the slanting trail.

"No time for that. We have fighting to do."

CHAPTER VII
When Hok Came to Bay

As Maie had mounted upward, pursued by a leash of Cos's soldiery, Hok had seen, understood, and prepared. Quickly he had gathered as many big rocks as he could find, heaping them at the very top of the sloping trail. Now he began to hurl them. The heavy missiles, propelled by all his oaken strength, made themselves felt even through hammered helmets and linked breastplates of bronze. One or two of the foremost pursuers fell, badly hurt. The others paused, and Hok launched his chief dissuader—a rounded boulder, a leg's length in diameter.

A heave and a shove started it, and down trail it bounded and plunged, sweeping three men along with it.

The others flung spears at Hok and Maie. The girl took a bronze point in her upper arm, but Hok dodged one shaft, caught another as was his wont, and threw it back to transfix an enemy. That was enough to halt a second volley. The soldiers hung back, cagey and nervous. Hok flourished his diamond-headed club.

"Come and fight!" he taunted them. "You are easier to kill than flies!"

More were approaching from behind, but those at the forefront tried to shove their comrades back. It caused a press not many men's lengths beneath the place where Hok stood to hold the trail. Thus things might have hung in abeyance for an indefinite time; but Maie, behind Hok, looked up from cherishing her wound. She screamed.

"Hok! The priest! Beware—"

Hok spun around. The eagled-faced man who had served Ghirann had crept up, his robes kilted in one hand, a bronze axe in the other. He struck, but not soon enough. Hok stooped under the downward sweep of the axe, caught him at the waist with an encircling arm. Plunging back toward the trail, he found the soldiers rushing up toward him.

He hurled the priest, like a billet of wood. The man's body mowed two men from the head of the trail, then flew from the path into the abyss. A shriek trailed upward as the wretch vanished. But others had gained the top of the barrier, were deploying to attack Hok as hunters might attack a lion or bear.

Hok made a lightning decision, shot out a hand to catch Maie, and ran swiftly back toward the mountain. His flying feet outdistanced the none-too-eager servitors of Cos, and there was considerable margin between him and his enemies as he gained the mouth of the cave where the thunder weapon was made.

At his roars and club-flourishes, the score and more of

toiling slaves wailed and scurried out like rats surprised by a hungry ferret. Hok motioned to Maie.

"Into the cave," he directed quickly. "It is full of the thunder stuff. We can fight off nations."

They ran in, gazing around in the light of the fire. Maie uttered a despairing groan, and shook her dark head.

"It will not serve us," she said. "Look!"

Lifting her unwounded arm, she pointed to the great heaps of powdered black material that almost filled the back of the cave. "The thunder dust is loose, not in round balls," she said. "We cannot throw it. I might have known that Cos would not let the weapon be finished anywhere but in his palace—up here an enemy might come and gain advantage over him."

"We can still defend this cave," said Hok, and sprang back to the entrance. His big bulk almost filled it.

The first rush of men was upon him, and his heavy diamond club hummed as it struck once, twice, smashing two craniums. The bodies fell across each other, and Hok caught up a weapon in his left hand, one of the cleaver-like swords of Cos's bodyguard. He flailed at the oncoming band with both weapons, cutting a third man almost in half and breaking the arm of still another. The rest gave back. They had to.

"Spears!" roared someone, and Hok dropped the Wise Stone from his right hand in time to snatch yet again a whistling shaft, reverse it, and send it through the body of its hurler. Then he dropped to one knee, quickly dragging the bodies of his dead into a protecting heap in front of him. The press of soldiers—there were at least sixty or seventy by now—again drew back, staring in panic. About Hok and his dead hung a certain atmosphere of uncertain, superhuman horror.

"He is invulnerable," muttered one.

"Yes—was he not sent to be eaten by Ghirann? Could not even Ghirann finish him?" And the murmurs grew.

Then there was more commotion, and into the heart of the group hurried a figure with gold on head and arms, with a dark face and a lopsided black beard—Cos, the tyrant. His men below had beaten the undisciplined throng of rebels and were driving it through the lower levels of the city, and he had come aloft to see what happened on the barrier. His eyes blazed as he stared into the cavern, and saw Maie staunching the blood on her arm.

"Who hurt the woman?" he bawled. "I want her."

"You can never have me," Maie cried back to him.

Cos gestured angrily. "Why do you all stand like fools? Go into the cave and fetch her out."

"They are sick of trying," Hok informed him.

Cos gave new orders: "Throw no more spears. Capture Maie alive, but cut that big savage to pieces."

"He is a devil," protested a white-faced soldier, who felt that he had had more than enough of fighting with Hok.

"Do you fear him more than you fear me?" demanded Cos angrily. "Charge him!"

A full dozen obeyed. Hok, meeting them, was hard put to it to defend himself against a rain of blows, much less speed returns. But help came. Maie, catching up a hoe-like tool from the floor of the cave, rushed pluckily. She came to Hok's right side, and with a sweeping stroke brought down a guardsman. Others turned blindly upon her, striking and stabbing, and Hok in turn belabored them. Once again there was a reeling backward from the cave-mouth, now half-blocked with bodies. Cos, safely out of reach, was again able to see what had happened, and he cursed wildly.

"Fools! You have killed her!"

It was true. Maie, the fair chieftainess whom a ruler had coveted, lay dead. Her body was stabbed through with spears, her head was bitten open by a chopping sword. There was silence. Hok and Cos gazed at each other above the heap of mangled bodies, as fixedly as though they were the only two men left in the world.

"You have been the reason for her death," said Cos, in a cold voice of accusation.

Hok wagged his bright-thatched head. "That is a lie, as is almost every word you speak. It is you who made her die. A quick death, and now she is happy with the Sky-Dwellers—safe out of your hands, Cos the liar and coward.''

"Ghirann shall punish you," gritted the ruler of Tlanis.

Again Hok made a sign of negation. "Can Ghirann punish his punisher? Look yonder in that cave, that is half-full of water. Ghirann, whom you called your brother, lies pounded to nothing. And I did it—I! Hok, who brings woe to you and yours!"

Somebody moved through the crowd to Cos's side. It was the red-kilted imbecile who had been a servitor of Ghirann and Ghirann's priest. The foolish head was wagging, to corroborate Hok's story.

Cos turned back to the cave chieftain. His soft red mouth broke open in an ugly grin.

"Your life is forfeit, stone-chipper, before you bring more calamity on us," he said in a voice that choked. His hand reached out, the fingers snapped. Someone gave him what he wanted—a bomb, with hanging fuse. Another offered a blazing lamp to kindle it.

But a frantic chorus of protests rose. "No, master! No! Throw nothing! He will seize and throw it back!"

"That is the truth," Hok assured Cos. "I have been doing it all day."

The tyrant of Tlanis gazed wildly about him. "Someone must charge him," he said. "Charge and hold him, so that he cannot catch the thing. Who goes?"

Only one dared rush upon death—the madman, who was too foolish to fear. He leaped forward and at Hok, grappling with monkeyish strength. For the moment Hok was busy tearing him free, then swung the Wise Stone against the idiot head. In the meantime, Cos laughed as Death laughs, ignited his fuse, and whirled the bomb backward for a cast.

Hok saw, and with his left hand threw something on his own account—the bronze chopping-sword he had caught up. It sang in the air like a deadly insect, and struck home. Cos remained briefly upon his feet, but of his head remained only the black beard, the grinning red mouth. The rest flew away like a nut falling overripe from its tree.

In death, his hand still moved to throw the bomb, but it went high. Diving beneath it, Hok landed in the thick of his enemies.

The lump of explosive intended for him went sailing, all a-sputter, into the cave he had quitted.

He broke a skull, another, with the Wise Stone. As he whipped it up for a third blow, he heard a voice shriek:

"Fly! Fly! The cave is full of thunder dust—it will take fire—kill us all—"

And Hok, remembering that the bomb had fallen in the one place where it would wreak the most damage, stopped fighting and ran. He clove a way through the press as a knife speeds through water, and began to run northward along the causeway. So did some others. But it was too late.

The bomb exploded. Then came a greater explosion—the great hoard of thunder dust. Then a third—the volcano itself. And the doom of Tlanis was sealed.

CHAPTER VIII
Home Is the Hunter

Hok had thought only of getting away. The soldiers of Tlanis had thought only of returning to their city under the barrier. This difference of desire resulted in his escape and their destruction.

As Hok raced northward along the rocky shore, the voice of the bombarded mountain bellowed behind him, filling the earth and the sky with noise. The shock of the first explosion made him stagger, the shock of the second threw him flat. He scrambled up again, shaking off the dizziness. The air was suddenly full of pungent vapors. The volcano was spewing smoke and fire.

For the cave-full of explosive had acted as a greater bomb than any man of that age could conceive. It drove deep into the heart of the mountain, liberating a rush of red-hot lava.

The warriors of Tlanis dashed along their sloping trail to

the levels below. Thus hidden under the overhang of the barrier's height, they did not see the destruction that was upon them until the immemorial sturdiness of rocks dissolved and dashed them down, forty or fifty of them at once.

For the new upward rush of the subterranean fires had split open the slopes of the hollow mountain. Water from the sea flung itself upon a world of molten rock, fluffing away into live steam. The tortured rocks and slopes shook and writhed, like a huge animal in pain, then disintegrated.

Probably many in Tlanis—the merchants, the nobles, the soldiers, the beggars—died before they knew that the wall above them had changed from stone to water, and was descending to crush before it overwhelmed. Others did see, shrieked and ran. They were overtaken and obliterated before they could reach the gates. Tlanis, built for an age, was being washed away like a scattering of leaves in a spring freshet. The blue teemings of ocean, crowding through the widening rent in the barrier, deployed to flow out and down valley.

Hok, still running like an antelope, realized that the waves no longer beat against the shore at his left hand. They raced to his rear, to the south, scrambling and fighting like live things to find and pass through the hole where the mountain had burst. The sand-plugged stones under his feet ground and gritted together. They, too, would go before long.

Hok's mind, trained to face and deal with danger, told him that he had best get away from this sea-assailed rampart. He did not slack his windy speed, but his eyes quested ever and again to the right, the landward. And eventually he found what he sought—a sloping ledge that dropped away, like that other one now disintegrated and drowned, that had given descent toward Tlanis. Hok raced down it, sprang at the end into a lofty treetop, and swarmed down to the brown soil of the valley. He resumed his running, ever to the north and the higher ground. At length he came out on the brow of a rise, and stopped to look.

The sea had taken possession of the valley's bottom. It rushed in a fierce, foul torrent, full of uprooted trunks and leafage, masses of turf and muck, the bodies of trapped an-

imals, either slack or struggling—yes, and the bodies of men.
Overhead flew screaming clouds of frantic birds. Beyond all
this Hok could see the barrier, its gap now torn as wide as
the whole of City of Tlanis had been, and widening. There
was the greatest swirl, through which still burst the angry jets
of steam and smoke from the riven volcano.

The water rose visibly as he paused. He dare not stop to
see more.

But, as he turned away to run still farther, a sound broke
forth beside him that made him jump, then turn gladly. It was
a whinny, the voice of a horse—one of the horses of Tlanis,
a servant and worshipper of man.

It came trotting to him, trailing a broken halter—a trembling brown beast with wide, worried eyes, glad all over to
see a man still alive, already trusting Hok to avert danger and
death for them both. Hok held out his open hand, and the
animal put a soft nose into it.

"Shall we go together?" asked Hok, as though the beast
could understand. He thrust the handle of the Wise Stone into
his belt, seized the end of the halter, and vaulted upon the
willing back. Then, with drumming heels, he urged his steed
away to higher ground still.

On he rode, until the poor horse panted and stumbled, and
the sun dropped down. The day was dying, and Hok took
time to remember that at mid-morning he had first set eyes
on Tlanis. A day's adventure and strife beyond imagination—
and would he live to see the sun again?

Horse and man camped because they could budge no further among hills that gave like buttresses upon the slopes of
mountains. Hok slept, exhausted; but twice he awoke, shuddering, from ill dreams, and the gray dawn showed him that
all the upward slope over which he had galloped was
drowned, with the sea come in to fill, from horizon to horizon, that vast valley which had known the rule of Cos and
the worship of Ghirann. The water still climbed after him.

A second day he urged his horse to the slope, and a second
day the sea crept in pursuit, but more slowly. At noon of the

third day, he was aware of no chase. The sea was finding its depth, was content with its conquered lands.

He came to a forest of pines and beeches, a forest he thought he knew. Not far away would be his own country.

At once he dismounted from the brown horse. He drew off the halter that was its badge of servitude, and started away on foot. There came a clop-clop of hoofs. He was being followed.

Turning, he faced the animal. "Go and be free," he bade it solemnly. "I cannot take you to my people. They do not use horses, except to eat."

The horse gazed as though it understood, but made to follow again. Hok shouted, and it came to a halt.

"I tell you to go another way," he said sternly. "My country is bad for horses. Not only men will eat you, but lions, bears, tigers, Gnorrls. You are safe from me, because you helped me escape. But not even I can protect you."

Again he walked away, for a good hundred paces among the trees. Then he glanced back. The horse remained where his voice had last halted it, as though it was loath to bid him goodbye.

When Hok returned, after some days, to his home in the bluff-surrounded cave that fronted the half-moon beach and the river from whose brink he had driven the Gnorrl people, all his tribe came to stare respectfully.

"You have not been gone more than a moon," remarked Zorr, his father-in-law. "Yet you have many new scars. Was there a fight?"

"There was a fight," replied Hok. He felt like deferring the story until he had rested.

Oloana came forward, curiosity mingled with the adoration in her eyes. "What is that thing on your wrist, the thing that shines?" she asked.

Hok undid the string of beads.

"It is gold," he said. "A woman called Maie gave it to me."

"A pretty woman?" demanded Oloana quickly.

"Not as pretty as you," Hok assured her, with something

like marital diplomacy. "She is dead. I kept her gift for you. It is to be worn on the neck."

Oloana donned the bauble, and asked other questions, but Hok never had much to say about Maie, then or later. Today her name, as Mu or Mou, or Maya, is a name of mystery.

Zhik arrived from the hunt, to greet his brother heartily, and to him Hok presented the bronze dagger that he had taken from the priest of Ghirann. For himself he kept, forever after, the Wise Stone in its wooden handle, as a war-club hard enough to crush the toughest skulls of man or beast.

And finally he came to his cave, and sat alone by the fire in the entrance. It was quiet there, and he began to yawn. A patter of feet sounded from the gloomy interior. There emerged a plump little entity, with a shock of hair as pale as frosted barley grass. In one chubby fist was clutched a toy spear of wood.

"My son," said Hok.

"Father," came the solemn response. "Will you tell me a story?"

Hok drew the boy to his knee.

"I will tell you," he began, "a story which you must remember as a great marvel. When you have children, tell it to them, and they will tell it to their children. It is the story of Tlanis, the home of many strange and wonderful things, and of how the sea drowned it and them."

IV.

JACK WILLIAMSON

INTRODUCTION

Born April 29, 1908 in Bisbee, Arizona, Jack Williamson now resides in Portales, New Mexico, and at age 80 he is still writing industriously and attending science fiction conventions. Must be something to what they say about that Southwestern climate. After all, his first story was published in 1928, and six decades as a writer is tough to match.

With some forty books to his credit, Williamson is generally regarded as a science fiction writer, his high reputation firmly assured by such books as the dystopian classic, *The Humanoids* (1949); his outstanding collaboration with James E. Gunn, *Star Bridge* (1955); and his earlier Legion of Space series, quintessential space opera. Williamson, however, has also left his mark on the fantasy genre. At the start, his inspiration was A. Merritt, *the* master of the science-fantasy-adventure yarn, and Williamson's early stories show this influence. The best example of this phase is the excellent lost-race adventure, *Golden Blood*, serialized in *Weird Tales* in 1933. A splendid heroic fantasy novel, *The Reign of Wiz-*

ardry, was serialized in *Unknown* in 1940. The December 1940 issue of *Unknown Fantasy Fiction* would also run Williamson's best known fantasy novel, *Darker Than You Think*—certainly among the top five werewolf novels ever written. And, a decade earlier, Williamson wrote the novella, "Wolves of Darkness."

During its initial thirty-one-year run, *Weird Tales* had the occasional rival in the weird-fantasy field: *Ghost Stories*, *Tales of Magic and Mystery*, *Strange Stories*, and (to an extent) *Unknown*. *Weird Tales* easily outlasted the competition. The most serious threat to *Weird Tales'* supremacy was a short-lived pulp entitled *Strange Tales*. Backed by the money of the then-mighty Clayton Magazines, editor Harry Bates launched *Strange Tales* in 1931 with the professed intention of blowing *Weird Tales* off the stands. After all, Clayton's new science fiction pulp, *Astounding Stories*, was already grabbing the market from such competition as *Amazing Stories* and *Wonder Stories*. Paying far better rates—and paying on schedule—Bates was able to lure a number of the *Weird Tales* stalwarts, as well as attract competent writers from other pulp genres. It was a brave effort, but this was also the Depression. Clayton Magazines went bottom up, and *Strange Tales* folded in 1933 with only seven issues. *Astounding Stories* was continued by another publisher and still exists today under its later title, *Analog*. One wonders what might have happened had Street & Smith also elected to salvage *Strange Tales*.

"Wolves of Darkness" appeared in the January 1932 issue of *Strange Tales*, earning a striking cover by H. W. Wesso. In certain instances the reader will note a presage of *Darker Than You Think*, but this novella is far more than a youthful dry run of that famous novel. "Wolves of Darkness" is an unabashed horror thriller, written in the most florid language of the pulps. Can you say "ululation"? How many times?

While Williamson was soon to develop his mature polished style, the youthful exuberance displayed here makes "Wolves of Darkness" a pure pulp classic. It is also a headlong-paced chiller told with a bloodthirsty zeal that modern horror writers can envy. No ancient swordplay here, but this tale of other dimensions, evil powers, derring-do, desperate courage and heroism certainly fits the model for the *Echoes of Valor* series. And one more thing: This is not a story that you're going to forget.

WOLVES OF DARKNESS
by Jack Williamson

CHAPTER I
The Tracks in the Snow

Involuntarily I paused, shuddering, on the snow-covered station platform. A strange sound, weird, and somehow appalling, filled the ghostly moonlight of the winter night. A quavering and distant ululation, which prickled my body with chills colder than the piercing bite of the motionless, frozen air.

That unearthly, nerve-shredding sound, I knew, must be the howling of the gray prairie or *lobo* wolves, though I had not heard them since childhood. But it carried a note of elemental terror which even the trembling apprehensions of boyhood had never given the voice of the great wolves. There was something sharp, broken, about that eery clamor, far-off and deeply rhythmic as it was. Something—and the thought brought a numbing chill of fear—which suggested that the dreadful ululation came from straining human throats!

Striving to shake the phantasy from me, I hastened across the icy platform, and burst rather precipitately into the dingy waiting room. It was brilliantly lit with unshaded electric bulbs. A red-hot stove filled it with grateful heat. But I was less thankful for the warmth than for the shutting out of that far-away howling.

Beside the glowing stove a tall man sat tense over greasy cards spread on the end of a packing box which he held between his knees, playing solitaire with strained, feverish attention. He wore an ungainly leather coat, polished slick with wear. One tanned cheek bulged with tobacco, and his lips were amber-stained.

He seemed oddly startled by my abrupt entrance. With a sudden, frightened movement, he pushed aside the box, and sprang to his feet. For a moment his eyes were anxiously upon me; then he seemed to sigh with relief. He opened the stove door, and expectorated into the roaring flames, then sank back into his chair.

"Howdy, Mister," he said, in a drawl that was a little strained and husky. "You sort of scairt me. You was so long comin' in that I figgered nobody got off."

"I stopped to listen to the wolves," I told him. "They sound weird, don't they?"

He searched my face with strange, fearful eyes. For a long time he did not speak. Then he said briskly, "Well, Mister, what kin I do for ye?"

As I advanced toward the stove, he added, "I'm Mike Connell, the station agent."

"My name is Clovis McLaurin," I told him. "I want to find my father, Dr. Ford McLaurin. He lives on a ranch near here."

"So you're Doc McLaurin's boy, eh?" Connell said, warming visibly. He rose, smiling and shifting his wad of tobacco to the other cheek, and took my hand.

"Yes," I said. "Have you seen him lately? Three days ago I had a strange telegram from him. He asked me to come at once. It seems that he's somehow in trouble. Do you know anything about it?''

Connell looked at me queerly.

"No," he said at last. "I ain't seen him lately. None of 'em off the ranch ain't been in to Hebron for two or three weeks. The snow is the deepest in years, you know, and it ain't easy to git around. I dunno how they could have sent a telegram, though, without comin' to town. And they ain't none of us seen 'em!''

"Have you got to know Dad?" I inquired, alarmed more deeply.

"No, not to say real well," the agent admitted. "But I seen him and Jetton and Jetton's gal often enough when they come into Hebron, here. Quite a bit of stuff has come for 'em to the station, here. Crates and boxes, marked like they was scientific apparatus—I dunno what. But a right purty gal, that Stella Jetton. Purty as a picture.''

"It's three years since I've seen Dad," I said, confiding in the agent in hope of winning his approval and whatever aid he might be able to give me in reaching the ranch, over the unusual fall of snow that blanketed the West Texas plains. "I've been in medical college in the East. Haven't seen Dad since he came out here to Texas three years ago.''

"You're from the East, eh?"

"New York. But I spent a couple of years out here with my uncle when I was a kid. Dad inherited the ranch from him.''

"Yeah, old Tom McLaurin was a friend of mine," the agent told me.

It was three years since my father had left the chair of astrophysics at an eastern university, to come here to the lonely ranch to carry on his original experiments. The legacy from his brother Tom, besides the ranch itself, had included a small fortune in money, which had made it possible for him to give up his academic position and to devote his entire time to the abstruse problems upon which he had been working. Being more interested in medical than in mathematical science, I had not followed Father's work completely, though I used to help him with his experiments, when he had to perform them in a cramped flat, with pitifully limited equipment. I knew, however, that he had worked out an extension of Weyl's non-Euclidian geometry in a direction quite different from those chosen by Eddington and Einstein—and whose implications, as regards the structure of our universe, were stupendous. His new theory of the wave-electron, which completed the wrecking of the Bohr planetary atom, had been as sensational.

The proof his theory required was the exact comparison of the velocity of beams of light at right angles. The experiment required a large, open field, with a clear atmosphere, free from dust or smoke; hence his choosing the ranch as a site upon which to complete the work.

Since I wished to remain in college, and could help him no longer, he had employed as an assistant and collaborator, Dr. Blake Jetton, who was himself well known for his remarkable papers upon the propagation of light, and the recent modifications of the quantum theory.

Dr. Jetton, like my father, was a widower. He had a single child, a daughter named Stella. She had been spending several months of each year with them on the ranch. While I had not seen her many times, I could agree with the station agent that she was pretty. As a matter of fact I had thought her singularly attractive.

Three days before, I had received the telegram from my father. A strangely worded and alarming message, imploring me to come to him with all possible haste. It stated that his life was in danger, though no hint had been given as to what the danger might be.

Unable to understand the message, I had hastened to my rooms for a few necessary articles—among them, a little automatic pistol—and had lost no time in boarding a fast train. I had found the Texas Panhandle covered with nearly a foot of snow—the winter was the most severe in several years. And that weird and terrible howling had greeted me omi-

nously when I swung from the train at the lonely village of
Hebron.

"The wire was urgent—most urgent," I told Connell. "I
must get out to the ranch to-night, if it's at all possible. You
know of any way I could go?"

For some time he was silent, watching me, with dread in
his eyes.

"No, I don't," he said presently. "Ten mile to the ranch.
And they ain't a soul lives on the road. The snow is nigh a
foot deep. I doubt a car would make it. Ye might git Sam
Judson to haul you over tomorrow in his wagon."

"I wonder if he would take me out to-night?" I inquired.

The agent shook his head uneasily, peered nervously out
at the glistening, moonlit desert of snow beyond the windows, and seemed to be listening anxiously. I remembered
the weird, distant howling I had heard as I walked across the
platform, and could hardly restrain a shiver of my own.

"Naw, I think not!" Connell said abruptly. "It ain't
healthy to git out at night around here, lately."

He paused a moment, and then asked suddenly, darting a
quick, uneasy glance at my face, "I reckon you heard the
howlin'?"

"Yes. Wolves?"

"Yeah—anyhow, I reckon so. Queer. Damn queer! They
ain't been any loafers around these parts for ten years, till we
heard 'em jest after the last blizzard." ("Loafer" appeared
to be a local corruption of the Spanish word *lobo* applied to
the gray prairie wolf, which is much larger than the coyote,
and was a dreaded enemy of the rancher in the Southwest
until its practical extermination.)

"Seems to be a reg'lar pack of the critters rovin' the
range," Connell went on. "They've killed quite a few cattle
in the last few weeks, and—" he paused, lowering his voice,
"and five people!"

"The wolves have killed people!" I exclaimed.

"Yeah," he said slowly. "Josh Wells and his hand were
took two weeks ago, come Friday, while they was out ridin'
the range. And the Simms' are gone. The old man and his

woman and little Dolly. Took right out of the cow-pen, I reckon, while they was milkin'. It ain't two mile out of town to their place. Rufe Smith was out that way to see 'em Sunday. Cattle dead in the pen, and the smashed milk buckets lying in a drift of snow under the shed. And not a sign of Simms and his family!''

"I never heard of wolves taking people that way!" I was incredulous.

Connell shifted his wad of tobacco again, and whispered, "I didn't neither. But, Mister, these here ain't ordinary wolves!''

"What do you mean?" I demanded.

"Wall, after the Simms' was took, we got up a sort of posse, and went out to hunt the critters. We didn't find no wolves. But we did find tracks in the snow. The wolves is plumb gone in the daytime!

"Tracks in the snow," he repeated slowly, as if his mind were dwelling dazedly upon some remembered horror. "Mister, them wolf tracks was too tarnation far apart to be made by any ordinary beast. The critters must 'a' been jumpin' thirty feet!

"And they warn't all wolf tracks, neither. Mister, part was wolf tracks. And part was tracks of bare human feet!''

With that, Connell fell silent, staring at me strangely, with a queer look of utter terror in his eyes.

I was staggered. There was, of course, some element of incredulity in my feelings. But the agent did not look at all like the man who has just perpetrated a successful wild story, for there was genuine horror in his eyes. And I recalled that I had fancied human tones in the strange, distant howling I had heard.

There was no good reason to believe that I had merely encountered a local superstition. Widespread as the legends of lycanthropy may be, I have yet to hear a whispered tale of werewolves related by a West Texan. And the agent's story had been too definite and concrete for me to imagine it an idle fabrication or an ungrounded fear.

"The message from my father was very urgent," I told

Connell presently. "I *must* get out to the ranch to-night. If the man you mentioned won't take me, I'll hire a horse and ride."

"Judson is a damn fool if he'll git out to-night where them wolves is!" the agent said with conviction. "But there's nothing to keep ye from askin' him to go. I reckon he ain't gone to bed yet. He lives in the white house, jest around the corner behind Brice's store."

He stepped out upon the platform behind me to point the way. And as soon as the door was opened, we heard again that rhythmic, deep, far-off ululation, that weirdly mournful howling, from far across the moonlit plain of snow. I could not repress a shudder. And Connell, after pointing out to me Sam Judson's house, among the straggling few that constituted the village of Hebron, got very hastily back inside the depot, and shut the door behind him.

CHAPTER II
The Pack that Ran by Moonlight

Sam Judson owned and cultivated a farm nearly a mile from Hebron, but had moved his house into the village so that his wife could keep the post-office. I hurried toward his house, through the icy streets, very glad that Hebron was able to afford the luxury of electric lights. The distant howling of the wolf-pack filled me with a vague and inexplicable dread. But it did not diminish my determination to reach my father's ranch as soon as possible, to solve the riddle of the strange and alarming telegram he had sent me.

Judson came to the door when I knocked. He was a heavy man, clad in faded, patched blue overalls, and brown flannel shirt. His head was almost completely bald, and his naked scalp was tanned until it resembled brown leather. His wide face was covered with a several week's growth of black beard. Nervously, fearfully, he scanned my face.

He led me to the kitchen, in the rear of the house—a small, dingy room, the walls covered with an untidy array of pots and pans. The cook stove was hot; he had, from appearances, been sitting with his feet in the oven, reading a newspaper, which now lay on the floor.

He had me sit down, and, when I took the creaking chair, I told him my name. He said that he knew my father, Dr. McLaurin, who got his mail at the post-office which was in the front room. But it had been three weeks, he said, since anyone had been to town from the ranch. Perhaps because the snow made traveling difficult, he said. There were five persons now staying out there, he told me. My father and Dr. Jetton, his daughter, Stella, and two hired mechanics from Amarillo.

I told him about the telegram, which I had received three days before. And he suggested that my father, if he had sent it, might have come to town at night, and mailed it to the telegraph office with the money necessary to send it. But he thought it strange that he had not spoken to anyone, or been seen.

Then I told Judson that I wanted him to drive me out to the ranch, at once. At the request his manner changed; he seemed frightened!

"No hurry about starting to-night, is there, Mr. McLaurin?" he asked. "We can put you up in the spare room, add I'll take ye over in the wagon to-morrow. It's a long drive to make at night."

"I'm very anxious to get there," I said. "I'm worried about my father. Something was wrong when he telegraphed. Very much wrong. I'll pay you enough to make it worth while."

"It ain't the money," he told me. "I'd be glad to do it for a son of Doc McLaurin's. But I reckon you heard—the wolves?"

"Yes, I heard them. And Connell, at the station, told me something about them. They've been hunting men?"

"Yes." For a little time Judson was silent, staring at me with strange eyes from his hairy face. Then he said, "And that ain't all. Some of us seen the tracks. And they's men runnin' with 'em!''

"But I must get out to see my father," I insisted. "We should be safe enough in a wagon. And I suppose you have a gun?''

"I have a gun, all right," Judson admitted. "But I ain't anxious to face them wolves!''

I insisted, quite ignorant of the peril into which I was dragging him. Finally, when I offered him fifty dollars for the trip, he capitulated. But he was going, he said—and I believed him—more to oblige a friend than for the money.

He went into the bedroom, where his wife was already asleep, roused her, and told her he was going to make the trip. She was rather startled, as I judged from the sound of her voice, but mollified when she learned that there was to be a profit of fifty dollars.

She got up, a tall and most singular figure in a purple flannel nightgown, with nightcap to match, and busied herself making us a pot of coffee on the hot stove, and finding blankets for us to wrap about us in the farm wagon, for the night was very cold. Judson, meanwhile, lit a kerosene lantern, which was hardly necessary in the brilliant moonlight, and went to the barn behind the house to get ready the vehicle.

Half an hour later we were driving out of the little village, in a light wagon, behind two gray horses. Their hoofs broke through the crust of the snow at every step, and the wagon wheels cut into it steadily, with a curious crunching sound. Our progress was slow, and I anticipated a tedious trip of several hours.

We sat together on the spring seat, heavily muffled up, with blankets over our knees. The air was bitterly cold, but there was no wind, and I expected to be comfortable enough. Judson had strapped on an ancient revolver, and we had a repeating rifle and a double barrel shotgun leaning against our knees. But despite our arms, I could not quite succeed in quieting the vague fears raised by the wolf-pack, whose quavering, unearthly wail was never still.

Once outside the village of Hebron, we were surrounded on all sides by a white plain of snow, almost as level as a table-top. It was broken only by the insignificant rows of posts which supported wire fences; these fences seemed to be Judson's only land-marks. The sky was flooded with ghostly opalescence, and a million diamonds of frost glittered on the snow.

For perhaps an hour and a half, nothing remarkable happened. The lights of Hebron grew pale and faded behind us. We passed no habitation upon the illimitable desert of snow. The eery, heart-stilling ululation of the wolves, however, grew continually louder.

And presently the uncanny, wailing sounds changed position. Judson quivered beside me, and spoke nervously to the gray horses, plodding on through the snow. Then he turned to face me, spoke shortly.

"I figger they're sweeping in behind us, Mr. McLaurin."

"Well, if they do, you can haul some of them back, to skin tomorrow," I told him. I had meant it to sound cheerful. But my voice was curiously dry, and its tones rang false in my ears.

For some minutes more we drove on in silence.

Suddenly I noticed a change in the cry of the pack.

The deep, strange rhythm of it was suddenly quickened. Its eery wailing plaintiveness seemed to give place to a quick, eager yelping. But it was still queerly unfamiliar. And there was something weirdly ventriloquial about it, so that we could not tell precisely from which direction it came. The rapid, belling notes seemed to come from a dozen points scattered over the brilliant, moonlit waste behind us.

The horses became alarmed. They pricked up their ears, looked back, and went on more eagerly. I saw that they were trembling. One of them snorted suddenly. The abrupt sound jarred my jangled nerves, and I clutched convulsively at the side of the wagon.

Judson held the reins firmly, with his feet braced against the end of the wagon box. He was speaking softly and soothingly to the quivering grays; but for that, they might already have been running. He turned to me and muttered:

"I've heard wolves. And they don't sound like that. Them ain't ordinary wolves!"

And as I listened fearfully to the terrible baying of the pack, I knew that he was right. Those strange ululations had an unfamiliar, an alien, note. There was a weird, terrible something about the howling that was not of this earth. It is hard to describe it, because it was so utterly foreign. It comes to me that if there are wolves on the ancient, age-dead deserts of Mars, they might cry in just that way, as they run some helpless creature to merciless death.

Malevolent were those belling notes, foul and hateful. Rioting with an infernal power of evil alien to this earth. Strong with the primal wickedness of the cosmic wastes.

"Reckon they are on the trail," Judson said suddenly, in a low, strained voice. "Look behind us."

I turned in the spring seat, peered back over the limitless flat desolation of sparkling, moonlit snow. For a few minutes I strained my eyes in vain, though the terrible belling of the unseen pack grew swiftly louder.

Then I saw leaping gray specks, far behind us across the snow. By rights, a wolf should have floundered rather slowly through the thick snow, for the crust was not strong enough to hold up so heavy an animal. But the things I saw—fleet, formless gray shadows—were coming by great bounds, with astounding speed.

"I see them," I told Judson tremulously.

"Take the lines," he said, pushing the reins at me, and snatching up the repeating rifle.

He twisted in the seat, and began to fire.

The horses were trembling and snorting. Despite the cold, sweat was raining from their heaving bodies. Abruptly, after Judson had begun to shoot, they took the bits in their teeth and bolted, plunging and floundering through the snow, dragging the wagon. Tug and jerk at the reins as I would, I could do nothing with them.

Judson had soon emptied the rifle. I doubt that he had hit any of the howling animals that ran behind us, for accurate shooting from the swaying, jolting wagon would have been impossible. And our wildly bounding pursuers would have been difficult marks, even if the wagon had been still.

Judson dropped the empty rifle into the wagon box, and turned a white, frightened face toward me. His mouth was open, his eyes protruding with terror. He shouted something incoherent, which I did not grasp, and snatched at the reins. Apparently insane with fear, he cursed the leaping grays, and lashed at them, as if thinking to outrun the pack.

For a little time I clung to the side of the rocking wagon. Then the snorting horses turned suddenly, almost breaking the wagon tongue. We were nearly upset. The spring seat was dislodged from its position, and fell into the wagon box. I was thrown half over the side of the wagon. For another agonized moment I tried to scramble back. Then the grays plunged forward again, and I was flung into the snow.

I broke through the thin crust. The thick, soft snow beneath checked the force of my fall. In a few moments I had floundered to my feet, and was clawing madly at my face, to get the white, powdery stuff away from my eyes.

The wagon was already a hundred yards away. The fear-maddened horses were still running, with Judson standing erect in the wagon, sawing wildly at the reins, but powerless to curb them. They had been turning abruptly when I was thrown out.

Now they were plunging back toward the weirdly baying pack!

Judson, screaming and cursing, crazed with terror, was being carried back toward the dimly seen, gray, leaping shapes whose uncanny howling sobbed so dreadfully through the moonlight.

Horror came over me, like a great, soul-chilling wave. I felt an insane desire to run across the snow, to run and run until I could not hear the wailing of the strange pack. With an effort I controlled myself, schooled my trembling limbs, swallowed to wet my dry throat.

I knew that my poor, floundering run could never distance the amazingly fleet gray shapes that bounded through the silver haze of moonlight toward the wagon. And I reminded myself that I had a weapon, a .25 caliber automatic pistol, slung beneath my shoulder. Something about the strange message from my father had made me fasten on the deadly little weapon, and slip a few extra clips of ammunition into my pockets.

With trembling hands, I pulled off a glove and fumbled inside my garments for the little weapon.

At last I drew out the heavy little automatic, gratefully warm with the heat of my body, and snapped back the slide to be sure that a cartridge was in the chamber. Then I stood there, in a bank of powdery snow that came nearly to my knees, and waited.

The dismal, alien howling of the pack froze me into a queer paralysis of fear. And then I was the horrified spectator of a ghastly tragedy.

The wagon must have been four hundred yards from me, across the level, glistening snow, when the dim gray shapes of the baying pack left the trail and ran straight across toward it. I saw little stabs of yellow flame, heard sharp reports of guns, and the thin, whistling screams of bullets. Judson, I suppose, had dropped the reins and was trying to defend himself with the rifle and shotgun, and his old-fashioned revolver.

The vague gray shapes surrounded the wagon. I heard the scream of an agonized horse—except for the unearthly howling of that pack, the most terrible, nerve-wracking sound I know. A struggling mass of faintly seen figures seemed to surround the wagon. There were a few more shots, then a shriek, which rang fearfully over the snow, bearing an agony of pain and terror that is inconceivable. . . . I knew it came from Judson.

After that, the only sound was the strange, blood-congealing belling of the pack—an awful outcry that had not been stilled.

Soon—fearfully soon—that alien ululation seemed to be drawing nearer. And I saw gray shapes come bounding down the trail, away from the grim scene of the tragedy—toward me!

CHAPTER III
The Wolf and the Woman

I can give no conception of the stark, maddened terror that seized me when I knew that the gray animals were running on my trail. My heart seemed to pause, until I thought I would grow dizzy and fall. Then it was thumping loudly in my throat. My body was suddenly cold with sweat. My muscles knotted until I was gripping the automatic with painful force.

I had determined not to run, for it was madness to try to escape the pack. But my resolution to stand my ground was nothing in the face of the fear that obsessed me.

I plunged across the level waste of snow. My feet broke through the thin crust. I floundered along, with laboring lungs. The snow seemed tripping me like a malevolent demon. Many times I stumbled, it seemed. And twice I sprawled in the snow, and scrambled desperately to my feet, and struggled on again, sobbing with terror, gasping in the cold air.

But my flight was cut short. The things that ran behind me could travel many times faster than I. Turning, when I must have gone less than a hundred yards, I saw them drawing near behind me, still vague gray shapes in the moonlight. I now perceived that only two had followed.

Abruptly I recalled the little automatic in my hand. I raised it, and emptied it, firing as rapidly as I could. But if I hit either of those bounding gray figures, they certainly were invulnerable to my bullets.

I had sought in my pocket for another clip, and was trying

with quivering fingers to slip it into the gun, when those things came near enough, in a milky haze of moonlight, to be seen distinctly. Then my hands closed in rigid paralysis upon the gun—I was too astounded and unstrung to complete the operation of loading.

One of those two gray shapes was a wolf. A gaunt prairie wolf, covered with long, shaggy hair. A huge beast, he must have stood three feet high at the shoulder. He was not standing now, however, but coming toward me with great leaps that covered many yards. His great eyes glowed with a weird, greenish, unnatural light—terrible and strange and somehow hypnotic.

And the other was a girl.

It was incredible. It numbed and staggered my terror-dazed mind. At first I thought it must be a hallucination. But as she came nearer, advancing with long, bounding steps, as rapidly as the gray wolf, I could no longer discredit my eyes. I recalled the weird suggestion of a human voice I had caught in the unearthly cry of the pack; recalled what Connell and Judson had told me of human footprints mingled with those of wolves in the trail the pack had left.

She was clad very lightly, to be abroad in the bitter cold of the winter night. Apparently, she wore only a torn, flimsy slip, of thin white silk, which hung from one shoulder, and came not quite to her knees. Her head was bare, and her hair, seeming in the moonlight to be an odd, pale yellow, was short and tangled. Her smooth arms and small hands, her legs, and even her flashing feet, were bare. Her skin was white, with a cold, leprous, bloodless whiteness. Almost as white as the snow.

And her eyes shone green.

They were like the gray wolf's eyes, blazing with a terrible emerald flame, with the fire of an alien, unearthly life. They were malevolent, merciless, hideous. They were cold as the cosmic wastes beyond the light of stars. They burned with an evil light, with a malicious intelligence, stronger and more fearful than that of any being on earth.

Across her lips, and her cheeks of alabaster whiteness, was a darkly red and dripping smear, almost black by moonlight.

I stood like a wooden man, nerveless with incredulous horror.

On came the girl and the wolf, springing side by side through the snow. They seemed to have preternatural strength, an agility beyond that of nature.

As they came nearer, I received another shock of terror.

The woman's face was familiar, for all its dreadful pallor and the infernal evil of the green, luminous eyes, and the red stain on her lips and cheeks. She was a girl whom I had known. A girl whom I had admired, whom I had even dreamed that I might come to love.

She was Stella Jetton!

This girl was the lovely daughter of Dr. Blake Jetton, whom, as I have said, my father had brought with him to this Texas ranch, to assist with his revolutionary experiments.

It came to me that she had been changed in some fearful way. For this could be no sane, ordinary human girl—this strange, green-eyed being, half-clad, white-skinned, who ran over the moonlit snow beside a gaunt gray wolf, with dripping red upon her fearfully pallid skin!

"Stella!" I cried.

More a scream of frightened, anguished unbelief, than a human voice, the name came from my fearparched throat. I was startled at my own call, hoarse, inchoate, gasping.

The huge gray wolf came directly at me, as if it were going to spring at my throat. But it stopped a dozen feet before me, crouching in the snow, watching me with alert and strange intelligence in its dreadful green eyes.

And the woman came even nearer, before she paused, standing with bare feet in the snow, and stared at me with terrible eyes like those of the wolf—luminous and green and filled with an evil, alien will.

The face, ghastly white, and fearfully red-stained as it was, was the face of Stella Jetton. But the eyes were not hers! No, the eyes were not Stella's!

They were the eyes of some hideous monstrosity. The eyes of some inconceivable, malevolent entity, from some frozen hell of the far-off, night-black cosmic void!

Then she spoke. The voice had some little of its old, familiar ring. But there was a new, strange note in it. A note that bore the foreign, menacing mystery of the eyes and the leprous skin. A note that had a suggestion of the dismal, wailing ululation of the pack that had followed us.

"Yes, Stella Jetton," the dreadful voice said. "What are you called? Are you Clovis McLaurin? Did you receive a telegram?"

She did not know me, apparently. Even the wording of her sentences was a little strange, as if she were speaking a language with which she was not very familiar. The delightful, human girl I had known was fearly changed: it was as if her fair body had been seized by some demoniac entity.

It occurred to me that she must be afflicted with some form of insanity, which had given her the almost preternatural strength which she had displayed in running with the wolf-pack. Cases of lycanthropy, in which the sufferer imagines himself a wolf—or sometimes a tiger or some other animal—and imitates its actions, have been common cnough in the annals of the insane. But if this is lycanthropy, I thought, it must indeed be a singular case.

"Yes, I'm Clovis McLaurin," I said, in a shaken voice. "I got Dad's telegram three days ago. Tell me what's wrong—why he worded the message as he did!"

"Nothing is wrong, my friend," this strange woman said. "We merely desired your assistance with certain experiments, of a great strangeness, which we are undertaking to perform. Your father now waits at the ranch, and I came to conduct you to him."

This singular speech was almost incredible. I could accept it only on the assumption that the speaker suffered from some dreadful derangement of the mind.

"You came to meet me?" I exclaimed, fighting the horror that almost overwhelmed me. "Stella, you mustn't be out in the cold without more wraps. You must take my coat."

I began to strip off the garment. But, as I had somehow expected, she refused to accept it.

"No, I do not need it," her strange voice told me. "The cold does not harm this body. And you must come with us, now. Your father waits for us at the house, to perform the great experiment."

She said *us*! It gave me new horror to notice that she thus classed the huge gaunt wolf with herself.

Then she sprang forward with an incredible agility, leaping through the snow in the direction in which Judson and I had been traveling. With a naked, dead-white arm, she beckoned me to follow. And the great, gray wolf sprang behind me.

Nerved to sudden action, I recalled the half-loaded automatic in my hand. I snapped the fresh clip into position, jerked back the slide mechanism to get a cartridge into the breech, and then emptied the gun into that green-orbed wolf.

A strange composure had come over me. My motions were calm enough, almost deliberate. I know that my hand did not shake. The wolf was standing still, only a few yards away. It is unlikely that I missed him at all, impossible that I missed him with every shot.

I know that I hit him several times, for I heard the bullets drive into his gaunt body, saw the animal jerk beneath their impact, and noticed gray hairs float from it in the moonlight.

But he did not fall. His terrible green eyes never wavered in their sinister stare of infernal evil.

Just as the gun was empty—it had taken me only a few seconds to fire the seven shots—I heard an angry, wolfish snarl from the woman, from the strange monster that Stella Jetton had become. I had half turned when her white body came hurtling at me like a projectile.

I went down beneath her, instinctively raising an arm to guard my throat. It is well that I did, for I felt her teeth sinking into my arm and shoulder, as we fell together into the snow.

I am sure that I screamed with the horror of it.

I fought at her madly, until I heard her strange, non-human voice again.

"You need not be afraid," it said. "We are not going to kill you. We wish you to aid with a greatly remarkable experiment. For that reason, you must come with us. Your father waits. The wolf is our friend, and will not harm you. And your weapon will not hurt it."

A curious, half-articulate yelp came from the throat of the great wolf, which had not moved since I shot at it, as if it had understood her words and gave affirmation.

The woman was still upon me, holding me flat in the snow, her bared, bloody teeth above my face, her fingers sunk clawlike into my body with almost preternatural strength. A low, bestial, growling sound came from her throat, and then she spoke again.

"You will now come with us, to the house where your father waits, to perform the experiment?" she demanded in that terrible voice, with its suggestion of the wolf-pack's weird cry.

"I'll come," I agreed, relieved somewhat to discover that the strange pair of beasts did not propose to devour me on the spot.

The woman—I cannot call her Stella, for except in body, she was not Stella!—helped me to my feet. She made no objection when I bent, and picked up the automatic, which lay in the snow, and slipped it into my coat pocket.

She and the gaunt gray wolf, which my bullets had so strangely failed to kill, leaped away together over the moonlit snow. I followed, floundering along as rapidly as I could, my mind filled with confused and terror-numbed conjecture.

There was now no doubt remaining in my mind that the woman thought herself a member of the wolf-pack, no doubt that she actually was a member. A curious sympathy certainly seemed to exist between her and the great gaunt wolf beside her.

It must be some strange form of lunacy, I thought, though I had never read of a lycanthrope whose symptoms were exaggerated to the terrible extent that hers appeared to be. It is well known that maniacs have unnatural strength, but her feats of running and leaping across the snow were almost beyond reason.

But there was that about her which even the theory of insanity did not explain. The corpse-like pallor of her skin; the terrible green luminosity of her eyes; the way she spoke—as if English were an unfamiliar tongue to her, but half mastered. And there was something even more indefinite: a strangeness that smacked of the alien life of forbidden universes!

The pace set for me by the woman and the wolf was mercilessly rapid. Stumble along as best I could, I was unable to move as fast as they wished. Nor was I allowed to fall behind, for when I lagged, the wolf came back, and snarled at me menacingly.

Before I had floundered along many miles, my lungs were aching, and I was half blind with fatigue. I stumbled and sprawled in the soft snow a last time. My tortured muscles refused to respond when I tried to rise. I lay there, ready to endure whatever the wolf might do, rather than undergo the agony of further effort.

But this time the woman came back. I was half unconscious, but I realized vaguely that she was lifting me, raising me to her shoulders. After that, my eyes were closed; I was too weary to watch my surroundings. But I knew dimly, from my sensations of swaying, that I was being carried.

Presently the toxins of exhaustion overcame my best efforts to keep my senses. I fell into the deep sleep of utter fatigue, forgetting that my limbs were growing very cold, and that I was being borne upon the back of a woman endowed with the instincts of a wolf and the strength of a demon: a woman who, when I had last seen her, had been all human and lovable!

CHAPTER IV
A Strange Homecoming

Never can I forget the sensations of my awakening. I opened my eyes upon gloom relieved but faintly by dim red light. I lay upon a bed or couch, swathed in blankets. Hands that even to my chilled body seemed ice-cold were chafing my arms and legs. And terrible greenish orbs were swimming above in the terrible crimson darkness, staring down at me, horribly.

Alarmed, recalling what had happened in the moonlight as a vague, hideous nightmare, I collected my scattered senses, and struggled to a sitting position among the blankets.

It is odd, but the first definite thing that came to my confused brain was an impression of the ugly green flowers in monotonous rows across the dingy, brown-stained wall paper. In the red light that filled the room they appeared unpleasantly black, but still they awakened an ancient memory. I knew that I was in the dining room of the old ranch house, where I had come to spend two years with my uncle, Tom McLaurin, many years before.

The weirdly illuminated chamber was sparsely furnished. The couch upon which I lay stood against one wall. Opposite was a long table, with half a dozen chairs pushed under it. Near the end of the room was a large heating stove, with a full scuttle of coal and a box of split pine kindling behind it.

There was no fire in the stove, and the room was very cold. My breath was a white cloud in that frosty atmosphere. The dim crimson light came from a small electric lantern standing on the long table. It had been fitted with a red bulb, probably for use in a photographer's dark room.

All those impressions I must have gathered almost subconsciously, for my horrified mind was absorbed with the persons in the room.

My father was bending over me, rubbing my hands. And Stella was chafing my feet, which stuck out beneath the blankets.

And my father was changed as weirdly, as dreadfully, as the girl, Stella!

His skin was a cold, bloodless white—white with the pallor of death. His hands, against my own, felt fearfully cold—as cold as those of a frozen corpse. And his eyes, watching me with a strange, terrible alertness, shone with a greenish light.

His eyes were like Stella's—and like those of the great gray wolf. They were agleam with the fire of cosmic evil, with the light of an alien, hellish intelligence!

And the woman—the dread thing that had been lovely Stella—was unchanged. Her skin was still fearfully pallid, and her eyes strange and luminously green. The stain was still on her pale face, appearing black in the somber crimson light.

There was no fire in the stove. But, despite the bitter cold of the room, the woman was still clad as she had been before, in a sheer slip of white silk, half torn from her white body. My father—or that which had once been my father—wore only a light cotton shirt, with the sleeves torn off, and a pair of ragged trousers. His feet and arms were bare.

Another fearful thing I noticed. My breath, as I said, condensed in white clouds of frozen crystals in the frigid air. But no white mists came from Stella's nostrils, or from my father's.

From outside, I could hear the dismal, uncanny keening of the running pack. And from time to time the two looked uneasily toward the door, as if anxious to go to join them.

I had been sitting up, staring confusedly and incredulously about, before my father spoke.

"We are glad to see you, Clovis," he said, rather stiffly, and without emotion, not at all in his usual, jovial, affectionate manner. "You seem to be cold. But you will presently be normal again. We have surprising need of you, in the performance of an experiment, which we cannot accomplish without your assistance."

He spoke slowly, uncertainly, as a foreigner might who has attempted to learn English from a dictionary. I was at a loss to understand it, even if I assumed that he and Stella both suffered from a mental derangement.

And his voice was somehow whining; it carried a note weirdly suggestive of the howling of the pack.

"You will help us?" Stella demanded in the same dreadful tones.

"Explain it! Please explain everything!" I burst out. "Or I'll go crazy! Why were you running with the wolves? Why are your eyes so bright and green, your skins so deathly white? Why are you both so cold? Why the red light? Why don't you have a fire?"

I babbled my questions, while they stood there in the strange room, and silently stared at me with their horrible eyes.

For minutes, perhaps, they were silent. Then an expression of crafty intelligence came into my father's eyes, and he spoke again in those fearful tones, with their ring of the baying pack.

"Clovis," he said, "you know we came here for purposes of studying science. And a great discovery has been ours to make; a huge discovery relating to the means of life. Our bodies, they are changed, as you appear to see. Better machines they have become; stronger they are. Cold harms them not, as it does yours. Even our sight is better, so bright lights we no longer need.

"But we are yet lacking of perfect success. Our minds were changed, so that we do not remember all that once it had been ours to accomplish. And it is you whom we desire to be our assistant in replacing a machine of ours, that has been broken. It is you that we wish to aid us, so that to all humanity we may bring the gift of the new life, that is ever strong, and knows not death. All people we would change with the new science that it has been ours to discover."

"You mean you want to make the human race into monsters like yourselves?" I cried.

My father snarled ferociously, like a beast of prey.

"All men will receive the gift of life like ours," his strange voice said. "Death will be no more. And your aid is required by us—and it we will have!" There was intense, malefic menance in his tones. "It is yours to be our aid. You will refuse not!"

He stood before me with bared teeth and with white fingers hooked like talons.

"Sure, I'll help you," I contrived to utter, in a shaken voice. "I'm not a very brilliant experimenter, however." It appeared that to refuse would be a means of committing very unpleasant suicide.

Triumphant cunning shone in those menacing green eyes, the evil cunning of the maniac who has just perpetrated a clever trick. But it was even more than that; it was the crafty look of supreme evil in contemplation of further victory.

"You can come now, in order to see the machine?" Stella demanded.

"No," I said hastily, and sought reasons for delay. "I am cold. I must light a fire and warm myself. Then I am hungry, and very tired. I must eat and sleep." All of which was very true. My body had been chilled through, during my hours on the snow. My limbs were trembling with cold.

The two looked at each other. Unearthly sounds passed between them, incoherent, animal whinings. Such, instead of words, seemed to be their natural speech; the English they spoke seemed only an inaccurately and recently learned tongue.

"True," my father said to me again, in a moment. He looked at the stove. "Start a fire if you must. What you need is there?" He pointed inquiringly toward coal and kindling, as if fire were something new and unfamiliar to him.

"We must go without," he added. "Light of fire is hurtful to us, as cold is to you. And in other room, called—" he hesitated perceptibly, "kitchen, will be food. There we will wait."

He and the white girl glided silently from the room.

Shivering with cold, I hurried to the stove. All the coals in it were dead; there had been no fire in it for many hours, none, perhaps, for several days. I shook down the ashes, lit a ball of crumpled newspaper with a match I found in my pocket, dropped it on the grate, and filled the stove with pine and coal. In a few minutes I had a roaring fire, before which I crouched gratefully.

In a few minutes the door was opened slowly. Stella, first peering carefully, apparently to see if these was light in the room, stepped cautiously inside. The stove was tightly closed, no light escaped from it.

The pallid, green-eyed woman had her arms full of food, a curious assortment that had evidently been collected in the kitchen in a haphazard manner. There were two loaves of bread, a slab of raw bacon, an unopened can of coffee, a large sack of salt, a carton of oatmeal, a can of baking powder, a dozen tins of canned foods, and even a bottle of stove polish.

"You eat this?" she inquired, in her strangely animal voice, dropping the articles on the table.

It was almost ludicrous; and too, it was somehow terrible. She seemed to have no conception of human alimentary needs.

Comfortably warm again, and feeling very hungry, I went over to the table, and examined the odd assortment. I selected a loaf of bread, a tin of salmon, and one of apricots, for my immediate use.

"Some of these things are to be eaten as they are," I ventured, wondering what her response would be. "And some of them have to be cooked."

"Cooked?" she demanded quickly. "What is that?"

Then, while I was silent, dazed with astonishment, she added a terrible question.

"Does it convey that they must be hot and bleeding from the animal?"

"No!" I cried. "No. To cook a food one heats it. Usually adding seasonings, such as salt. A rather complicated process, requiring considerable skill."

"I see," she said. "And you must consume such articles, to keep your body whole?"

I admitted that I did, and then remarked that I needed a can cutter, to get at the food in the tins. First inquiring about the appearance of the implement, she hurried to the kitchen, and soon returned with one.

Presently my father came back into the room. Both of them watched me with their strange green eyes as I ate. My appetite failed somewhat, but I drew the meal out as long as possible, in order to defer whatever they might intend for me after I had finished.

Both of them asked many questions. Questions similar to Stella's query about cooking, touching subjects with which an ordinary child is familiar. But they were not stupid questions—no, indeed! Both of them evinced a cleverness that was almost preternatural. They never forgot, and I was astounded at their skill in piecing together the facts I gave them, to form others.

Their green eyes watched me very curiously when, unable to drag out the pretense of eating any longer, I produced a cigarette and sought a match to light it. Both of them howled, as if in agony, when the feeble yellow flame of the match flared up. They covered their strange green eyes, and leaped back, cowering and trembling.

"Kill it!" my father snarled ferociously.

I flicked out the tiny flame, startled at its results.

They uncovered their terrible green eyes, blinking. It was several minutes before they seemed completely recovered from their amazing fear of the light.

"Make light no more when we are near," my father growled at me. "We will tear your body if you forget!" His teeth were bared; his lips curled like those of a wolf; he snarled at me frightfully.

Stella ran to an east window, raised the blind, peered nervously out. I saw that the dawn was coming. She whined strangely at my father. He seemed uneasy, like an animal at bay. His huge green eyes rolled from side to side. He turned anxiously to me.

"Come," he said. "The machine which we with your aid

will repair is in the cellar beneath the house. The day comes. We must go."

"I can't go," I said. "I'm dog tired; been up all night. I've got to rest, before I work on any machine. I'm so sleepy I can't think."

He whined curiously at Stella again, as if he were speaking in some strange wolf-tongue. She replied in kind, then spoke to me.

"If rest is needful to the working of your body, you may sleep till the light is gone. Follow."

She opened the door at the end of the room, led me into a dark hall, and from it into a small bedroom. It contained a narrow bed, two chairs, a dresser, and wardrobe trunk.

"Try not to go," she snarled warningly, at the door, "or we will follow you over the snow!"

The door closed and I was alone. A key grated ominously in the lock. The little room was cold and dark. I scrambled hastily into the bed, and for a time I lay there, listening.

The dreadful howling of the wolf-pack, which had never stilled through all the night, seemed to be growing louder, drawing nearer. Presently it ceased, with a few sharp, whining yelps, apparently just outside the window. The pack had come here, with the dawn!

As the increasing light of day filled the little room, I raised myself in the bed to scrutinize its contents again. It was a neat chamber, freshly papered. The dresser was covered with a gay silk scarf, and on it, in orderly array, were articles of the feminine toilet. A few dresses, a vivid beret, and a bright sweater were hanging under a curtain in the corner of the room. On the wall was a picture—of myself!

It came to me that this must be Stella's room, into which I had been locked to sleep until night had come again. But what weird and horrible thing had happened to the girl since I had seen her last?

Presently I examined the windows with a view to escape. There were two of them, facing the east. Heavy wooden bars had been fastened across them, on the outside, so close together that I could not hope to squeeze between them. And a survey of the room revealed no object with which they could be easily sawed.

But I was too sleepy and exhausted to attempt escape. At thought of the ten weary miles to Hebron, through the thick, soft snow, I abandoned the idea. I knew that, tired as I already was, I could never cover the distance in the short winter day. And I shuddered at the thought of being caught on the snow by the pack.

I lay down again in Stella's clean bed, about which a slight fragrance of perfume still lingered, and was soon asleep. My slumber, though deep, was troubled. But no nightmare could be as hideous as the reality from which I had found a few hours' escape.

CHAPTER V
The Machine in the Cellar

I slept through most of the short winter day. When I woke it was sunset. Gray light fell athwart the illimitable flat desert of snow outside my barred windows, and the pale disk of the moon, near the full, was rising in the darkening eastern sky. No human habitation was in view, in all the stretching miles of that white waste. I felt a sharp sense of utter loneliness.

I could look for no outside aid in coping with the strange and alarming situation into which I had stumbled. If I were to escape from these dread monsters who wore the bodies of those dearest to me, it must be by my own efforts. And in my hands alone rested the task of finding from what evil malady they suffered, and how to restore them to their old, dear selves.

Once more I examined the stout wooden bars across the windows. They seemed strongly nailed to the wall on either side. I found no tool that looked adequate to cutting them. My matches were still in my pocket, however, and it occurred to me that I might burn the bars. But there was no

time for such an undertaking before the darkness would bring
back my captors, nor did I relish the thought of attempting
to escape with the pack on my trail.

I was hungry again, and quite thirsty also.

Darkness fell, as I lay there on the bed, among the intimate
belongings of a lovely girl for whom I had owned tender
feelings—waiting for her to come with the night, amid her
terrible allies, to drag me to I knew not what dread fate.

The gray light of the day faded imperceptibly into pale
silvery moonlight.

Abruptly, without warning, the key turned in the lock.

Stella—or the alien entity that ruled the girl's fair body—
glided with sinister grace into the room. Her green eyes were
shining, and her skin was ghastly white.

"Immediately you will follow," came her wolfish voice.
"The machine below awaits the aid for you to give in the
great experiment. Quickly come. Your weak body, it is
rested?"

"All right," I said. "I've slept, of course. But now I'm
hungry and thirsty again. I've got to have water and something to eat before I tinker with any machine."

I was determined to postpone whatever ordeal lay before
me as long as possible.

"Your body you may satisfy again," the woman said. "But
take not too long!" she snarled warningly.

I followed her back to the dining room.

"Get water," she said, and glided out the door.

The stove was still faintly warm. I opened it, stirred the
coals, dropped in more fuel. Soon the fire was roaring again.
I turned my attention to the food I had left. The remainder
of the salmon and apricots had frozen on the plates, and I set
them over the stove to warm.

Soon Stella was back with a water bucket containing a
bulging mass of ice. Apparently surprised that I could not
consume water in a solid form, she allowed me to set it on
the stove to thaw.

While I waited, standing by the stove, she asked innumerable questions, many of them so simple they would have been

laughable under less strange conditions, some of them concerning the latest and most recondite of scientific theories, her mastery of which seemed to exceed my own.

My father appeared suddenly, his corpse-white arms full of books. He spread them on the table, curtly bid me come look with him. He had Einstein's *The Meaning of Relativity*, Weyl's *Gravitation und Elektricität*, and two of his own privately printed works. The latter were *Space-Time Tensors* and the volume of mathematical speculation entitled *Interlocking Universes* whose bizarre implications created such a sensation among those savants to whom he sent copies.

My father began opening these books, and bombarding me with questions about them, questions which I was often unable to answer. But the greater part of his queries related merely to grammar, or the meaning of words. The involved thought seemed easy for him to understand; it was the language which caused him difficulty.

His questions were exactly such as might be asked by a super-intellectual being from Mars, if he were attempting to read a scientific library without having completely mastered the language in which its books were written.

And his own books seemed as unfamiliar to him as those of the other scientists. But he ran through the pages with amazing speed, pausing only to ask an occasional question, and appeared to gain a complete mastery of the volume as he went.

When he released me, the food and water were warm. I drank, and then ate bread and salmon and apricots, as deliberately as I dared. I invited the two to share the food with me, but they declined abruptly. The volley of questions continued.

Then suddenly, evidently concluding that I had eaten enough, they started toward the door, commanding me to follow. I dared not do otherwise. My father paused at the end of the table and picked up the electric lantern, whose dimly glowing red bulb supplied the only light in the room.

Again we traversed the dark hall, and went out through a door in the rear of the frame building. As we stepped out upon the moonlit snow, I shuddered to hear once more the distant, wailing ululation of the pack, still with that terrible note which suggested strained human vocal organs.

A few feet from us was the door of a cellar. The basement had evidently been considerably enlarged, quite recently, for huge mounds of earth lay about us, filling the back yard. Some of them were covered with snow, some of them black and bare.

The two led the way down the steps into the cellar, my father still carrying the electric lantern, which faintly illuminated the midnight space with its feeble, crimson glow.

The cellar was large, neatly plastered. It had not been itself enlarged, but a dark passage sloped down beside the door, to deeper excavations.

In the center of the floor stood the wreck of an intricate and unfamiliar mechanism. It had evidently been deliberately smashed—I saw an ax lying beside it, which must have been the means of the havoc. The concrete floor was littered with the broken glass of shattered electron tubes. The machine itself was a mass of tangled wires and twisted coils and bent magnets, oddly arranged outside a great copper ring, perhaps four feet in diameter.

The huge copper ring was mounted on its edge, in a metal frame. Before it was a stone step, placed as if to be used by one climbing through the ring. But, I saw, it had been impossible for one actually to climb through, for on the opposite side was a mass of twisted apparatus—a great parabolic mirror of polished metal, with what appeared to be a broken cathode tube screwed into its center.

A most puzzling machine. And it had been very thoroughly wrecked. Save for the huge copper ring, and the heavy stone step before it, there was hardly a part that was not twisted or shattered.

In the end of the cellar was a small motor-generator—a little gasoline engine connected to a dynamo—such as is sometimes used for supplying isolated homes with electric light and power. I saw that it had not been injured.

From a bench beside the wall, my father picked up a brief

case, from which he took a roll of blue prints, and a sheaf of papers bound in a manila cover. He spread them on the bench and set the red lantern beside them.

"This machine, as you see, has been, most unfortunately for us, wrecked," he said. "These papers tell the method of construction to be followed in the erection of such machines. Your aid we must have in deciphering what they convey. And the new machine will bring such great, strong life as we have to all your world."

"You say 'your world'!" I cried. "Then you don't belong to this earth? You are a monster, who has stolen the body of my father!"

Both of them snarled like beasts. They bared their teeth and glowered at me with their terrible green eyes. Then a crafty look came again into the man's sinister orbs.

"No, my son," came his whining, animal tones. "A new secret of life have we discovered. Great strength it gives to our bodies. Death we fear no longer. But our minds are changed. Many things we do not remember. We must require your aid in reading this which we once wrote—"

"That's the bunk!" I exclaimed, perhaps not very wisely. "I don't believe it. And I'll be damned if I'll help repair the infernal machine, to make more human beings into monsters like you!"

Together they sprang toward me. Their eyes glowed dreadfully against their pallid skins. Their fingers were hooked like claws. Saliva drooled from their snarling lips, and naked teeth gleamed in the dim crimson radiance.

"Aid us you will!" cried my father. "Or your body will we most painfully destroy., We will eat it slowly, while you live!"

The horror of it broke down my reason. With a wild, terror-shaken scream, I dashed for the door.

It was hopeless, of course, for me to attempt escape from beings possessing such preternatural strength.

With startling, soul-blasting howls, they sprang after me together. They swept me to the cellar's floor, sinking their teeth savagely into my arms and body. For a few moments I struggled desperately, writhing and kicking, guarding my throat with one arm and striking blindly with the other.

Then they held me helpless. I could only curse, and scream a vain appeal for aid.

The woman, holding my arms pinioned against my sides, lifted me easily, flung me over her shoulder. Her body, where it touched mine, was as cold as ice. I struggled fiercely but uselessly as she started with me down the black, inclined passage, into the recent excavations beneath the cellar's floor.

Behind us, my father picked up the little red lantern, and the blue prints and sheets of specifications, and followed down the dark, slanting passage.

CHAPTER VI
The Temple of Crimson Gloom

Helpless in those preternaturally strong, corpse-cold and corpse-white arms, I was carried down narrow steps, to a high, subterranean hall. It was filled with a dim blood-red light, which came from no visible source, its angry, forbidding radiance seeming to spring from the very air. The walls of the underground hall were smooth and black, of some unfamiliar ebon substance.

Several yards down that black, strangely illuminated passage I was carried. Then we came into a larger space. Its black roof, many yards above, was groined and vaulted, supported by a double row of massive dead-black pillars. Many dark, arched niches were cut into its walls. This greater hall, too, was sullenly illuminated by a ghastly scarlet light, which seemed to come from nowhere.

A strange, silent, awful place. A sort of cathedral of darkness, of evil and death. A sinister atmosphere of nameless terror seemed breathed from its very midnight walls, like the stifling fumes of incense offered to some formless god of horror. The dusky red light might have come from unseen tapers burned in forbidden rites of blood and death. The dead silence itself seemed a tangible, evil thing, creeping upon me from ebon walls.

I was given little time to speculate upon the questions that it raised. What was the dead-black material of the walls? Whence came the lurid, bloody radiance? How recently had this strange temple of terror been made? And to what demoniac god was it consecrated? No opportunity had I to seek answers to those questions, nor time even to recover from my natural astonishment at finding such a place beneath the soil of a Texas ranch.

The emerald-eyed woman who bore me dropped me to the black floor, against the side of a jet pillar, which was round and two feet thick. She whined shrilly, like a hungry dog. It was evidently a call, for two men appeared in the broad central aisle of the temple, which I faced.

Two men—or, rather, malevolent monstrosities in the bodies of men. Their eyes shone with green fires alien to our world, and their bodies, beneath their tattered rags of clothing, were fearfully white. One of them came toward me with a piece of frayed manila rope, which must have been a lasso they had found above.

Later it came to me that these two must be the mechanics from the city of Amarillo, who, Judson had told me on the evening of our fatal drive, had been employed here by my father. I had not yet seen Dr. Blake Jetton, Stella's father, who had been the chief assistant of my own parent in various scientific investigations—investigations which, I now began to fear, must have borne dreadful fruit!

While the woman held me against the black pillar, the men seized my arms, stretched them behind it, and tied them with the rope. I kicked out, struggled, cursed them, in vain. My body seemed but putty to their fearful strength. When my hands were tied behind the pillar, another length of the rope was dropped about my ankles and drawn tight about the ebon shaft.

I was helpless in this weird, subterranean temple, at the mercy of these four creatures who seemed to combine infernal super-intelligence with the strength and the nature of wolves.

"See the instrument which we are to build!" came the snarling voice of my father. Standing before me, with the roll of blue prints in his livid hands, he pointed at an object that I had not yet distinguished in the sullen, bloody gloom.

In the center of the loftly, central hall of this red-lit temple, between the twin rows of looming, dead-black pillars, was a long, low platform of ebon stone. From it rose a metal frame—wrought like the frame of the wrecked machine I had seen in the cellar, above.

The frame supported a huge copper ring in a vertical position. It was far huger than the ring in the ruined mechanism; its diameter was a dozen feet or more. Its upper curve reached far toward the black, vaulted roof of the hall, glistening queerly in the ghastly red light. Behind the ring, a huge, parabolic mirror of silvery, polished metal had been set up.

But the device was obviously unfinished.

The complex electron tubes, the delicate helixes and coils, the magnets, and the complicated array of wires, whose smashed and tangled remains I had observed about the wreck of the other machine, had not been installed.

"Look at that!" cried my father again. "The instrument that comes to let upon your earth the great life that is ours. The plan on this paper, we made. From the plan, we made the small machine, and brought to ourselves the life, the strength, the love of blood—"

"The love of blood!" My startled, anguished outcry must have been a shriek, for I was already nearly overcome with the brooding terror of my strange surroundings. I collapsed against the ropes, shaken and trembling with fear.

The light of strange cunning came once more into the glaring green eyes of the thing that had been my father.

"No, fear not!" he whined on. "Your language, it is new to me, and I speak what I do not intend. Be not fearing—if you will do our wish. If you do not, then we will taste your blood.

"But the new life came only to few. Then the machine broke, because of one man. And our brains are changed, so that we remember not to read the plans that we made. Your aid is ours, to restore a new machine. To you and all your world, then, comes the great new life!"

He stepped close to me, his green eyes burning malevolently. Before my eyes he unrolled one of the sheets which bore plans and specifications for the strange electron tubes, to be mounted outside the copper ring. From his lips came the curious, wolfish whine with which these monsters communicated with one another. One of the weirdly transformed mechanics stepped up beside him, carrying in dead-white hands the parts of such a tube—filaments, plate, grid, screens, auxiliary electrodes, and the glass tube in which they were to be sealed. The parts evidently had been made to fit the specifications—as nearly as these entities could comprehend those specifications with their imperfect knowledge of English.

"We make fit plans for these parts," my father whined. "If wrong, you must say where wrong. Describe how to put together. Speak quick, or die slowly!" He snarled menacingly.

Though I am by no means a brilliant physicist, I saw easily enough that most of the parts were useless, though they had been made with amazing accuracy. These beings seemed to have no knowledge of the fundamental principles underlying the operation of the machine they were attempting to build, yet, in making these parts, they had accomplished feats that would have been beyond the power of our science.

The filament was made of metal, well enough—but was far too thick to be lit by any current, without that current wrecking the tube in which it were used. The grid was nicely made—of metallic radium! It was worth a small fortune, but quite useless in the electron tube. And the plate was evidently of pure fused quartz, shaped with an accuracy that astounded me; but that, too, was quite useless.

"Parts wrong?" my father barked excitedly in wolfish tones, his glowing green eyes evidently having read something in my face. "Indicate how wrong. Describe to make correct!"

I closed my lips firmly, determined to reveal nothing. I knew that it was through the wrecked machine that my father and Stella had been so dreadfully altered. I resolved that I would not aid in changing other humans into such hellish monsters. I was sure that this strange mechanism, if completed, would be a threat against all humanity—though, at the time, I was far from conceiving the full, diabolic significance of it.

My father snarled toward the woman.

She dropped upon all fours, and sprang at me like a wolf, her beastly eyes gleaming green, her bare teeth glistening in the sullen red light, and she was hideously howling!

Her teeth caught my trousers, tore them from my leg from the middle of the right thigh downward. Then they closed into my flesh, and I could feel her teeth gnawing . . . gnawing. . . .

She did not make a deep wound, though blood, black in the terrible red light, trickled from it down my leg toward the shoe—blood which, from time to time, she ceased the gnawing to lick up appreciatively. The purpose of it was evidently to cause me the maximum amount of agony and horror.

For minutes, perhaps, I endured it—for minutes that seemed ages.

The pain itself was agonizing: the steady gnawing of teeth into the flesh of my leg, toward the bone.

But that agony was less than the terror of my surroundings. The strange temple of black, with its black floor, black walls, black pillars, vaulted black ceiling. The dim, sourceless, blood-red light that filled it. The dreadful stillness—broken only by my groans and shrieks, and by the slight sound of the gnawing teeth. The demoniac monster standing before me in the body of my father, staring at me with shining green eyes, holding the plans and the parts that the mechanic had brought, waiting for me to speak. But the most horrible thing was the fact that the gnawing demon was the body of dear, lovely Stella!

She was now digging her teeth in with a crunching sound. I writhed and screamed with agony. Sweat rolled from my body. I tugged madly against my bonds, strove to burst the rope that held my tortured leg.

Fierce, eager growls came wolf-like from the throat of the gnawing woman. Her leprously pallid face was once more smeared with blood, as it had been when I first saw her. Occasionally she stopped the unendurable gnawing, to lick her lips with a dreadful satisfaction.

Finally I could stand it no longer. Even if the fate of all the earth depended upon me—as I thought it did—I could endure it no longer.

"Stop! Stop!" I screamed. "I'll tell you!"

Rather reluctantly, the woman rose, licking her crimson lips.

My father—I find myself continually calling the monster by that name, but it was *not* my father—again held the plans before my face, and displayed upon his palm the tiny parts for the electron tube.

It took all my will to draw my mind from the throbbing pain of the fresh wound in my leg. But I explained that the filament wire would have to be drawn much finer, that the radium would not do for the grid, that the plate must be of a conducting metal, instead of quartz.

He did not easily understand my scientific terms. The name tungsten, for instance, meant nothing to him until I had explained the qualities and the atomic number of the metal. That identified it for him, and he appeared really to know more about the metal than I did.

For long hours I answered his questions, and made explanations. A few times I thought of refusing to answer, again. But the memory of that unendurable gnawing always made me speak.

The scientific knowledge and skill displayed in the construction of the machine's parts, once the specifications were properly understood, astounded me. The monsters that had stolen these human bodies seemed to have remarkable scientific knowledge of their own, particularly in chemistry and certain branches of physics—though electricity and magnetism, and the modern theories of relativity and equivalence, seemed new to them, probably because they came from a world whose natural phenomena are not the same as ours.

They brought, from one of the chambers opening into the great hall, an odd, glistening device, consisting of connected bulbs and spheres of some bright, transparent crystal. First, a lump of limestone rock, which must have been dug up in the making of this underground temple, was dropped into a large lower globe. Slowly it seemed to dissolve, forming a heavy, iridescent, violet-colored gas.

Then, whenever my father or one of the others wished to make any object—a metal plate or grid, a coil of wire, an insulating button, anything needed in building the machine— a tiny pattern of it was skilfully formed of a white, soft, wax-like substance.

The white pattern was placed in one of the crystal bulbs, and the heavy violet gas—which must have been disassociated protons and electrons from the disrupted limestone—was allowed to fill the bulb through one of the numerous transparent tubes.

The operator watched a little gauge, and at the right instant, removed from the bulb—not the pattern, but the finished object, formed of any desired element!

The process was not explained to me. But I am sure that it was one of building up atoms from the constituent positive and negative electrons. A process just the reverse of disintegration, by which radium decomposes into lead. First such simple atoms as those of hydrogen and helium. Then carbon, or silicon, or iron. Then silver, if one desired it, or gold! Finally radium, or uranium, the heaviest of metals. The object was removed whenever the atoms had reached the proper number to form the element required.

With this marvelous device, whose accomplishments exceeded the wildest dreams of the alchemist, the construction of the huge machine in the center of the hall proceeded with amazing speed, with a speed that filled me with nothing less than terror.

It occurred to me that I might delay the execution of the monsters' dreadful plan by a trick of some kind. Racking my weary and pain-clouded brain, I sought for some ruse that might mislead my clever opponents. The best idea that came to me was to give a false interpretation of the word "vacuum." If I could keep its true meaning from my father, he would leave the air in the tubes, and they would burn out when the current was turned on. When he finally asked the meaning of the word, I said that it signified a sealed or enclosed space.

But he had been consulting scientific works, as well as my meager knowledge. When the words left my lips, he sprang at me with a hideous snarl. His teeth sought my throat. But for a very hurried pretense of alarmed stupidity, my part in the dreadful adventure might have come to a sudden end. I protested that I had been sincere, that my mind was weary and I could not remember scientific facts, that I must eat and sleep again.

Then I sagged forward against the ropes, head hanging. I refused to respond, even to threats of further torture. And my exhaustion was scarcely feigned, for I had never undergone a more trying day—a day in which one horror followed close upon another.

Finally they cut me loose. The woman carried me out of the sullen crimson light of the temple, up the narrow passage, and into the house again; I was almost too weak to walk alone. As we came out upon the snow, the distant, keening cry of the weird pack broke once more upon my startled ears.

The pale disk of the moon was rising, cold and silvery, in the east, over the illimitable plain of snow. It was night again! I had been in the subterranean temple for more than twenty-four hours.

CHAPTER VII
When I Ran from the Pack

Again I was in the little room that had been Stella's, among her intimate possessions, catching an occasional suggestion of her perfume. It was a small room, clean and chaste, and I had a feeling that I was invading a sacred place. But I had no choice in the matter, for the windows were barred, and the door locked behind me.

Stella—or, I should say, the werewoman—had let me stop in the other room to eat and drink again. She had even let me find the medicine cabinet and get a bottle of antiseptic to use in the wound on my leg.

Now, sitting on the bed in a shaft of cold, argent moonlight, I applied the stinging liquid, and then bound the place with a bandage torn from a clean sheet.

Then I got to my feet and went to the window: I was determined to escape if escape were possible, or end my life if it were not. I had no intention of going back alive to the hellish red-lit temple.

But the quavering, dismal howling of the pack came faintly to my ears, as I reached the window, setting me trembling with horror. I gazed fearfully across the fantastic desert of silvery snow, bright in the opalescent haze of moonlight.

Then I glimpsed moving green eyes, and I cried out.

Below the window was a huge, lean gray wolf, pacing deliberately up and down, across the glistening snow. From time to time he lifted his head, stared straight at my windows with huge, malevolent eyes.

A sentinel set to watch me!

With my hopeless despair came a leaden weight of weariness. I felt suddenly exhausted, physically and mentally. I stumbled to the bed, crept under the covers without troubling to remove my clothing, and fell almost instantly asleep.

I awoke upon a gray, cold day. A chill wind was whistling eerily about the old house, and the sky was gloomy with

steel-blue clouds. I sprang out of bed, feeling much re-
freshed by my long sleep. For a moment, despite the dreary
day, I was conscious of an extraordinary sense of relief; it
seemed, for the merest instant, as if all that had happened
to me was a horrible nightmare, from which I was waking.
Then recollection came, with a dull pain in my wounded
leg.

I wondered why I had not been carried back into the terrible temple of blood-red gloom before the coming of day;
perhaps I must have been sleeping too soundly to be roused.

Recalling the gray wolf, I looked nervously out at the window. It was gone, of course; the monsters seemed unable to
endure the light of day, or any other save the terrible crimson
dusk of the temple.

I wrapped a blanket about my shoulders, for it was extremely cold, and I set about at once to escape from the
room. I was determined to win my liberty or die in the attempt.

First I examined the windows again. The bars outside them,
though of wood, were quite strong. My utmost strength failed
to break any one of them. I could find nothing in the room
with which they might be cut or worn in twain, without hours
of labor.

Finally I turned to the door. My kicks and blows failed to
make any impression upon its sturdy panels. The lock seemed
strong, and I had neither skill nor tools for picking it.

But, while I stood gazing at the lock, an idea came to me.

I still had the little automatic, and two extra clips of ammunition. My captors had shown only disdain for the little
weapon, and I had rather lost faith in it after its puzzling
failure to kill the gray wolf.

Now I backed to the other side of the room, drew it, and
deliberately fired three shots into the lock. When I first tried
the door again, it seemed as impassable as ever. I worked
upon it, twisting the knob, again and again. There was a
sudden snap, and the door swung open.

I was free. If only I could reach a place of safety before
darkness brought out the weird pack!

* * *

In the old dining room I paused to drink, and to eat scantily. Then I left the house by the front door, for I dared not go near the mouth of that hell-burrow behind the house, even by day. In fearful, desperate haste, I set out across the snow.

The little town of Hebron, I knew, lay ten miles away, directly north. Few landmarks were visible above the thick snow, and the gray clouds hid the sun. But I plodded along beside a barbed wire fence, which I knew would guide me.

Slowly the time-yellowed ranch house, an ugly, rambling structure with a gray shingle roof, dwindled upon the white waste behind me. The outbuildings, resembling the house, though looking smaller, more ancient and more dilapidated, drew toward it to form a single brown speck upon the endless desolation of the snow-covered plain.

The crust upon the snow, though frozen harder than upon the ill-fated night of my coming, was still too thin to support my weight. It broke beneath my feet at every step, and I sank ankle-deep in the soft snow beneath.

My progress was a grim, heartbreaking struggle. My strength had been drained by the nerve-racking horrors and exhausting exertions of the past few days. Soon I was gasping for breath, and my feet felt leaden-heavy. There was a dull, intolerable ache in the wound on my leg.

If the snow had been hard enough to support my weight, so that I could run, I might have reached Hebron before dark. But, sinking deep into it at every step, it was impossible for me to move rapidly.

I must not have covered over half the distance to Hebron, when the gloom of the gray, cheerless day seemed to settle upon me. I realized, with a chill of fatal horror, that it had not been early morning when I set out; my watch had stopped, and since the leaden clouds had obscured the sun, I had no gauge of time.

I must have slept through half the day or more, exhausted as I had been by the day and night of torture in the dark temple. Night was upon me, when I was still far short of my destination.

Nearly dead with fatigue, I had more than once been almost on the point of stopping to rest. But terror lent me fresh strength. I plodded on as fast as I could, but forcing myself to keep from running, which would burn up my energy too soon.

Another mile, perhaps, I had covered, when I heard the weird, blood-congealing voice of the pack.

The darkness, for a time, had been intense, very faintly relieved by the ghostly gleam of the snow. But the clouds had lightened somewhat, and the light of the rising moon shone through them, casting eldritch shadows of silver on the level snow.

At first the dreadful baying was very distant, low and moaning and hideous with the human vocal note it carried. But it grew louder. And there was something in it of sharp, eager yelping.

I knew that the pack which had run down Judson and me had been set upon my trail.

The terror, the stark, maddening, soul-searing horror that seized me, is beyond imagination. I shrieked uncontrollably. My hands and body felt alternately hot and fevered, and chilled with a cold sweat. A harsh dryness roughened my throat. I reeled dizzily, and felt the pounding of my pulse in all my body.

And I ran.

Madly, wildly. Ran with all my strength. Ran through the thick snow faster than I had thought possible. But in a few moments, it seemed I had used up all my strength.

I was suddenly sick with fatigue, swaying, almost unable to stand. Red mists, shot with white fire, danced in front of my eyes. The vast plain of snow whirled about me fantastically.

And on and on I staggered. When each step took all my will. When I felt that I must collapse in the snow, and fought with all my mind for the strength to raise my foot again.

All the time, the fearful baying was drawing nearer, until

the wailing, throbbing sound of it drummed and rang in my brain.

Finally, unable to take another step, I turned and looked back.

For a few moments I stood there, swaying, gasping for breath. The weird, nerve-blasting cry of the pack sounded very near, but I could see nothing. Then, through the clouds, a broad, ghostly shaft of moonlight fell athwart the snow behind me. And I saw the pack.

I saw them! The pinnacle of horror!

Gray wolves, leaping, green-eyed and gaunt. And strange human figures among them, racing with them. Chill, soulless emerald orbs staring. Bodies ghastly pallid, clad only in tattered rags. Stella, bounding at the head of the pack.

My father, following. And other men. All green-orbed, leprously white. Some of them frightfully mutilated.

Some so torn they should have been dead!

Judson, the man who had brought me out from Hebron, was among them. His livid flesh hung in ribbons. One eye was gone, and a green fire seemed to sear the empty socket. His chest was fearfully lacerated. And the man was—eviscerated!

Yet his hideous body leaped beside the wolves.

And others were as dreadful. One had no head. A black mist seemed gathered above the jutting, lividly white stump of his neck, and in it glowed malevolently—two green eyes!

A woman ran with them. One arm was torn off, her naked breasts were in ribbons. She ran with the rest, green eyes glowing, mouth wide open, baying with other members of the pack.

And now I saw a horse in that grotesque company. A powerful, gray animal, he was, and he came with tremendous leaps. Its eyes, too, were glowing green—glowing with the malignant fire of an evil intelligence not normally of this earth. This was one of Judson's animals, changed as dreadfully as he and all the others had been. Its mouth yawned open, with yellow teeth glistening, and it howled madly with the pack.

Swiftly, hideously, they closed in upon me. The weird host sprang toward me from all directions—gray wolves, men, and horse. Eyes glaring, teeth bared, snarling, the hellish horde came closer.

The horror of it was too much for my mind. A merciful wave of darkness overcame me as I felt myself reeling to fall upon the snow.

CHAPTER VIII
Through the Disk of Darkness

I awoke within the utter stillness of a tomb. For a little time I lay with eyes closed, analyzing the sensations of my chilled, aching body, conscious of the dull, throbbing pain from my wounded leg. I shuddered at recollection of the fearful experiences of the past few days, endured again the overwhelming horror of the moment when the pack—wolves and men and horse, frightfully mutilated, eyes demoniacally green—had closed in upon me on the moonlit snow. For some time I did not dare to open my eyes.

At last, nerving myself against the new horrors that might surround me, I raised my lids.

I looked into the somber, crimson radiance of the ebon-pillared temple. Beside a dull jet wall I lay, upon a pile of rags, with a blanket thrown carelessly over me. Beyond the row of massive, black, cylindrical pillars, I saw the great, strange machine, with the huge copper ring glistening queerly in the dim, bloody light. The polished mirror behind it seemed flushed with a living glow of molten rubies, and the many electron tubes, now mounted in their sockets, gleamed redly. The mechanism appeared to be near completion; livid, green-orbed figures were busy about it, moving with a swift, mechanical efficiency. It struck me abruptly that they moved more like machines than like living beings. My father, Stella, the two mechanics.

For many minutes I lay very still, watching them covertly. Evidently they had brought me down into this subterranean chamber, so that I would have no chance to repeat my escape. I speculated upon the possibility of creeping along the wall to the ascending passage, dashing through it. But there was little hope that I could do it unseen. And I had no way of knowing whether it might be night or day; it would be folly to run out into the darkness. I felt the little automatic still under my arm; they had not troubled to remove a weapon which they did not fear.

Suddenly, before I had dared to move, I saw my father coming across the black floor toward me. I could not repress a tremor, at closer sight of his deathly pallid body and sinister, baleful greenish eyes. I lays still, trying to pretend sleep.

I felt his ice-cold fingers close upon my shoulder; roughly I was drawn to my feet.

"Further assistance from you must be ours," whined his wolfish voice. "And not again will you be brought back living, should you be the fool to run!" His whine ended with an ugly snarl.

He dragged me across toward the fantastic mechanism that glistened in the grim, bloody radiance.

I quailed at the thought of being bound to the black pillar again.

"I'll help!" I cried. "Do anything you want. Don't tie me up, for God's sake! Don't let her gnaw me!" My voice must have become a hysterical scream. I fought to calm it, cudgeled my brain for arguments.

"It would kill me to be tied again," I pleaded wildly. "And if you leave me free, I can help you with my hands!"

"Be free of bonds, then," my father whined. "But also remember! You go, and we bring you back not alive!"

He led me up beside the great machine. One of the mechanics, at a shrill, wolfish whine from him, unrolled a blue print before me. He began to ask questions regarding the

wiring to connect the many electron tubes, the coils and helixes and magnets, all ranged about the huge copper ring.

His strange brain seemed to have no conception of the
nature of electricity; I had to explain the fundamentals. But
he grasped each new fact with astounding quickness, seemed
to see the applications instinctively.

It soon developed that the great mechanism was practically
finished; in an hour, perhaps, the wiring was completed.

"Now what yet is to be constructed?" my father whined.

I realized that no provision had been made for electricity
to light the tubes and energize the magnets. These beings
apparently did not even know that a source of power was
necessary. This, I thought, was another chance to stop the
execution of their hellish plan.

"I don't know," I said. "So far as I can see, the machine
now fits the specifications. I know nothing else to do."

He snarled something to one of the mechanics, who produced the bloody rope with which I had previously been
bound. Stella sprang toward me, her lips curled in a leering
animal snarl, her white teeth gleaming.

Uncontrollable terror shook me, weakened my knees until
I reeled.

"Wait! Stop!" I screamed. "I'll tell if you won't tie me!"
They halted.

"Speak!" my father barked. "Quickly describe!"

"The machine must have power. Electricity?"

"From what place comes electricity?"

"There is a motor generator up in the cellar, where the
other machine is. That might do."

He and the monster that had been Stella hurried me down
the black-pillared hall, and up the inclined passage to the old
cellar. He carried the red-glowing electric lantern. In the cellar I showed them the generator and attempted a rough explanation of its operation.

Then he and the woman bent and caught the metal base of
the unit. With their incredible strength, they lifted it quite
easily and carried it toward the passage. They made me walk
ahead of them as we returned to the machine in the black

hall—blasting another hope for a chance to make a dash for the open.

Just as they were placing the heavy machine—gasoline engine and dynamo, which together weighed several hundred pounds—on the black platform beside the strange, gigantic mechanism, there came an interruption that, to me, was terrifying.

From the passage came the rustle of feet, and mingled whining, snarling sounds such as the monsters seemed to use for communication. And in the vague, blood-red light, between the tall rows of great black pillars, appeared the pack!

Huge, gaunt wolves there were. Frightfully mutilated men—Judson, and the others that I had seen. The gray horse. All their eyes were luminously green—alight with a dreadful, malevolent fire.

Human lips were crimsoned. Scarlet smeared the gray wolves' muzzles, and even the long nose and gray jaws of the horse. And they carried—the catch!

Over Judson's livid, lacerated shoulders was hung the torn, limp, bleeding body of a woman—his wife! One of the gaunt gray wolves had the hideously mangled body of a man across his back, holding it in place with jaws turned sidewise. Another had the body of a spotted calf. Two more carried in red-dripping jaws the lax gray bodies of coyotes. And one of the men bore upon his shoulder the remains of a huge gray wolf.

The dead, torn, mutilated specimens were dropped in a horrible heap in the wide central aisle of the jet-pillared temple, near the strange machine, like an altar of death. Dark blood flowed from it over the black floor, congealing in thick, viscid clots.

"To these we bring life," my father snarled at me, jerking his head toward the dreadful, mangled heap.

Shuddering and dazed with horror, I sank on the floor, covering my eyes. I was nauseated, sick. My brain was reeling, fogged, confused. It refused to dwell upon the meaning of this dreadful scene.

The mad, fearful, demoniac thing that had been my father

jerked me roughly to my feet, dragged me toward the motor generator, and began plying me with questions about its operation, about how to connect it with the strange mechanism of the copper ring.

I struggled to answer his questions, trying vainly to forget my horror in the work.

Soon the connection was completed. Under my father's directions, I examined the gasoline engine, saw that it was supplied with fuel and oil. Then he attempted to start it, but failed to master the technique of choking the carburetor. Under constant threat of the blood-darkened rope and the werewoman's gnawing fangs, I labored with the little motor until it coughed a few times, and fell to firing steadily.

Then my father made me close the switch, connecting the strange machine with the current from the generator. A faint, shrill humming came from the coils. The electron tubes glowed dimly.

And a curtain of darkness seemed suddenly drawn across the copper ring. Blackness seemed to flow from the queer tube behind it, to be reflected into it by the polished mirror. A disk of dense, utter darkness filled the ring.

For a few moments I stared at it in puzzled wonder.

Then, as my eyes became slowly sensitized, I found that I could see through it—see into a dread, nightmare world.

The ring had become an opening into another world of horror and darkness.

The sky of that alien world was unutterably, inconceivably black; blacker than the darkest midnight. It had no stars, no luminary; no faintest gleam relieved its terrible, oppressive intensity.

A vast reach of that other world's surface lay in view, beyond the copper ring. Low, worn, and desolate hills, that seemed black as the somber sky. Between them flowed a broad and stagnant river, whose dull and sullen waters shone with a vague and ghostly luminosity, with a pale glow that was somehow unclean and noisome, like that of decaying foul corruption.

And upon those low and ancient hills, that were rounded like the bloated breasts of corpses, was a loathsome vegetation. Hideous, obscene travesties of normal plants, whose leaves were long, narrow, snake-like, with the suggestion of ugly heads. With a dreadful, unnatural life, they seemed to writhe, lying in rotting tangles upon the black hills, and dragging in the foul, lurid waters of the stagnant river. Their thin reptilian, tentacular vines and creepers glowed with a pale and ghastly light, lividly greenish.

And upon a low black hill, above the evil river, and the rotting, writhing, obscene jungle, was what must have been a city. A sprawled and hideous mass of red corruption. A foul splash of dull crimson pollution.

This was no city, perhaps, in our sense of the word. It seemed to be a sort of cloud of foul, blood-hued darkness, trailing repulsive tentacles across the low black hill; a smear of evil crimson mist. Mad and repulsive knobs and warts rose about it, in grotesque mockery of spires and towers. It was motionless. And I knew instinctively that unclean and abominable life, sentience, reigned within its hideous scarlet contamination.

My father mounted to the black stone step between the copper ring, and stood there howling weirdly and hideously, into that world of darkness—voicing an unclean call!

In answer, the sprawled, nightmare city seemed to stir. Dark things—masses of fetid, reeking blackness—seemed to creep from its ugly protuberances, to swarm toward us through the tainted filth of the writhing, evilly glowing vegetation.

The darkness of evil concentrate, creeping from that nightmare world into ours!

For long moments the utter, insane horror of it held me paralyzed and helpless. Then something nerved me with the abrupt, desperate determination to revolt against my fearful masters, despite the threat of the bloody rope.

I tore my eyes from the dreadful attraction that seemed to draw them toward the foul, sprawled city of bloody darkness, in that hideous world of unthinkable evil.

Realization came to me that I stood alone, unguarded. The green eyes of the monsters about me were fixed in avid fascination upon the ring through which that nightmare world was visible. None of them seemed aware of me.

If only I could wreck the machine, before those creeping horrors of darkness came through into our world! I started forward instinctively, then paused, realizing that it might be difficult to do great damage to it with my bare hands, before the monsters saw me and attacked.

Then I thought of the little automatic in my pocket, which I had been permitted to keep with me. Even though its bullets could not harm the monsters, they might do considerable damage to the machine.

I snatched it out and began firing deliberately at the dimly glowing electron tubes. As the first one was shattered, the image of that hideous, nightmare world flickered and vanished. The huge, polished mirror was once more visible beyond the copper ring.

For the time being, at least, those rankling shapes of black and utter evil were shut out of our world!

As I continued to fire, shattering the electron tubes and the other most delicate and most complicated parts of the great mechanism, a fearful, soul-chilling cry came from the startled monsters in human and animal bodies.

Suddenly the creatures sprang toward me, over the black floor, howling hideously.

CHAPTER IX
The Hypnotic Revelation

It was the yellow, stabbing spurts of flame from the automatic that saved me. At first the fearfully transformed beasts and men had leaped at me, howling with the agony that light seemed to cause them. I kept on firing, determined to do all the damage possible before they bore me down.

And abruptly they fell back away from me, wailing dreadfully, hiding their unearthly green eyes, slinking behind the
massive black pillars.

When the gun was empty, some of them came toward me
again. But still they seemed shaken, weakened, uncertain of
movement. In nervous haste, I fumbled in my pockets for
matches—I had not realized before how they were crippled
by light.

I found only three, all, apparently, that I had left.

The weird monsters, recovered from the effect of the gun
flashes, were leaping across toward me, through the sullen,
blood-red gloom, as I struggled desperately to make a light.

The first match broke in my fingers.

But the second flared into yellow flame. The monsters,
almost upon me, sprang back, wailing in agony again. As I
held the tiny, feeble flame aloft, they cowered, howling, in
the flickering shadows cast by the huge, ebon pillars.

My confused, horror-dazed mind was abruptly cleared and
sharpened by hope of escape. With the light to hold them
back, I might reach the open air.

And to my quickened mind it came abruptly that it must
be day above. It was morning, and the pack had been driven
back to the burrow by the light of the coming sun!

As swiftly as I could, without extinguishing the feeble flame
of the match with the wind of my motion, I advanced down
the great hall. I kept in the middle of the wide central aisle,
afraid that my enemies were slinking along after me in the
shadows of the pillars.

Before I reached the passage which led to the surface, a
stronger breath of air caught the feeble orange flame. It flickered out. Dusky crimson gloom fell about me once more,
with baleful green eyes moving in it, in the farther end of the
temple. The howling rose again, angrily. I heard swiftly padding feet.

Only one of the three matches was left.

I bent, scratched it very carefully on the black floor and
held it above my head.

A new wailing of pain came from the monsters; they fell back again.

I found the end of the passage, rushed through it, guarding the precious flame in a cupped hand.

In the great hall behind me, the blood-chilling wail of the pack rose again. I heard the monsters surging toward the passage.

By the time I had reached the old cellar, from whose wall the slanting tunnel had been dug, the match was almost consumed. I turned, let its last dying rays shine down the passage. Dreadful cries of agony and terror came again; I heard the monsters retreating from the tunnel.

The match suddenly went out.

In mad haste I dashed across the cellar's floor and blundered heavily into the wall. I found the steps that led to the surface and rushed up them desperately.

I heard the howling pack running up the passage, moving far swifter than I was able to do.

At last my hand touched the under surface of the wooden door, above the steps. Beyond, I knew, was the golden light of day.

And at the same instant, corpse-cold fingers closed about my ankle, in a crushing, powerful grasp.

Convulsively, I thrust upward with my hand.

The door flew up, slammed crashingly beside the opening. Above was soft, brilliant azure sky. In it the white morning sun blazed blindingly. Its hot radiance brought tears to my eyes, accustomed as they were to the dim crimson light of the temple.

Fearful, agonized animal wailing sounds came again from behind me.

The grasp on my ankle tightened convulsively, then relaxed.

Looking back, I saw Stella on the steps at my feet, cowering, writhing as if in unbearable agony, animal screams of pain coming from her lips. It seemed that the burning sunlight had struck her down, that she had been too much weakened to retreat as those behind her had done.

Abruptly she seemed to me a lovely, suffering girl—not a strange demoniac monster. Pity for her—even, perhaps, love—came over me in a tender wave. If I could save her, restore her to her true, dear self!

I ran back down the steps, seized her by the shoulders, started to carry her up into the light. Deathly cold and deathly white her body still was. And still it had a vestige of that unnatural strength.

She writhed in my arms, snarling, slashing at my body with her teeth. For a moment her green eyes smoldered malevolently at me. But as the sunlight struck them she closed them, howling with agony, and tried to shield them with her arm.

I carried her up the steps, into the brilliant sunlight.

First I thought of closing the cellar door, and trying to fasten it. Then I realized that the light of day, shining down the passage, would hold back the monsters more effectually than any locked door.

It was still early morning. The sun had been up no more than an hour. The sky was clear, and the sunshine glittered with blinding, prismatic brilliance on the snow. The air, however, was still cold; there had been no thawing, nor would there be until the temperature had moderated considerably.

As I stood there in the blaze of sunlight, holding Stella, a strange change came over her. The fierce snarling and whining sounds that came from her throat slowly died away. Her writhing, convulsive struggles weakened, as though a tide of alien life were ebbing from her body.

There was a sudden last convulsion. Then her body was lax, limp.

Almost immediately, I noticed a change in color. The fearful, corpse-like pallor slowly gave place to the normal pinkish flush of healthy life. The strange, unearthly chill was gone; I felt a glow of warmth where her body was against mine.

Then her breast heaved. She breathed. I felt the slow throbbing of her heart. Her eyes were still closed as she lay inert in my arms, like one sleeping. I freed one of my hands and gently lifted a long-lashed lid.

The eye was clear and blue—normal again. The baleful, greenish fire was gone!

In some way, which I did not then understand, the light of day had purified the girl, had driven from her the fierce, unclean life that had possessed her body.

"Stella! Dear Stella! Wake up!" I cried. I shook her a little. But she did not rouse. Still she seemed sleeping heavily.

Realizing that she would soon be chilled, in the cold air, I carried her into the house, into her own room, where I had been imprisoned, and laid her on the bed, covering her with blankets. Still she appeared to be sleeping.

For an hour, perhaps, I tried to rouse her from the profound syncope or coma in which she lay. I tried everything that experience and the means at hand made available. And still she lay insensible.

A most puzzling situation, and a surprising one. It was almost as if Stella—the real Stella—had been dispossessed of her body by some foul, alien being. The alien, evil life had been killed by the light, and still she had not returned.

At last it occurred to me to try hypnotic influence—I am a fair hypnotist, and have made a deep study of hypnotism and allied mental phenomena. A forlorn hope, perhaps, since her coma appeared so deep. But I was driven to clutch at any straw.

Exerting all my will to recall her mind, placing my hand upon her smooth brow, or making slow passes over her still, pale, lovely face, I commanded her again and again to open her eyes.

And suddenly, when I was almost on the point of new despair, her eyelids flickered, lifted. Of course, it may have been a natural awakening, though a most unusual one, instead of the result of my efforts. But her blue eyes opened and stared up at me.

But still she was not normally awake. No life or feeling

was revealed in the azure depths of her eyes. They were clouded, shadowed with sleep. Their opening seemed to have been a mechanical answer to my commands.

"Speak. Stella, my Stella, speak to me!" I cried.

Her pale lips parted. From them came low, sleep-drugged tones.

"Clovis." She spoke my name in that small, colorless voice.

"Stella, what has happened to you and my father?" I cried.

And here is what she told me, in that tiny, toneless voice. I have condensed it somewhat, for many times her voice wandered wearily, died away, and I had to prompt her, question her, almost force her to continue.

"My father came here to help Dr. McLaurin with his experiment," she began, slowly, in a low monotone. "I did not understand all of it, but they sought for other worlds besides ours. Other dimensions, interlocking with our own. Dr. McLaurin had been working out his theory for many years, basing his work upon the new mathematics of Weyl and Einstein.

"Not simple is our universe. Worlds upon worlds lie side by side, like the pages of a book—and each world unknown to all the others. Strange worlds touching, spinning side by side, yet separated by walls not easily broken down.

"In vibration is the secret. For all matter, all light, all sound, all our universe, is of vibration. All material things are formed of vibrating particles of electricity—electrons. And each world, each universe, has its own order of vibration. And through each, all unknown and unseen, are the myriad other worlds and universes vibrating, each with an order of its own.

"Dr. McLaurin knew by mathematics that these other worlds must exist. It was his wish to explore them. Here he came, to be alone, with none to pry into his secrets. Aided by my father, and other men, he toiled through years to build his machine.

"A machine, if successful, would change the vibration rate of matter and of light. To change it from the order of our dimension, to those of others. With it, he might see into those myriad other worlds in space beside our own, might visit them.

"The machine was finished. And through its great copper ring, we saw another world. A world of darkness, with midnight sky. Loathsome, lividly green plants writhed like reptilian monstrosities upon its black hills. Evil, alien life teemed upon it.

"Dr. McLaurin went through into that dark world. The horror of it broke down his mind. A strange madman, he came back. His eyes were green and shining, and his skin was very white.

"And things he brought back with him—clinging, creeping things of foul blackness, that stole the bodies of men and beasts. Evil, living things, that are the masters of the black dimension. One crept into me, and took my body. It ruled me, and I know only like a dim dream what it made my body do. To it, my body was but a machine.

"Dim dreams. Terrible dreams. Dreaming of running over the snow, hunting for wolves. Dreams of bringing them back, for the black things to flow into, and make live again. Dreams of torturing my father, whom no black thing took, at first.

"Father was tortured, gnawed. My body did it. But I did not do it. I was far away. I saw it only dimly, like a bad dream. One of the black creatures had come into my body, taken it from me.

"New to our world were the black things. Light slays them, for it is a force strange to their world, against which they have no armor. And so they dug a deep place, to slink into by day.

"The ways of our world they knew not; nor the language; nor the machines. They made Father teach them; teach them to speak; to read books; to run the machine through which they came. They plan to bring many of their evil kind through the machine, to conquer our world. They plan to make black clouds to hide the sun forever, so our world will be as dark as their own. They plan to seize the bodies of all men and animals, to use as machines to do that thing.

"When Father knew the plan, he would not tell them more. So my body gnawed him—while I looked on from afar, and could not help. Then he pretended to be in accord with them. They let him loose. He smashed the machine with an ax, so no more evil things could come through. Then he blew off his head with a gun, so they could not torture him, and make him aid them again.

"The black things could not themselves repair the machine. But in letters they learned of Clovis McLaurin, son of Dr. McLaurin. He, too, knew of machines. They sent for him, to torture him as Father had been tortured. Again my mind was filled with grief, for he was dear to me. But my body gnawed him, while he aided the black things to build a new machine.

"Then he broke it. And then . . . then. . . ."

Her tiny, toneless voice died wearily away. Her blue eyes, still clouded with shadowed sleep, stared up unseeingly. Deep indeed was her strange trance.

She had even forgotten that it was I to whom she spoke!

CHAPTER X
The Creeping Darkness

An amazing and terrible story, was Stella's. In part, it was almost incredible. Yet, much as I wished to doubt it, and much as I wished to discount the horror that it promised our fair earth, I knew that it must be true.

Prominent scientists have speculated often enough of the possibility of other worlds, other planes, side by side with our own. For there is nothing solid or impenetrable about the matter of our universe. The electron is thought to be only a vibration in the ether. And in all probability, there are vibrating fields of force, forming other electrons, other atoms, other suns and planets, existing beside our world, yet not making their existence known. Only a tiny band of the vibrations in the spectrum is visible to our eyes as light. If our eyes were turned to other bands, above the ultra-violet, or below the infra-red, what new, strange worlds might burst upon our vision?

No, I could not doubt that part of Stella's story. My father had studied the evidence upon the existence of such worlds invisible to us, more deeply than any other man, had published his findings, with complete mathematical proof, in his startling work, *Interlocking Universes*. If those parallel worlds were to be discovered, he was the logical man to make the discovery. And I could not doubt that he had made it—for I had seen that world of dread nightmare, beyond the copper ring!

And I had seen, in that dark, alien world, the city of the creeping things of blackness. I could well believe the part of the story about those strangely malignant entities stealing the bodies of men and animals. It offered the first rational solution of all the astounding facts I had observed, since the night of my coming to Hebron.

And it came to me suddenly that soon the monstrous beings would have the machine repaired; they would need no further aid from me. Then other hordes of the black shapes would come through. Come to seize our world, Stella had said, to enslave humanity, to aid them in making our world a planet of darkness like the grim sphere they left. It seemed mad, incredible—yet I knew it was true!

I must do something against them! Fight them—fight them with light! Light was the one force that destroyed them. That had freed Stella from her dread bondage. But I must obtain better means of making light than a few matches. Lamps would do; a searchlight, perhaps.

And I was determined to take Stella to Hebron, if she were able to go. I must go there to find the supplies I needed, and yet I could not bear the thought of leaving her for the monstrosities to find when night fell again, to seize her fair body again for their foul ends.

I found that at my command she would move, stand, and walk, though slowly and stiffly, like a person walking in sleep.

It was still early morning, and I thought there might be time for her to walk to Hebron, with me to support her steps, before the fall of darkness.

I investigated her possessions in the room, found clothing for her: woolen stockings, strong shoes, knickers, sweater, gloves, cap. Her efforts to dress herself were slow and clumsy, like those of a weary child, trying to pull off his clothing when half asleep, and I had to aid her.

She seemed not to be hungry. But when we stopped in the dining room, where the remainder of the food still lay on the table, I made her drink a tin of milk. She did it mechanically. As for myself, I ate heartily, despite ill-omened recollections of how I had eaten at this table on the eve of my first attempt to escape.

We set out across the snow, following along by the wire fence as I had done before. I could distinguish my old footprints and the mingled tracks of wolf, man, and horse, in the trail the pursuing pack had left. We followed that trail with greater ease now, for the soft snow had been packed by the running feet.

I walked with an arm about Stella's waist, sometimes half-carrying her, speaking to her encouragingly. She responded with slow, dull mechanical efforts. Her mind seemed far away; her blue eyes were misty with strange dreams.

As the hours of weary struggle went by, with her warm body against mine, it came to me that I loved her very much, and that I would give my life to save her from the dread fate that menaced us.

Once I stopped, and drew her unresisting body fiercely to me, and brought my mouth close to her pale lips, that were composed, and a little parted, and perfumed with sleep. Her blue eyes stared at me blankly, still clouded with sleep, devoid of feeling or understanding. Suddenly I knew that it would be wrong to kiss her so. I pushed her pliant body back, and led her on across the snow.

The sun reached the zenith, and began declining slowly westward.

As the evening wore on, Stella seemed to tire—or perhaps it was only that her trance-like state became deeper. She responded more slowly to my urgings that we must hurry. When, for a few moments, my encouraging voice was silent, she stood motionless, rigid, as if lost in strange vision.

I hurried her on desperately, commanding her steadily to keep up her efforts. My eyes were anxiously on the setting sun. I knew that we would have scant time to reach the village before the fall of night; haste was imperative.

At last, when the sun was still some distance above the white horizon, we came within sight of the town of Hebron. A cluster of dark specks, upon the limitless plain of glittering snow. Three miles away, they must have been.

Still the girl seemed to sink deeper into the strange sea of sleep from which only hypnotic influence had lifted her. By the time we had covered another mile, she refused to respond to my words. She was breathing slowly, regularly; her body was limp, flaccid; her eyes had closed. I could do nothing to rouse her.

The sun had touched the snow, coloring the western world with pale rose and purple fires. Darkness was not far away.

Desperately, I took the limp, relaxed body of the girl upon my shoulders and staggered on beneath the burden. It was no more than two miles to Hebron; I had hopes of getting there with her before dark.

But the snow was so deep as to make the effort of even unburdened walking exhausting. And my body was worn out, after the terrible experiences I had lately undergone. Before I had tottered on half a mile, I realized that my effort was hopeless.

Dusk had fallen. The moon had not yet risen, but the snow gleamed silvery under the ghostly twilight that still flooded the sky. My ears were straining fearfully for the voice of the dreadful pack. But a shroud of utter silence hung about me. I was still plodding wearily along, carrying Stella.

Abruptly I noticed that her body, against my hands, was becoming strangely cold. Anxiously, I laid her down upon the snow, to examine her—trembling with a premonition of the approaching horror.

Her body was icy cold. And it had again become ghastly, deathly white. White as when I had seen her running over the snow with the gaunt gray wolf!

But her limbs, strangely, did not stiffen; they were still pliant, relaxed. It was not the chill of death comig over her; it was the cold of that alien life, which the sunlight had driven from her, returning with the darkness!

I knew that she would soon be a human girl no longer, but a weird wolf-woman, and the knowledge chilled my soul with horror! For a few moments I crouched beside her inert body, pleading wildly with her to come back to me, crying out to her almost insanely.

Then I saw the hopelessness of it, and the danger. The monstrous life would flow into her again. And she would carry me back to hateful captivity in the subterranean temple, to be a slave of the monsters—or perhaps a member of their malefic society.

I must escape! For her sake. For the world's. It would be better to abandon her now, and go on alone, than have her carry me back. Perhaps I would have another chance to save her.

And I must somehow render her helpless, so that she could not pursue me, when the dread life returned to her body.

I snatched off my coat, and then my shirt. In anxious haste, I tore the shirt into strips, which I twisted rapidly into cords. I drew her ankles together, passed the improvised bonds about them, knotted them tightly. I turned the frightfully pallid, corpse-cold girl upon her face, crossed the lax arms behind her back, and fastened her wrists together with another rope of twisted cloth. Then, by way of extra precaution, I slipped the belt from my trousers and buckled it firmly about her waist, over the crossed wrists, pinioning them.

Finally I spread on the snow the coat I had taken off, and laid her upon it, for I wanted her to be as comfortable as possible.

Then I started off toward Hebron, where a little cluster of

white lights shone across the snow, through the gray, gathering dusk. I had gone but a few steps when something made me pause, look back, fearfully.

The inert, deathly pallid body of the girl still lay upon the coat. Beyond it, I glimpsed a strange and dreadful thing, moving swiftly through the ghostly, gray twilight.

Incredible and hideous was the thing I gazed upon. I can hardly find words to describe it; I can give the reader no idea of the weird, icy horror that grasped my heart with dread fingers as I saw it.

It was a mass of darkness, flowing over the snow. A creeping cloud of foul *blackness*, shapeless and many-tentacled. Its form changed continually as it moved. It had no limbs, no features—only the inky, snake-like, clinging extensions of its blackness, that it thrust out to move itself along. But deep within it were two bright green points—like eyes. Green baleful orbs, aflame with fiendish malevolence!

It was alive, this living darkness. It was unlike any higher form of life. But it has since come to me that it resembled the amoeba—a single-cell animal, a flowing mass of protoplasmic slime. Like the amoeba this darkness moved by extended narrow pseudopods from its mass. And the green eyes of horror, in which its unearthly life appeared to be concentrated, perhaps correspond to the vacuoles or nuclei of the protozoan animals.

I realized, with a paralyzing sensation of horror unutterable, that it was one of the monsters from that world of black nightmare, beyond the copper ring. And that it was coming to claim again Stella's body, to which it was still connected by some tainted bond.

Though it seemed only to creep or flow, it moved with a terrible swiftness—far faster, even, than the wolves.

In a moment after I saw it, it had reached Stella's body. It paused, hung over her, a thick, viscid, clinging cloud of unclean blackness with those greenish, fearful eyes staring from its foul mass. For a moment it hid her body, with its creeping, sprawling, ink-black and shapeless masses, crawling over her like horrid tentacles.

Then it *flowed* into her body.

It seemed to stream through her nostrils, into her mouth. The black cloud hanging over her steadily diminished. The infernal green orbs remained above, in the writhing darkness, until the last. And then they seemed to sink into her eyes.

Abruptly, her pallid body came to terrible life.

She writhed, straining at her bonds with preternatural strength, rolling from the coat into the snow, hideously convulsed. Her eyes were open again—and they shone, not with their own life, but with the dreadful fire of the green, malevolent orbs that had sunk into them.

Her eyes were the eyes of the creeping blackness.

From her throat came the soul-numbing, wolfish baying, that I had already heard under such frightful circumstances. It was an animal cry, yet it had an uncanny human note that was terrifying.

She was calling to the pack!

That sound nerved my paralyzed limbs. For the few moments that it had taken the monstrous thing of blackness to flow into Stella's body, I had stood motionless, transfixed with the horror of it.

Now I turned and ran madly across the snow toward the dancing lights of Hebron. Behind me the werewoman still writhed in the snow, trying to break her bonds, howling weirdly—summoning the pack!

Those twinkling lights seemed to mock me. They looked very near across the ghostly, gleaming plain of snow. They seemed to dance away from me as I ran. They seemed to move like fireflies, pausing until I was almost upon them, then retreating, to scintillate far across the snow.

I forgot my weariness, forgot the dull, throbbing pain of the unhealed wound in my leg. I ran desperately, as I had never run before. Not only was my life at stake, but Stella's and my father's. Even, I had good reason to fear, the lives of all humanity.

Before I had covered half the distance, I heard behind me the voice of the pack. A weird, wailing, far-off cry which grew swiftly louder. The werewoman had called, and the pack was coming to free her.

On I ran. My steps seemed so pitifully short, despite my agony of effort, so pitifully slow. My feet sank deep into the snow which seemed to cling to them with maleficent demon-fingers. And the lights that seemed so near appeared to be dancing mockingly away before me.

Sweat poured from my body. My lungs throbbed with pain. My breath came in quick, agonized gasps. My heart seemed to hammer against the base of my brain. My mind seemed drowning in a sea of pain. And on I ran.

The lights of Hebron became unreal ghost-fires, false will-o'-the-wisps. They quivered before me in a blank world of gray darkness. And I labored on toward them, through a dull haze of agony. I saw nothing else. And nothing I did I hear, but the moaning of the pack.

I was so weary that I could not think. But I suddenly became aware that the pack was very near. I think I turned my head and glanced back for a moment. Or it may be that I remember the pack only as I saw it in imagination. But I have a very vivid picture of gaunt gray wolves leaping and baying hideously, and pallid, green-eyed men running with them, howling with them.

Yet on I ran, fighting the black mists of exhaustion that closed about my brain. Heartbreaking inertia seemed to oppose every effort, as if I were swimming against a resisting tide. On and on I ran, with eyes for nothing, thought for nothing, except the lights before me, the dancing, mocking lights of Hebron, that seemed very near, and always fled before me.

Then suddenly I was lying in the soft snow with my eyes closed. The yielding couch was very comfortable to my exhausted body. I lay there, relaxed. I did not even try to rise; my strength was utterly gone. Blackness came upon me—unconsciousness that even the howling of the pack could not keep away. The weird ululation seemed to grow fainter and I knew no more.

CHAPTER XI
A Battle of Light and Darkness

"**P**retty near all in, ain't you, Mister?" a rough voice penetrated to my fatigue-drugged mind. Strong hands were helping me to my feet. I opened my eyes and stared confusedly about me. Two roughly clad men were supporting me. And another, whom I recognized as the station agent, Connell, held a gasoline lantern.

Before me, almost at hand, were the lights of Hebron, which had seemed to dance away so mockingly. I saw that I had collapsed in the outskirts of the straggling village—so near the few street lights that the pack had been unable to approach me.

"That you, McLaurin?" Connell demanded in surprise, recognizing my face. "We figgered they got you and Judson."

"They did," I found voice to say. "But they carried me off alive. I got away."

I was too nearly dead with exhaustion to answer their questions. Only vaguely do I recall how they carried me into a house, and undressed me. I went to sleep while they were examining the wound on my leg, exclaiming with horror at the marks of teeth. After I was sleeping they dressed it again, and then put me to bed.

It was noon of the following day when I awoke. A nervous boy of perhaps ten years was sitting by the bed. His name, he said, was Marvin Potts, son of Joel Potts, owner of a general store in Hebron. His father had been one of the men who had found me when their attention was attracted by the howling of the pack. I had been carried into the Potts home.

The boy called his mother. She, finding that I was hungry, soon brought me coffee, biscuits, bacon, and fried potatoes. I ate with good appetite, though I was far from recovered from my desperate run to escape the pack. While I was eating, still lying in bed, raised on an elbow, my host came in. Connell, the station agent, and two other men were with him.

All were anxious to hear my story. I told it to them briefly, or as much of it as I thought they would believe.

From them I learned that the weird pack had found several more human victims. A lone ranch house had been raided on the night before and three men carried from it. They told me, too, that Mrs. Judson, frantic with grief over the loss of her husband, had gone out across the snow to seek him and had not come back. How well I recalled now that she had found him! Bitterly I reproached myself for having urged the man to risk the night trip with me.

I inquired if any steps had been made to hunt the wolves.

The sheriff, I learned, had organized a posse, which had ventured out from Hebron several times. Abundant tracks of men and wolves, running side by side, had been found. There had been no difficulty in following the trail. But, I gathered, the hunters had not been very eager for success. The snow was deep; they could not travel rapidly, and they had owned no intention of meeting the pack by night. The trails had never been followed more than six or seven miles from Hebron. The sheriff had returned to the county seat, twelve miles down the railroad, promising to return when the snow had melted enough to make traveling easier. And the few score inhabitants of Hebron, though deeply disturbed by the fate of their neighbors who had been taken by the pack, had been too much terrorized to undertake any determined expedition on their own account.

When I spoke of getting someone to return with me to the ranch, quick evasions met me. The example of Judson's fate was very strongly in the minds of all present. None cared to risk being caught away from the town by night. I realized that I must act alone, unaided.

Most of that day I remained in bed, recuperating. I knew that I would need my full strength for the trial that lay before me. I investigated the available resources, however, and made plans for my mad attempt to strike at the menace that overhung humanity.

With the boy, Marvin, acting as my agent, I purchased an

ancient buggy, with a brown nag and harness, to carry me back to the ranch house; my efforts to rent a vehicle, or to hire someone to take me back, had proved signal failures. I had him also to arrange to procure for me other equipment.

I had him buy a dozen gasoline lanterns, with an abundant supply of mantles, and two five-gallon tins, full of gasoline. Finding that the Hebron High School boasted a meager supply of laboratory equipment, I sent the boy in search of magnesium ribbon, and sulphur. He returned with a good bundle of the thin, metallic strips, cut in various lengths. I dipped the ends of each strip in molten sulphur, to facilitate lighting.

He bought me two powerful electric flashlights, with a supply of spare bulbs and batteries, extra ammunition for my automatic, and two dozen sticks of dynamite, with caps and fuses.

Next morning I woke early, feeling much recovered. The shallow, gnawed wound in my leg was fast healing, and had ceased to pain me greatly. As I sat down to a simple breakfast with the Potts family, I assured them confidently that, on this day, I was going to return to the den of the strange pack, from which I had escaped, and put an end to it.

Before we had finished eating, I heard the hail of the man from whom the buggy had been bought, driving up to deliver it and collect the ample price that Marvin Potts had agreed that I would pay. The boy went out with me. We took the vehicle, and together made the rounds of Hebron's few stores, collecting the articles he had bought for me on the day before—the lanterns, the supply of gasoline, the electric search-lights, and the dynamite.

It was still early morning when I left the boy at the end of the street, rewarding him with a bill, and drove alone through the snow, back toward the lonely ranch house where I had experienced such horrors.

The day, though bright, was cold. The snow had never begun to thaw; it was still as thick as ever. My brown nag plodded along slowly, his feet and the buggy's tires crunching through the crusted snow.

As Hebron vanished behind me, and I was surrounded only by the vast, glittering sea of unbroken snow, fear and dread came upon me—a violent longing to hurry to some crowded haunt of men. My imagination pictured the terrors of the night, when the weird pack would run again upon the snow.

How easy would it be to return, take the train for New York, and forget the terrors of this place! No, I knew that I could never forget. I could never forget the threat of that dread, night-black world beyond the copper ring, the fact that its evil spawn planned to seize our world and make it a sphere of rotting gloom like their own.

And Stella! Never could I forget her. I knew now that I loved her, that I must save her or perish with her.

I urged the pony on, across the lonely and illimitable desert of sunlit snow.

It was somewhat past noon when I reached the ranch house. But I still had a safe margin of daylight. Immediately I set about my preparations.

There was much to do: unpacking the boxes piled on the buggy; filling the dozen gasoline lanterns, pumping them up with air, burning their mantles, and seeing that they operated satisfactorily; attaching caps and fuses to the sticks of dynamite, testing my powerful flashlights; loading the little automatic and filling the extra clips; stowing conveniently in my pockets an abundance of matches, ammunition, extra batteries for the electric torches, the strips of magnesium ribbon.

The sun was still high when the preparations were completed. I took time then to put the pony in the stable behind the old house. I locked the door, and barricaded the building, so that, if any dread change converted the animal into a green-eyed monster, it would find itself imprisoned.

Then I went through the old house, carrying a lighted lantern. It was silent, deserted. All the monsters were evidently below. The door of the cellar was closed, all crevices chinked against light.

I lit my dozen powerful lanterns and arranged them in a circle about it.

Then I threw back the door.

A weird and fearful howl came from the dark passage below it! I heard the rush of feet, as the howling thing retreated down the tunnel. From below came angry growls, shrill feral whines.

A physical wave of nauseating horror broke chillingly over me, at the thought of invading that red-lit temple-burrow, where I had endured such unnamable atrocities of horror. I shrank back, trembling. But at the thought of my own father and lovely, blue-eyed Stella, down in that temple of terror, ruled by foul monsters, I recovered my courage.

I stepped back toward the yawning black mouth of the den that these monsters had built.

The lanterns I had first intended to leave in a ring about the mouth of the burrow, except one to carry with me. Now it occurred to me that they would prevent the escape of the monsters more effectively if scattered along the passage. I gathered up six of them, three in each hand, and started down the steps.

Their powerful white rays illuminated the old cellar with welcome brilliance. I left one of them there, in the center of the cellar's floor. And three more of them I set along the slanting passage that led down into the deeper excavation.

I intended to set the two that remained on the floor of the temple, and perhaps return to the surface for others. I hoped that the light would drive the alien life from all of the pack, as it had from Stella. When they were unconscious, I could carry out Stella and my father, and any of the others that seemed whole enough for normal life. The great machine, and the temple itself, I intended to destroy with the dynamite.

I stepped from the end of the passage, into the vast, black, many-pillared hall. The intense white radiance of the faintly humming lanterns dispelled the terrible, blood-red gloom. I heard an appalling chorus of agonized animal cries; weird, feral whines and howls of pain. In the farther end of the long hall, beyond the massive ebon pillars, I saw slinking, green-orbed forms, crowding into the shadows.

I set the two lanterns down on the black floor and drew

one of the powerful flashlights from my pocket. Its intense, penetrating beam probed the shadows beyond the huge columns of jet. The cowering, howling shapes of men and wolves shrieked when it touched them, and fell to the black floor.

Confidently I stepped forward, to search out new corners with the brilliant finger of light.

Fatal confidence! I had underestimated the cunning and the science of my enemies. When I first saw the black globe, my foot was already poised above it. A perfect sphere of utter blackness, a foot-thick globe that looked as if it had been turned from midnight crystal.

I could not avoid touching it. And it seemed to explode at my touch. There was a dull, ominous *plop*. And billowing darkness rushed from it. A black gas swirled up about me and shrouded me in smothering gloom.

Wildly I turned, dashed back toward the passage that led up to open air and daylight. I was utterly blinded. The blazing lanterns were completely invisible. I heard one of them dashed over by my blundering feet.

Then I stumbled against the cold temple wall. In feverish haste I felt along it. In either direction, as far as I could reach, the wall was smooth. Where was the passage? A dozen feet I blundered along, feeling the wall. No, the passage must be in the other direction.

I turned. The triumphant, unearthly baying of the pack reached my ears; the padding of feet down the length of the temple. I rushed along the wall, stumbled and fell over a hot lantern.

And they were upon me. . . .

The strange, sourceless, blood-hued radiance of the temple was about me once more. The thick, black pillars thrust up beside me, to support the ebon roof. I was bound, helpless, to one of those cold, massive columns, as I had once been before, with the same bloody rope.

Before me was the strange mechanism that opened the way to that other plane—the Black Dimension—by changing the vibration frequencies of the matter of one world, to those of the other, interlocking universe. The red light gleamed like blood on the copper ring, and the huge mirror behind it. I saw with relief that the electron tubes were dead, the gasoline engine silent, the blackness gone from the ring.

And before the ring had been erected a fearful altar, upon which reposed the torn, mangled, and bleeding bodies of men and women, of gaunt gray wolves, and little coyotes, and other animals. The pack had found good hunting, on the two nights that I had been gone!

The corpse-white, green-orbed, monstrous things, the frightfully changed bodies of Stella and my father and the others, were about me.

"Your coming back is good," the whining, feral tones of the thing in my father's body rang dreadfully in my ears. "The manufacturer of electricity will not run. You return to make it turn again. The way must be opened again, for new life to come to these that wait." He pointed a deathly white arm to the pile of weltering bodies on the black floor.

"Then the new life to you also we will bring. Too many times you run away. You become one with us. And we seek a man who will act as we say. But first must the way be opened again.

"From our world will the life come. To take the bodies of men as machines. To make gas of darkness like that you found within this hall, to hide all the light of your world, and make it fit for us."

My mind reeled with horror at thought of the inconceivable, unthinkable menace risen like a dread specter to face humanity. At the thought that soon I, too, would be a mere machine. My body, cold and white as a corpse, doing unnamable deeds at the command of the thing of darkness whose green eyes would blaze in my sockets!

"Quickly tell the method to turn the maker of electricity," came the maleficent snarl, menacing, gloating, "or we gnaw the flesh from your bones, and seek another who will do our will!"

CHAPTER XII
Spawn of the Black Dimension

I agreed to attempt to start the little gasoline engine, hoping for some opportunity to turn the tables again. I was certain that I could do nothing so long as I was bound to the pillar. And the threat to find another normal man to take my place as teacher of these monsters from that alien world brought realization that I must strike soon.

Presently they were convinced that they required more than verbal aid in starting the little motor. One of the mechanics unbound me, and led me over to the machine, keeping a painful grip upon my arm with ice-cold fingers.

Unobtrusively, I dropped a hand to feel my pockets. They were empty!

"Make not light!" my father snarled warningly, having seen the movement.

They had awakened to the necessity of searching my person. Glancing about the red-lit temple, I saw the articles they had taken from me, in a little pile against the base of a huge black pillar. The automatic, spare clips of ammunition, flashlights, batteries, boxes of matches, strips of magnesium ribbon. The two gasoline lanterns that I had brought into the great hall were there too, having evidently been extinguished by the black gas which had blinded me.

Two gray wolves stood alertly beside the articles, which must have been taken from me before I recovered consciousness after the onrush of the pack. Their strange green eyes stared at me balefully through the crimson gloom.

After fussing with the engine for a few moments, while my father kept his cold, cruelly firm grip upon my shoulder, and scores of hideous green orbs in the bodies of wolves and men watched my every move, I discovered that it had stopped for lack of fuel. They had let it run on after I wrecked the machine, until the gasoline was exhausted.

I explained to my father that it would not run without more gasoline.

"Make it turn to cause electricity," he said, repeating his menacing, wolfish snarl, "or we gnaw the flesh from your bones, and find another man."

At first I insisted that I could not get gasoline without visiting some inhabited place. Under the threat of torture however—when they dragged me back toward the bloody rope—I confessed that the fuel in the gasoline lanterns might be used.

They were suspicious. They searched me again, to be certain that I had upon my person no means of making a light. And the lanterns were examined very carefully for any means of lighting without matches.

Finally they brought me the lanterns. With my father grasping my arm, I poured the gasoline from them into the engine's fuel tank. Under any circumstances it would have been difficult to avoid spilling the liquid. I took pains to spill as much as seemed possible without rousing suspicion—contriving to pour a little pool of it under the exhaust, where a spark might ignite the fumes.

Then they made me start the engine. Coils hummed once more; the electron tubes lit. Blackness seemed to pour from the strange central tube, to be reflected into the great copper ring by the wide, polished mirror.

Again, I looked through the vast ring into the Black Dimension!

Before me lay a sky of gloom, of darkness unutterable and unbroken, stagnant, lurid waters, dimly aglow with the luminosity of foul decay; worn black hills, covered with obscene, writhing, reptilian vegetation that glowed vaguely and lividly green. And on one of those hills was the city.

A sprawled smear of red evil, it was, a splash of crimson darkness, of red corruption. It spread over the hill like a many-tentacled monster of dark red mist. Ugly masses rose from it, wart-like knobs and projections—ghastly travesties of minarets and towers.

It was motionless. And within its reeking, fetid scarlet

darkness, lurked things of creeping gloom—nameless hordes of things like that unthinkable monstrosity that I had seen flow into Stella's body. Green-eyed, living horrors of flowing blackness.

The monsters about me howled through the ring, into that black world—calling!

And soon, through the copper ring, came flowing a river of shapeless, inconceivable horror! Formless monsters of an alien universe. Foul beings of the darkness—spawn of the Black Dimension!

Fearful green eyes were swimming in clotted, creeping masses of evil darkness. They swarmed over the pile of dead things on the floor. And the dead rose to forbidden, nameless life!

Mutilated corpses, and the torn bodies of wolves sprang up, whining, snarling. And the eyes of each were the malevolent, glaring green eyes of the things that had flowed into them.

I was still beside the rhythmically throbbing little engine. As I shrank back in numbed horror from the fearful spectacle of the dead rising to unhallowed life, my eyes fell despairingly upon the little pool of gasoline I had spilled upon the black floor. It was not yet ignited.

I had some fleeting idea of trying to saturate my hand with gasoline and hold it in front of the exhaust, to make of it a living torch. But it was too late for that, and the ruthless, ice-cold fingers still clutched my arm painfully.

Then my father whined wolfishly.

A creepy, formless, obscene mass of blackness, with twin green orbs in it, glowing with mad, alien fires, left the river of them that poured through the ring and crept across to me.

"Now you become one like us!" came the whining voice.

The thing was coming to flow into my body, to make me its slave, its machine!

I screamed, struggled in the cruel hands that held me. In an insanity of terror, I cursed and pleaded—promised to give the monsters the world. And the creeping blackness came on.

I collapsed, drenched with icy sweat, quivering, nauseated with horror.

Then, as I had prayed it would do, the little engine coughed. A stream of pale red sparks shot from the exhaust. There was a sudden, dull, explosive sound of igniting vapor. A yellow flash lit the black-pillared temple.

A flickering column of blue and yellow flame rose from the pool of gasoline beside the engine.

The things of blackness were *consumed* by the light—they vanished!

The temple became a bedlam of shrill, agonized howls, of confused, rushing, panic-stricken bodies. The fierce grasp upon my arm was relaxed. My father fell upon the floor, writhing across the room toward the shelter of a black pillar, hiding his green eyes with an arm flung across them.

I saw that the gray wolves had deserted their post beside the articles of mine they had been guarding, at the foot of the massive black column. I left the flickering pillar of fire and dashed across to them.

In a moment my shaking hands had clutched upon one of the powerful electric flashlights. In desperate haste I found the switch and flicked it on. With the intense, dazzling beam, I swept the vast columned hall. The hellish chorus of animal cries of pain rose to a higher pitch. I saw gray wolves and ghastly white men cowering in the shadows of the massive pillars.

I snatched up the other searchlight and turned it on. Then, hastily gathering up pistol, ammunition, matches, and strips of magnesium ribbon, I retreated to a position beside the flaring gasoline.

This time I moved very cautiously, flashing the light before me to avoid stumbling into another bomb of darkness, like that which had been my undoing before. But I think my precaution was useless; I am sure, from what I afterward saw, that only one had been prepared.

As I got back to the engine, I noticed that it was still running, that the way to the Black Dimension, through the copper ring, was still open. I cut off the fuel, at the carburetor. The little engine coughed, panted, slowed down. The wall of darkness faded from the copper ring, breaking our connection with that hideous world of another interpenetrating universe.

Then I hastily laid the flashlights on the floor, laying them so they cast their broad, bright beams in opposite directions. I fumbled for matches, struck one to the end of a strip of magnesium ribbon, to which I had applied sulphur to make it easier to light.

It burst into sudden blinding, dazzling, white radiance, bright as a miniature sun. I flung it across the great black hall. It outlined a white parabola. Its intense light cut the shadows from behind the ebon pillars.

The cowering, hiding things howled in new agony. They lay on the black floor, trembling, writhing, fearfully contorted. Low, agonized whinings came from them.

Again and again I ignited the thin ribbons of metal and flung them flaming toward the corners of the room, to banish all shadow with their brilliant white fire.

The howling grew weaker, the whines died away. The wolves and the corpse-white men moved no more. Their fierce, twisting struggles of agony were stilled.

When the last strip of magnesium was gone, I drew the automatic, put a bullet through the little engine's gasoline tank, and lit a match to the thin stream of clear liquid that trickled out. As a new flaring pillar of light rushed upward, I hurried toward the passage that led to the surface, watching for another of those black spheres that erupted darkness.

I found the gasoline lanterns I had left in the tunnel still burning; the monsters had evidently found no way of putting them out.

On to the surface I ran. I gathered up the six lanterns I had left there—still burning brilliantly in the gathering dusk—and plunged with them back down the passage, into the huge, pillared temple.

The monsters were still inert, unconscious.

I arranged the powerful lanterns about the floor, so placed that every part of the strange temple was brilliantly illuminated. In the penetrating radiance, the monsters lay motionless.

Returning to the surface, I brought one of my full cans of gasoline, and two more of the lighted lanterns. I filled, pumped up, and lit the two lanterns from which I had drawn the gasoline.

Then I went about the black-walled temple, always keeping two lanterns close beside me, and dragged the lax, ice-cold bodies from their crouching postures, turning them so the faces would be toward the light. I found Stella, her lovely body still unharmed, except for its deathly pallor and its strange cold. And then I came upon my father. There was also the mangled thing that had been Judson, and the headless body that had been Blake Jetton, Stella's father. I gazed at many more lacerated human bodies and at the chill carcasses of wolves, of coyotes, of the gray horse, of a few other animals.

In half an hour, perhaps, the change was complete.

The unearthly chill of that alien life was gone from the bodies. Most of them quickly stiffened—with belated *rigor mortis*. Even my father was quite evidently dead. His body remained stiff and cold—though the strange chill had departed.

But Stella's exquisite form grew warm again; the soft flush of life came to it. She breathed and her heart beat slowly.

I carried her up to the old cellar, and laid her on its floor, with two lanterns blazing near her, to prevent any return of that forbidden life, while I finished the ghastly work left for me below.

I need not go into details. . . .

But when I had used half my supply of dynamite, no recognizable fragments were left, either of the accursed machine, or of the dead bodies that had been animated with such monstrous life. I planted the other dozen sticks of dynamite beside the great black pillars, and in the walls of the tunnel. . . .

The subterranean hall that I have called a temple will never be entered again.

When that work was done, I carried Stella up to her room, and put her very gently to bed. Through the night I watched her anxiously, keeping a bright light in the room. But there was no sign of what I feared. She slept deeply, but normally, apparently free from any taint of the monstrous life that had possessed her.

Dawn came after a weary night, and there was a rosy gleam upon the snow.

The sleeping girl stirred. Fathomless blue eyes opened, stared into mine. Startled eyes, eager, questioning. Not clouded with dream as when she had awakened before.

"Clovis!" Stella cried, in her natural, softly golden voice. "Clovis, what are you doing here? Where's Father? Dr. McLaurin?"

"You are all right?" I demanded eagerly. "You are well?"

"Well?" she asked, raising her exquisite head in surprise. "Of course I'm well. What could be the matter with me? Dr. McLaurin is going to try his great experiment to-day. Did you come to help?"

Then I knew—and a great gladness came with the knowledge—that all memory of the horror had been swept from her mind. She recalled nothing that had happened since the eve of the experiment that had brought such a train of terrors.

She looked suddenly past me—at the picture of myself upon the wall. These was a curious expression on her face; she flushed a little, looking very beautiful with heightened color.

"I didn't give you that picture," I accused her. I wished to avoid answering any questions, for the time being, about her father or mine, or any experiments.

"I got it from your father," she confessed.

I have written this narrative in the home of Dr. Friedrichs, the noted New York psychiatrist, who is a close friend of mine. I came to him as soon as Stella and I reached New York, and he has since had me stay at his home, under his constant observation.

He assures me that, within a few weeks, I shall be completely recovered. But sometimes I doubt that I will ever be entirely sane. The horrors of that invasion from another universe are graven too deeply upon my mind. I cannot bear to be alone in darkness, or even in moonlight. And I tremble when I hear the howling of a dog, and hastily seek bright lights and the company of human beings.

I have told Dr. Friedrichs my story, and he believes. It is because of his urging that I have written it down. It is an historical truism, my friend says, that all legend, myth, and folklore has a basis in fact. And no legends are wider spread than those of lycanthropy. It is remarkable that not only wolves are subjects of these legends, but the most ferocious wild animals of each country. In Scandinavia, for instance, the legends concern bears; on the continent of Europe, wolves; in South America, jaguars; in Asia and Africa, leopards and tigers. It is also remarkable that belief in possession of evil spirits, and belief in vampires, is associated with the widespread belief in werewolves.

Dr. Friedrichs thinks that through some cosmic accident, these monsters of the Black Dimension have been let into our world before; and that those curiously widespread legends and beliefs are folk-memories of horrors visited upon earth when those unthinkable monstrosities stole the bodies of men and of savage beasts, and hunted through the darkness.

Much might be said in support of the theory, but I shall let my experience speak for itself.

Stella comes often to see me, and she is more exquisitely lovely than I had ever realized. My friend assures me that her mind is quite normal. Her lapse of memory is quite natural, he says, since her mind was sleeping while the alien entity ruled her body. And he says there is no possibility that she will be possessed again.

We are planning to be married within a few weeks, as soon as Dr. Friedrichs says that my horror-seared mind is sufficiently healed.

V.

NICTZIN DYALHIS

INTRODUCTION

Nictzin Dyalhis (1880–1942) was then and forever shall remain one of the most enigmatic of the first-rank writers for *Weird Tales*. Despite a relatively small body of work, he was enormously popular with the readers, and, perhaps because almost nothing is known about the writer, Dyalhis has assumed legendary status. At my own small press imprint, Carcosa, I continually receive requests to reprint this author's stories—otherwise unavailable except from their original publication and a few almost-as-rare reprint anthologies. So then: here are three of the best and most sought-after stories of Nictzin Dyalhis. But first, ace science fiction/fantasy sleuth Sam Moskowitz here offers an introduction to the man and his work, apparently the only article ever written on this phantom author, in which Moskowitz recounts virtually everything that has ever been known about Nictzin Dyalhis—or likely ever will be known.

NICTZIN DYALHIS: MYSTERIOUS MASTER OF FANTASY

by Sam Moskowitz

Stories of sword-wielding heroic action set against a backdrop of sorcery and magic, though they have achieved unexampled heights of popularity in the past twenty years, are a very old facet of popular fiction. If we exempt the Norse legends, the genre can be traced to *Beowulf* (which was codified in the eighth century) and can claim *The Arabian Nights* (1450) as a legitimate ancestor. In the eighteenth century "Oriental Tales" became a very popular genre of English fiction. In 1786 the first all-fiction short-story magazine, *New Novelists Magazine or Little Novels* (issued by Harrison & Low, London), described its policy as being "to serve up to the Public, on terms proportionably advantageous, an elegant collection of the many beautiful little Tales and Stories scattered throughout innumerable voluminous miscellanies; which are frequently purchased with avidity, at a great expense, for the sake of a few pages only, the remainder being of no value to those who read for amusement." The magazine added types of stories of which "Oriental Tales'' of distinctly sword-and-sorcery content were prominently featured.

In the twentieth century *The Thief of Bagdad* by Achmed Abdullah (1924) has been filmed repeatedly with considerable success each time, but in general the genre languished until the current revival. If ever a prototype existed for today's tales of science and sorcery, excepting the Conan series by Robert E. Howard from which many are lineal descendants, it is ''The Sapphire Goddess'' by Nictzin Dyalhis from *Weird Tales*, February 1934. Occultism, magic, swordfights, dragons, a desperate journey, witch women, fighting aids, sorcerers, a beautiful enchanted maiden—all are woven into this one delightful novelette. It ranked first place in the issue by reader vote—no small achievement considering that Robert E. Howard's superb ''The Valley of the Worm'' was in the same issue, along with Edmond Hamilton's very effective ''The Man Who Returned,'' the second installment of David H. Keller's ''The Solitary Hunters'' (the other two installments would each win first place), and a fine Clark Ashton Smith story. Dyalhis was paid $125 for the 15,500 words and sold radio and serial rights. There is a light touch to ''The Sapphire Goddess'' and more than a seasoning of humor.

Virtually all the biographical information we possess concerning Nictzin Dyalhis comes from Willis Conover, Jr., an internationally known disc jockey who has spent most of his professional career working for the Voice of America. He obtained that position in 1954, and his shows are targeted to eighty countries with an estimated audience of thirty million. Virtually unknown in the United States, he has celebrity status abroad, even in the Soviet Union.

In the science fiction and fantasy world he is best known today for the editorial and artistic quality of his landmark volume, *Lovecraft at Last* (published in 1975), which reproduces his teenage correspondence with H.P. Lovecraft. In 1936 he flashed like a meteor across the rarefied atmosphere of the science fiction fan world with a small, superbly produced publication titled *Science-Fantasy Correspondent*, which in the two issues he edited (November–December 1936 and January–February 1937) showed the extent of his correspondence by including material by H. P. Lovecraft, David H. Keller, Robert Bloch, John Russell Fearn, Jack Williamson, Greye La Spina, Henry Kuttner and Arthur J. Burks. In 1975 he brought *Science-Fantasy Correspondent* back for a single issue in a new incarnation which reproduced some of the material from the original and had new material by Robert Aickman, H. P. Lovecraft, Robert E. Howard, Arthur C. Clarke, and Brian Aldiss.

As a teenager in the thirties, Conover resided at 27 High Street, Cambridge, in Dorchester County, Maryland—a community of 12,000 located on the Choptank River where it flows into Chesapeake Bay. In those days, Cambridge was probably best known for the Phillips Packing Company, a chicken and vegetable packing plant that had the distinction of producing a variety of five-cent cans of soup to compete with the more costly Campbell Soups at ten cents a can.

Cambridge was located about thirty highway miles from Jesterville in Wicomico County, Maryland—a village of 200 located about fifteen miles southwest of Salisbury, just where the Nanticoke River widens to terminate into Chesapeake Bay. The area was devoted to fishing and the raising of fruits and vegetables, with a number of processing plants for those products in the region. Dyalhis dwelled in Jesterville (named after a distributor of fresh and processed foods) in what Conover terms ''a shack.''

Conover had been impressed by ''The Sea-Witch'' by Nictzin Dyalhis (*Weird Tales*, December 1937) and wrote editor Farnsworth Wright asking for Dyalhis's address. He was thrilled to learn that Dyalhis lived such a respectively short distance from him, and he wrote asking to visit. He received a warm reply stating that, while Dyalhis did not have much to offer in the way of hospitality, he would most certainly be welcome. Conover took a bus from Cambridge to Salisbury and, since there was no public transportation to Jesterville, took a cab (they were very affordable during that dark Depression era). At first pass he missed the Dyalhis abode, expecting something more pretentious; but since there was nothing farther ahead, he had the cabbie swing back—and was in for something of a shock. The state of affluence of Dyalhis can be determined by the fact that his house had no running water, no plumbing, no electricity, no gas, and the only heat was provided by a potbellied stove. In the back there was a two-seater outhouse. The structure was situated on River Road, which followed the Nanticoke River. The rent was four dollars a month.

It was night when Conover first arrived, and he was greeted almost genially at the door by a short, thin man with a potbelly, a glass eye, no teeth, and wearing a worn cap over a balding head. Behind him was his wife, obviouly of Indian ancestry and considerably younger than Nictzin, who was then about 57 years of age and looked older. He had one daughter, whom Conover estimated to be about five or six years of age at the time.

This was one of several visits. At one of these the wife cooked a muskrat for dinner, which had a frightful odor, which tended to obscure any salutary memories of the meal. This was offset to some extent by sweet cider served with it as a beverage.

The youthful Conover later described Dyalhis as a man with "a wasted little old tubercular body." As to personality, on the negative side he was an "argumentive, opinionated man, employing profanity but not obscenity." For example, he pronounced "shit" as "shix." On the positive side Conover said he "housed a spirit as eager and ageless as an angel's—and as generous. But he was impatient with this world, because he had so often traveled more wonderful ways." His conversations were carried on alongside the stove, where he rolled his own cigarettes and spat into the fire. He talked incessantly, rarely permitting a word in edgewise.

There has been some confusion as to his nationality and origin. For example, in the January–February 1938 issue of *Fantascience Digest*, Conover specifically stated that Dyalhis was of Russian background. In the obituary he wrote of him (*Weird Tales*, September 1942), he said that the first name "Nictzin" was of Mexican Indian origin translated as "Flower of Youth," and the last name was Scotch-Irish from the Roman god "Flamen Dialis," believed to be the source of the later names of Dallas and Douglas. Mike Ashley in a biographical sketch in *Who's Who in Horror and Fantasy Fiction* (1977) was more specific, stating that Nictzin's father was a British sea captain who married a Mexican Indian woman. In a June 22, 1988 phone interview, Conover clarified this by stating that Dyalhis was born in the Americas and was a descendant of some Latin American Indian group.

Public records confirm that Nictzin Dyalhis was born June 4, 1880, son of Netulyani Teltorre and George Dyalhis, in Pima County, Arizona. This is west of Tucson and north of the Mexican border and contains the large Papago Indian Reservation. His mother had Indian blood and came from South America. His father was born in Pima County. Nictzin had a middle name which he rarely used: it was Wilston. If the records are to be believed, Dyalhis's father was an American and not British. This tends to question whether or not he was a sea captain.

Dyalhis believed in the occult and tried to practice it. He claimed his cabin was protected by friendly spirits and gave Conover at least one demonstration of special powers. He cut an arrow out of a newspaper, then stuck a needle into a bottle cork and pinned the arrow onto it. He then pointed his finger at the needle, and the paper arrow began to move. He explained this by asserting that he had summoned energy from the root of the spine, up to the head, and willed the paper to move. Conover states that there was no detectable flow of air or breeze in the room at the time.

Before coming to Maryland, Dyalhis said, he had worked for some technical company in sales, and he blamed his current destitution upon the failure of the company to live up to some promises it had made him.

Dyalhis's wife was a plain-looking woman, who was descended from the Toltecs, a Mexican Indian tribe that preceded the Aztecs. Validity of the Indian background of Dyalhis and his family seems confirmed by the stories of Mexican Indians which he sold to *Adventure* magazine in the very early twenties.

Since Dyalhis was born in 1880, and the *Adventure* stories are the earliest yet discovered written by him, he was in his forties at that time, and the details of his life previous to that are not known. Conover relates that he lived much of his early life in the Orient and "had known intimately its splendor and its squalor." He had dabbled in the Chinese occult and offered a blue dragon tattooed on a vein of his wrist, which he claimed was proof of membership in a Chinese occult society. He also claimed that he had visited Tibet when very few white men could make that statement and knew something of their alleged secrets. He asserted as well that he had viewed a voodoo ceremony in Haiti by staining his body a dark color to avoid standing out. Whether these stories are true or invented to entertain his youthful guest can only be surmised.

When he started his literary endeavors is open to question. He told Conover that he was a "close friend" of Rudyard Kipling, but where and in what context is not clear. Kipling lived in India and the United States as well as England. If the Kipling story is accurate, this may have preceded Dyalhis's writing period with *Adventure*.

With all of his travels to foreign countries, why he chose to settle in a desolate shack in a mosquito-ridden swampy area off Chesapeake Bay is as great a mystery as the rest of his life. Its high humidity was certainly not the place for a man who had suffered from tuberculosis. He would have been far better off in the Southwest, which would have been practical from the standpoint of his relationship to the Mexican Indians as well as his health.

As to his health, he wrote Conover the following letter in 1937:

> Last Sunday I woke up a whole lot nearer Hell than I like to remember. Old sister Pleurisy had me in her foul embrace squarely to the cardiac region.

Lasted all day, and I came close to hearing "Doesn't he look natural?" but made it through, thanks to the grittiest little woman who ever lived.

But there's a darker and more sinister side to the matter: vis; Knowing me well and unfavorably, The Great One doesn't want me . . . and the devil won't have me. . . . I said quite a lot of un-nice things about HIM in "The Eternal Conflict" and showed his brother up rather badly in "The Dark Lore"; so you can easily comprehend why I'm personally *non-grata* in the Pit.

Just the same, ol' sis P. will cuddle me once too often, and I'll succumb to her wiles.

Pleurisy is the inflammation of the lining that covers the lungs and the inner wall of the chest and is commonly associated with tuberculosis.

Pleurisy may well have preceded his death, for his wife wrote Conover that he died May 8, 1942 at 10:20 A.M. in Salisbury. At the time of his death he was a few weeks short of 62 years of age. The cause of his death was given as "chronic myocarditis," an inflammation of the heart muscle which can be caused by a great variety of reasons. His death occurred in Peninsula Hospital, Salisbury, Maryland. He was buried from St. Francis Church on May 11, 1942 in the Fruitland Cemetery, Fruitland, Maryland, a town adjoining Salisbury.

Nictzin Dyalhis was an utterly unique writer, who received very high ratings from the readers—but we have only been able to discover eleven stories over a nineteen-year period (added to these are three "fragments" which Conover says he has in his possession). The longest of these stories is "The Sapphire Goddess" at 15,500 words, and the bulk of them were paid for at about one cent a word—scarcely enough to keep a man and wife and daughter alive even at a rental of only four dollars a month. There was no welfare program during most of the period of Dyalhis's writing life, and he was not eligible for Social Security, which was only in effect a few years at the very end of his life. In the Chesapeake Bay area he could have fished, hunted, raised or picked fruits and vegetables. Undoubtedly he resorted to some of these options to replenish his larder.

Two stories discovered in *Adventure* for 1922 are "Who Keep the Desert Law" and "For Wounding Retaliation." A few words about the latter, which appeared in the issue for November 20, 1922, are in order, since it reflects Dyalhis's familiarity with the Southwest.

An 86-year-old Indian woman, Inez Chachalaka, riding a burro to the general store to buy some coffee, finds a Pima Indian baby asleep alongside the trail. She takes it home, leaving Indian signs as to what direction she has gone. An Indian family who has lost the baby follow the signs and are overjoyed at the recovery of their infant. The father wants to settle on a piece of ground near Inez's abode and brings the Indian agent out to arrange a purchase. The agent gets fresh with the Indian's pretty wife and ends up knocked cold with the Indian family heading for Mexico in their car.

The Indian agent is named Kyle and word of his misman-agement of his reservation begins to get around. One day, a large touring car drives up with an inspector from the United States government named Shane. He is an old friend of the Indian woman Inez, having rescued her from the Apaches when she was younger, and he can even speak the Pima lan-guage. She fills him in on the shortcomings of Kyle. Then with smoke signals she arranges to get the Indian who had knocked Kyle down back on the reservation. A plan is set up in which, after a battle, the men who under the kindly aus-pices of Kyle are selling bootleg whiskey to the Indians are killed or captured and everything is temporarily set right.

The style of writing throughout can best be described as flippant; the note of humor and irreverance in many of Dy-alhis's works is more strongly apparent here than in any other. The competence of the writing and the dialogue seem to in-dicate previous practice somewhere and a more than super-ficial knowledge of Indian mores is present.

Adventure, during that period, paid a minimum of two cents a word and would go as high as ten cents a word for a very famous author. Those were among the best rates paid in the pulp field at that time, though magazines like *Blue Book* or *Short Stories* would go to four or five cents a word for special authors by special arrangement.

With Dyalhis later claiming to Conover that he was involved in occult societies in China as a young man, we can understand why he became interested in *Weird Tales* as a market. He could not be unaware that they paid no more than one cent a word on publication, because editor Farnsworth Wright announced such rates in the writers' magazines. That could be excused on the basis that he wanted to write on subjects that the magazine featured, but what is more puzzling is that his first story for that publication, "When the Green Star Waned" (April 1925), was written as a straightforward and somewhat advanced science fiction story and not as a weird, occult or supernatural yarn. It would most certainly have been accepted by *Amazing Stories* had that magazine existed at the time. It definitely was not written for *Adventure*, which advertised in the writers' magazines that it wanted no pseudo-scientific or supernatural fiction.

The heroes of the story are highly civilized beings on the planet Venus (spelled Venhez) who have an instrument invented by the scientist Ron Ti, which can bring in close-up images and sounds from Earth (spelled Aerth) which is called the "Green Star," because that is the color it presents. The sounds stop coming in from Earth and the green color becomes lighter (the genesis of the story's title). Puzzled by this, Hul Jok, commander of the Forces for Planetary Defense (part of the Planetary Chain, made up of peoples of the inhabited worlds of the Solar System) leads a space formation to investigate.

They find the cities of Earth devastated, there is no sign of even animal life, and the vegetation is thinning out, resulting in the lightening of the planet's green color. What they do find are great protoplasmic "blobs" with a mouth and teeth, which will consume almost any life form. They destroy them with their "blastor" or disintegrator rays as they find them.

They finally discover the humans, utterly crushed and dispirited slaves, fed at will to the "blobs" by a silvery black race of creatures with advanced science, capable of altering shape at will, with a molecular structure so tenuous that they cannot be destroyed by the "blastors" though they can be still hurt by blows. They have subjected the Earth men by the hypnotic power of their wills, which the Venusians resist only with considerable effort. These creatures, able to levitate, have come from the dark side of Earth's moon and brought the "blobs" with them. They have an advanced science and attack the Venusians with silvery globes and electrical discharges, but those solid objects are destroyed by the blastors and ramming. What really inactivates them, though, are harmonious chords and melodies from musical instruments, and these are broadcast so that they are picked up. The Lunarians' globes are lured into space by a ruse and then rammed or blasted and the vacuum effectively accomplishes the death of the evil creatures, all except one which they take back with them to Venus.

The story has so many devices and gambits that later became standard in science fiction that it must be considered highly advanced for its period. It is written with a light touch, which includes humor, and completely captivated the readers of *Weird Tales*, for it was voted the single most popular story the magazine had printed up to that date! It was 9,250 words long and Dyalhis received $90 for it, above the going rate for the magazine. He sold all serial rights, retaining book and other sources of income. August Derleth later included it in his bulky historical science fiction anthology *Beyond Time & Space* (Pellegrini & Cudahy, 1950).

The logical thing for Dyalhis to have done at this point was to write a sequel, or failing in that, more straight science fiction, but instead, he turned to a tale of the occult and mysticism in its most rarefied and exalted form with "The Eternal Conflict" in *Weird Tales* for October 1925. The protagonist, a member of the occult order of the Secret Society of the Black Shrine dedicated to "The Goddess," has his intelligence projected from his still-living body to a luminescent city, not on any planet, somewhere in the farthest reaches of the universe. There he finds luminescent beings, like humans but not human, and confronts "The Goddess," a female form some thirty feet tall, who is "Love's Prototype," the personification of all love.

She has an enemy she cannot reach with her own powers, "The Lord of Hate" (yet, Dyalhis cannot help quipping, *he* loves too, since he "loves to hate"!). She wants the Earthman to act as her spy, since his race hates as well as loves and therefore can successfully penetrate the sanctums of her enemy. She also notes that the Earthmen are the great adventurers of the universe and that as one of them, he possesses the qualities to accomplish her mission. At this point it should be mentioned that Dyalhis does not seem to know the difference between our solar system and a galaxy.

The Earthman's ego travels through space and is reembodied in the kingdom of hatred as a being dwarfish, stunted and ugly. No sooner accomplished, than a monster pops up from the ground and swallows him. He conjures up a sharp metal rake and digs his way out of the creature's stomach. He doesn't get far before he is showered by powder from a poisonous plant. He plunges into a pool of water to rid himself of it and finds it is scathingly hot. Emerging, he is chased by a double-sized pack of wolflike creatures, only to be rescued by a man in armor, surrounded by a motley assortment of creatures from a variety of worlds. They rescued him not out of goodness but out of hatred for the wolflike creatures, for this is the world of hate, and they march him to a mighty city, much like one from the Middle Ages. They take him before the archdemon, who has a cultivated air. He tells the demon the truth, feeling that he will not be believed, but unexpectedly finds favor and good treatment.

The Prince of Evil, actually Lucifer, gives him a place at his side and takes him with him to the Conferences of the Lords of Wrong, the Princes of Evil. These vassals of Lucifer all take handsome forms. The Earthman finds that Lucifer has been toying with him; he has surmised his spying design and now subjects him to the most excruciating mental torture. He finds himself suspended in and then encased by particles. He is carried into space, first subjected to unbelievable heat, which turns to cold supplemented by intolerable compression, but he can only suffer and not die.

He is freed from his agony by The Goddess and gives his report. Lucifer demands him back but is defied. Lucifer with his minions attacks but is faced by many angelic creatures, many of whom are destroyed defending the Earthman, but it was the plan of The Woman of Light to bring Lucifer within range of her powers. A single flash of light from her hand turns him weak and sickly, and he flees with his minions and with her taunt hurled at him: "Lucifer, thou hast my pity."

The Earthman is sent once again to Lucifer to deliver *her* message that though he serves a purpose in the scheme of things he has overstepped his bounds and if he does so again "no worm squirming beneath the dust of the Green Star from whence I came can be so low as thou shalt be abased. *Heed yet the warning.*" Backed by the presence of The Goddess, Lucifer cringes on his throne.

The Earthman returns to his still living body in the Temple of The Black Shrine. He once again sees The Goddess and knows that ultimately he will be called again to serve her, but this time he will not return.

Today, the fundamentalist concepts of Heaven and Hell as presented in this story attain no willing suspension of disbelief, but once Dyalhis moved into the action of his adventures and of his tortures the story moved swiftly and engagingly enough to win first place as the best story in the issue, beating out the first of the Jules deGrandin stories by Seabury Quinn, "The Horror on the Links," which was in the same issue. Though the Dyalhis story was 14,700 words in length, he received only $100 for it, a lower rate than the first, but selling only first serial rights.

With the issue of July 1926, a magazine titled *Ghost Stories* was introduced, a direct competitor of *Weird Tales* published by Bernarr Macfadden, successful power behind *True Story Magazine* and *Physical Culture*. While *Weird Tales* was a pulp, this magazine was a large-sized, smooth-paper publication with the stories illustrated by photographs of living models posed to depict selected situations. Most of the stories in this magazine were formula tales involving a ghost, which lent an air of sameness to them. They also attempted to give the impression that they were true accounts, which by and large they were not. Why Dyalhis decided to write for the magazine is not clear, except that they did pay two cents a word upon acceptance. The April 1927 issue announced that he would have a story titled "My Encounter with Osric, The Troll," but when it appeared in the May, 1927 issue the title had been changed to "He Refused to Stay Dead." It was listed as a collaboration with Eric Marston, but immediately upon entering the story it turned out that Marston was the lead character, so it was but a weak ruse on the part of the magazine to give the impression that the story was true and that Dyalhis was the "ghost writer."

The blurb also belonged to some other story, for it was supposed to be a tale of wraiths that slip into the bodies of babes to consummate some task from a previous life, but it involves reincarnation of one of the characters and not the stated theme at all.

Eric Marston, an Englishman, formerly with Allenby in the Mesopotamian campaigns of World War I, obtains from a dying Arab a stone amulet inscribed in an unknown language. His girlfriend, Edwina, faints when she sees it, claiming she had lost it ages past in a previous life, and insists on wearing it.

Marston marries her and takes her to his ancestral home Falconwold, which claims a ghost dating back to the First Crusade. In those ancient days two dissolute brothers started to fight a duel when a mighty hand with an enormous sword intervened with a pyrotechnic display of arms so frightening that the brothers dropped their rapiers and clung to one another in supernatural fear.

Edwina believes that because the sword arm was unarmored it dates back *before* the First Crusade and begins research of the scrolls in the Falconwold library.

On the grounds they locate the burial mound of a Viking

named Thorwulf Sword Hand, whose spirit has been trapped in a vault by a metal plate placed on its entrance by Rolf the Friar, Chaplain to Count Hamo Falconer, and it is believed that the sword hand of ghostly legend is that of the Viking.

Marston has a dream in which he is Eric the Falcon and a strange ship is foundering on the surf outside his "castle." Everyone aboard is lost except one woman, an Arabian named Edwina, whom he weds. But she is captured when Norsemen invade his estate, and never seen again.

Now the tomb of Falconwold, which has the Seal of Suleiman on a metal plate, is opened by ripping the plate off, and seated therein is a Norseman in full armor, who comes to life on experiencing the inrush of air. The Norseman recognizes in Marston and his wife the reincarnation of Eric and his wife Edwina of ages past.

Marston seizes the Norseman's axe and a fight ensues in the tomb, then moves outside. Marston falls and loses the axe, but in falling his hand grasps something metallic which in desperation he flings into the face of his opponent. The Norseman when struck utters a cry, falls and dissolves into a skeleton. He has been struck by the silver plate which had imprisoned him for all these years.

The hair of both Marston and Edwina turns white from the experience, but mercifully she does not remember what happened.

The action scene following the opening of the tomb in this story is well done, but taken overall Dyalhis has complied to the ghost-story formula of the magazine, which greatly reduces the effectiveness of the story. All of the Dyalhis stories are difficult to find, but this one is probably to be the most difficult of all due to the rarity of the magazine.

"The Dark Lore," which received the cover of the August 1927 *Weird Tales* was a very powerful story which owes a great deal to Dante's *Inferno* (1307) and *The Monk* by M. G. Lewis (1796). The tale is that of Lura Veyle, told by her permission through an occultist. The evil woman, whose allurements are rejected by her sister's fiancée, through black magic causes his death in an automobile accident. Her sister dies of heartbreak as a result. Not satisfied, she conjures up the soul of the dead man, but then rejects it as too weak for her taste.

The angel Hesperus appears to her, a demonic spirit the equal of Lucifer. A host of lesser demons pays homage to her. Despite his undeniable appeal, she plays coy, giving him her mother's ring as a token. He leaves a necklace of ruby-colored stones, which seem to be sweating blood.

She finds she now is endowed with protective powers. When a statesman tries to put his arm around her, he dies of a heart attack.

Greatly impressed, she calls back the spirit of Hesperus without the use of occult preparation. He takes her to Hell and her body is interred, but she reemerges as solid flesh, learning that there are multiple layers of life, each "death" followed by a reappearance, but with each emergence a lessening of substance.

At first, she enjoys a life of wonder and revelry as Hesperus' queen, but finally Hesperus enters with a female from another planet. Infuriated, she tries to use the occult to revenge herself on Hesperus, but her efforts are futile.

Hesperus does not excuse this attempt. He denudes her of her clothes and gives her to a bestial servant, humanlike in appearance but with scales on his front and porcupine-like quills on his back. His face has lidless eyes and a beak like that of a turtle. He takes her on a flying monster back to his lair and subjects her to every form of debauchery. When he tires of her, he passes her on as a plaything to his fellow monstrosities. Eventually she is thrown from his tower and killed, passing into a new form.

Her agonies are just beginning. She is chased by twenty-foot-high skeleton creatures. Gaining strength, she grapples with and almost destroys one of them, but there are too many of them. To escape, she ventures out on a lake of ooze that will bear her weight only as long as she keeps moving. Polypods, great eight-limbed creatures, emerge from the ooze, catch and eat her. In a new incarnation as a "thinner" self, she finds her self walking on air, levitating and heading into a black pall from which emerges gargantuan laughter. She has the impression that she has arrived in the Great Void before the creation of the universe.

Cloaked in darkness, she feels she is alternately treading on piles of bones, squishy things, foul furry creatures and invisible beings. She is reduced to screams.

Then she encounters a host of fire beings followed by a floating group of three-headed women with thin snakes for hair, who catch her and kiss her while the serpents strike. Soon she is kissing them in return and feels herself gaining more substance while another face begins growing out of her head and her hair begins transforming itself into snakes. In desperation she concentrates her thoughts on her decent sister, but she is rent apart.

She becomes nothing but a spirit transferred through space, landing on a dying world where she acquires a new form. But now her own memories become a renewed torment.

When torment and despair seem eternal, a radiant being appears before her, and she learns that the spirit of her dead sister has interceded for a merciful end to her suffering. She is returned to the Earth body of an old, hunched, crinkled crone, where she tells her story.

As previously stated, discounting the difficult-to-accept occult and mystic premises of the narrative, what Dyalhis has done is lead the reader through his own concept of a sinner's experience in Hell with tremendous pace and vividness and with strong sexual overtones that were not uncommon in *Weird Tales* magazine. Despite this, "The Dark Lore" won only second place in readers' approval of stories in the issue, losing out to H. P. Lovecraft's "Pickman's Model." Dyalhis was elevated back up to a full one cent a word for his effort, receiving $122 for the story's 12,200 words.

The sequel to "When the Green Star Waned" was long overdue, and the readers finally received it in the September 1928 issue of *Weird Tales*: a story entitled "The Oath of Hul-Jok."

The same characters appear again, and the story opens when Hak Iri, a writer and recorder, receives a message from the great scientist Ron Ti that he is in trouble and is coming to him for answers. A similar message arrives from Hul Jok, the warlord, followed by related communications from all of his friends.

The problem rests with the captive Lunarian they had brought back from their successful battle on Earth. The same powers that his race utilized to bend the will of the Earthmen to them have been used on the *wives* of the assembled men. He has gotten them to release him, stolen a warship and taken off with seven of them.

The story is told with high humor, as the scientist installs a radar-like device which enables the Venusians to follow the stolen ship into space. They take with them a freed Earthman who learned, while a captive, to read Lunarian minds.

The captured ship heads back to Earth and they follow it. They are appalled to find that conditions there have not improved. A race of genetically shaped creatures patterned by the Lunarians is still on the planet with more advanced science and weapons than the Earthmen, who have nothing more than swords. The Venusians realize that when they freed the planet they only did half the job; they should have aided the Earthlings to get back on their feet.

The rescue ship crashes and when the men come to, they are all naked and in some underground cavern. Questioning them is a genetically engineered "woman" whose upper body is that of a female, but whose lower portion is that of a huge snake with reptilian legs. She is one-sixteenth Earth creature. Her "race," which is physically disharmonious in structure, has magnet rays that attract the metal swords of the Earthmen. The problem is that the attraction is so strong that the swords kill half of those with the magnetizers!

They have a genetic method for turning living flesh into metal statues, and their laboratories have also produced what they call Lyon-Cats, who are fierce lions from the waist up, used as guards. Their preferred delicacy is baked human.

By torturing some of the "mutations" the Venusians find that the Lunarian has landed. He prefers the snake women to the ones he has captured, and they will be sacrificed in nine days.

The Earthmen have ironworks, and with the aid of the Venusians they construct crumble-ray guns, which are sort of slow-action disintegrators. They recapture the Lunarian and use the technique of turning him into a metal statue, learning in the process that the metal piece will retain consciousness.

The story is a light-hearted action tale, laced through with satire and humor, reading swiftly and satisfyingly. The story ranked second in the issue to part two of the super-science novel "Crashing Suns" by Edmond Hamilton. It ran 15,533 words in length and Dyalhis received $155 for first American serial rights.

Beginning with "The Red Witch" in *Weird Tales* for April 1932, Nictzin Dyalhis ran the first of three novelettes that created his greatest popularity in the magazine. "The Red Witch" is a tale of reincarnation in which the moderns return to a prehistoric village of stone huts to experience a portion of a previous life whose circumstances manifest themselves in the present. Here the occult and mystical portions are much more convincing and Dyalhis's sense of humor gleams through the text, but not to the point of destroying the effectiveness of the story. His penchant for compelling, dramatic action is manifest. In reader preference, "The Red Witch" was only one vote behind "In the Vault" by H. P. Lovecraft for first place, and Dyalhis received $120 for the 12,000 words, selling only first American serial rights.

The impact of "The Sapphire Goddess" has already been described, and it wasn't until the December 1937 issue of *Weird Tales* that Dyalhis had another story, "The Sea-Witch." This was incontestably one of the finest stories in the entire history of *Weird Tales* magazine with elements of poignancy and human vulnerability replacing the satire and humor that peeked through so many other of Dyalhis's efforts. In a very real sense the lead character, the retired old man, is Dyalhis himself. Then 57 years of age, with only five more years to live, he was already physically a sick old man and realized it. It was a fantasy of wish-fulfillment, unattainable except in his writing. The concept of the ageless Sea-Witch, transcendentally more powerful than the old man who has befriended her, responding to his kindnesses with the attitude of a wistful girl who wishes she could erase some of the evil of her past and senses in the seemingly hopeless affection of the old man in the last phase of his life a source of comfort if not redemption, is superbly presented. This was a first-place story with the readers, with nothing else in an outstanding year even approaching it, and the story base on which Dyalhis's reputation will stand. It was 12,000 words in length and he received $120 for all serial and radio rights.

Only one other story by Dyalhis appeared before his career drew to a close; shortly after, his life would terminate as well. That story was "Heart of Atlantan," an 11,000-word novelette accepted by Farnsworth Wright in December 1939 shortly before that famous editor was terminated at *Weird Tales* following its adoption of a bimonthly publishing schedule. Wright had already made out a card that Dyalhis was to be paid $110 for the story, but for some undetermined reason both the story and the payment were held up until its appearance in the September 1940 number (which would have reached the newsstands in July 1940) and the rate was cut to one-half cent a word, Dyalhis receiving only $55 for the story. At that time *Weird Tales* was paying all other authors one cent a word, so the reason for the prejudicial treatment of Dyalhis is unclear.

In this story Dyalhis writes: "For the sins, follies and mistakes of earth, there is punishment provided, or atonement to be made. But for the sins spiritual there is retribution, grim, lasting, inexorable, and none dare say it will ever end." The narrator sits with his friend Leonard Carman discussing ancient civilizations whose nature is now lost, seemingly beyond penetrating. Carman claims he has a method of recovering information about them and calls in a hunchbacked, wry-necked, squint-eyed woman with a squashed nose, yellow fangs, a limp and muddy brown skin. She cannot read or write and her one redeeming feature is beautiful hands.

She is named Otilie and is asked to exhume information on lost Atlantis.

She starts with automatic writing, but gradually a faint aura resolves into the glowing form of a beautiful woman, who claims she is Tekla, who destroyed an entire continent. She was born of an evil king and queen who wanted a son and set her adrift in a boat, where she was picked up by a fisherman and brought to the priest Ixtlil, who raised her. When Earth tremors manifest themselves in the land, the old priest, who is said to possess the "magic" of the Shining Ones who came from the stars, subjects her to rays, gives her food concentrates in the form of tablets, and sends her out on the badlands toward the destination of a temple shaped in the form of a huge woman. In a trance, she sees the old priest who raised her, in fetters, taken before the evil king and queen and his heart cut out. Within the breast of the stone statue, a pulsating heart forms from a single crimson gem. She strikes it with a bronze mallet and it bursts into shards.

Abruptly, tremendous earthquake shocks result. She visualizes the evil king and queen assembled with their consorts amid ruins and water pouring down the streets, inundating the fleeing people. As for her, she remains in the stone chamber, taking the place of the shattered heart, but perpetually youthful.

She is advised by Carman to move her spirit into some youthful body and leave her present one where it is, in the temple. Otilie offers her body as a repository of Tekla's spirit. With the transfer, Otilie becomes beautiful. She rises and offers herself to the narrator, who is named Henri d'Armond. As he embraces her, there is a flash, and a great face surrounded by solemn figures appears. She vanishes and he passes out.

When he comes to, Carman is gone, he is blind, and Otilie tells him she has reverted to her old appearance. He marries her for the sake of convenience and gradually a vision comes to him, of Carman, who is the reincarnation of Ixtlil and Tekla, trapped eternally within "the pulsating heart of Atlantan."

Despite its length, the story is not well developed. It has all the ingredients of a good Dyalhis yarn but it needed still more length and greater clarity and logic, though his writing skills were sustained at a very high level.

Dyalhis' wife is now dead as well, but before he died he converted to Catholicism and was buried as a Catholic. Presumably his wife was either already a Catholic or also converted. Conover's last meeting with Dyalhis was on a strained note. On one of his visits he had borrowed the carbon copy of "When the Green Star Waned." He let an inordinate amount of time pass before returning it, which event took place in Salisbury a good distance from Dyalhis's home and required the sick man to walk in for the meeting. Dyalhis grasped the manuscript with some irritation and departed, and the two had no further contact either in person or by letter.

That was not the end of Conover's contact with the family. The wife wrote him when Dyalhis died, and in the late forties he received a phone call from the daughter. She had become a nun and entered a convent. She called Conover because he was the only person in the world who had known her when her father and mother were still alive, and it gave her a feeling of momentarily reestablishing contact with them by speaking to him.

There are many unanswered questions about Nictzin Dyalhis, a singular master of fantastic fiction. His life is a vague patchwork of intriguing hints with little documentation. The source of his livelihood is unclear; certainly it was not from his fantastic writing—which raises the question of whether he contributed a body of work that sustained him elsewhere that we do not know about, with fantasy little more than an occasional indulgence.

Certainly he could have sold more than he did to *Weird Tales*, and there is no question that he was desperate for even small sums of money; yet he did not. Perhaps he was a drinker, but we have no present evidence of that.

The theme that is present in most of his works is reincarnation. It is so persistent that despite the humor, the satire, the sly gibes found in the majority of his works, the experience of Conover seems to indicate that Dyalhis believed in it.

As he grew older, his writing displayed honest flashes of humanity, as though a previously assumed objectivity had softened. No unpublished manuscripts have emerged. Other writers from the old *Weird Tales* do not list him as a correspondent or an acquaintance, so no nostalgic memoirs make reference to him.

What we do know is that there are flashes of imaginative brilliance in his stories, and ''The Sea-Witch'' is an unquestioned masterpiece. We know that despite his limited output he richly deserves to be revived and sustained as a welcome addition to the fantasy field's unofficial Hall of Fame.

THE RED WITCH
by Nictzin Dyalhis

Is there a past, a present, and a future; or are they in reality all the same state, being merely differing phases of the same eternal "Now"?

Are our lives and deaths and the interludes between them naught but illusion; and are we ever the same beings, yet capable, even though we do not recognize the fact, of experiencing two or more states of consciousness of personal identity—I mean, under certain exceptional conditions?

Times there are when my recent terrific experience impels me to adopt that hypothesis. How else may I explain the events wherein I played so strange a part—together with another who is far dearer to me than aught else in the universe?

Am I Randall Crone, a scientist connected with a great public museum, or am I Ran Kron, a youthful warrior of a savage tribe in the eon-old Ice Age? Is my wife, Rhoda—the gently nurtured, highly cultured Rhoda Day—the modern product of this Twentieth Century; or is she Red Dawn, the flaming-haired daughter of a red-headed witch-priestess of a devil-worshipping tribe of skin-clad Anthropophagi in that same remote Ice Age?

What is true, and what false? By what strange laws are we governed, we mortals, that we can see neither ahead nor backward, and are only aware of a limited "Here"?

My brain reels as I seek to solve the mystery—and to what account? Truly has a great poet said:

> *Of all my seeking, this is all my gain—*
> *No agony of any mortal brain*
> *Shall wrest the secret of the life of man,*
> *The search has taught me that the search is vain!*

I first saw her in the museum where I was on duty, and hard-headed scientist that I prided myself on being, I admit that my heart did a flip-flop, and I knew I beheld the one woman for whom I'd ever truly care. But that is a mild word for the love I felt. Love, I say; and I mean just that. In the holy emotion that possessed me there was no faintest throb of passion, no taint of desire. Beautiful? Yes, the most superbly beautiful woman on earth, I thought then, and still do think, and will continue so to think long after wrinkles and gray hair and decrepitude shall cause others to say "Old Hag," should that ever come to pass.

For soul has spoken to soul, and we twain know that we belong to each other; and though menaced as we were by the frightful ghost of the implacable savage chieftain, Athak the Terrible, yet we have overcome his menace, and no longer has he the power to afflict and harass our love and happiness through his eon-old malicious hatred.

Yet while he still had the power, he surely availed himself of it, measure full and running over; as my beloved knew from her early childhood up to the time we were married; and as I myself had several samples of, after that event; although, thanks to some benignant power, Athak's final attack was his undoing. But I am in danger of anticipating and must set down my account in a more logical sequence.

As I have said: I loved Rhoda Day from the first; and later

I learned from her own lips that her feelings toward me were identical. At the time we neither of us knew why, but eventually we found out. Yet when I asked her to be my wife she burst into tears, sobbing:

"Oh, Randall, if only I could say 'Yes'; but—but—I—dare not!"

"Don't you care for me?"

"More than for life itself. . . ."

"Then why not—surely there must be some reason?"

"Oh, Randall, a terrible one. . . ."

"Tell me," I urged. But I coaxed for over an hour, holding her close in my arms, her head with its coronal of red-gold hair resting on my shoulder, her soft cheek against mine, before she finally gasped out fears in broken phrases.

I'll not attempt to render her exact words. It simply can not be done. We both were in the grip of one of life's greatest emotions, or to be precise, a whole storm of emotions; and at such times I do not think that memory reproduces exactly. But in substance, thus the matter stood:

From a child, she'd been cognizant that, no matter where she was, or what she did, always there seemed to be another present, invisible, but very real nevertheless. A very terrible presence, too, inspiring her with loathing and dread, although it did not seem antagonistic to her welfare or her life. Rather it seemed to gloat over her with an air of proprietorship which she found indescribably horrifying.

Times there were when the presence exercised a very real power to protect her; as for example—when in her eleventh year she had a nerve-shaking experience with an ill-natured brute of a dog that snarled and menaced her with bared fangs. She knew, irrefutably, that the beast would have sprung in another moment, and stood paralyzed with terror, unable to cry out for help.

She sensed a storm of ferocious wrath sweep past her, enveloping the dog; and—unbelievable as it appears—that dog died! Yet on its body was evident no mark of violence. Apparently the brute died in a paroxysm of terror. But even after that episode, for a long while she had no idea as to what the Presence was.

As she grew older, she noted more frequently that that same power, or force, or influence, was exerting itself in her behalf to guard her—sometimes too zealously—a something to fiercely possessive, and capable of emitting a wave of such malignant hostility that she was for the most part devoid of the friends such as a young girl usually has.

And as she ripened into the first flush of young womanhood, drawn by her beauty there was no lack of young men who sought to do her homage and court her with their attentions—but none of them ever sought long. Doubtless, the air of hostility they felt about her, enshrouding her like a garment, they attributed to her; believing her to be of a disagreeable, if not an actually repellent personality; instead of realizing that it was an alien nature, emanating from a source outside herself, and certainly quite apart from her desires.

At that same period she became aware that the Presence was even more strongly possessive in its attitude; and, worse, again and again it made her sense its proximity even in the sanctum of her own room. But up until the day we were assured of each other's feelings she had not seen the thing—whatever it was. That night, however, after retiring, she awoke with the hideous feeling of being not alone—awoke to see the two eyes staring down at her; eyes aflame with wrath; eyes set in a vague, nebulous blur that might or might not have borne the semblance of a human face.

Of course she was frightened. Any one would be, under the same circumstances. She was so frightened that, try as she would to call out and arouse the household, she could emit no sound louder than a moan, barely audible to herself. She could not even move a muscle; could only lie still in an agony of apprehension, staring wildly up into the blazing orbs not a yard above her face.

Oddly enough, the apparition contented itself with glaring at her, striving to impress something on her mind, indelibly. All the impression conveyed, however, was that in some manner she had angered the "Thing," although how, or why, she could not comprehend.

But as we met more frequently, and our minds as well as our hearts became more filled with each other, the unholy visitant, appearing nightly, became more and more enraged. It was easier to see, assuming density of form and features with its rapidly growing wrath. After such visits she felt as if she had been beaten, physically, with a thick stick, wielded by a strong hand and arm.

Always it strove to impress upon her consciousness a very definite command, but always it failed to make its will register. Yet with each visit it became more visible until it was easily seen to be a huge man, long-armed and thick-legged, inclining more to the blond type than to the swarthy; skin-clad, carrying a huge knotted club, and a great stone-bladed knife stuck through a narrow leather thong tied about his middle.

"He—he—looks so—*savage*," she shuddered.

I stared down at the lovely, tear-bedewed face, my mind in a queer jumble of commingled amazement and fear. Those wondrous blue eyes looked straight back into mine, reading my unspoken thought.

"Randall, my beloved," she said gravely, mastering her emotions with a superb manifestation of will-power, "it all sounds crazy enough, I know; but please do not think your Rhoda is crazy. *She isn't!* I know what I've been subjected to ever since I was old enough to remember anything."

Ashamed of my momentary suspicion, I hastened to make the only amends within my power.

"If you're crazy, then I'll go crazy, too," I stated seriously. "How soon will you marry me? You love me, and I love you. That being the case, to whom but me should you turn for sympathy, understanding, and protection; insofar as lies within my power to give them . . . why, Rhoda, what's a husband *good* for, if not to stand between his woman and the whole world, and the Powers of Hell, too, for that matter, if she needs his aid? Once married, we can be together at the very times when your danger is the greatest. I don't know what I can do, if anything; but I'll guarantee that whatever this skin-clad giant is up to, he'll have me to dispose of before he harms you. I want you, and you need me, and that brings us back where we were—*How soon do we get married?*"

"Randall! Randall! Stop urging me, or you'll sweep me off my feet! I can not and will not let you become involved——"

"Try keeping me out," I defied, my whole being aflame with loving sympathy and pity. Suddenly over me swept an unalterable certitude—that I was already involved, fully as much as was she. Nay, more: I felt that I always had been; only until then I had not known it. But in that one moment I knew that my fate and Rhoda's were one and the same; and that whatever this being was which menaced, it was likewise a menace to me, and would be so forevermore, unless in some manner as yet unguessed by me I could put an end to its unholy machinations. So I told her of my sudden conviction, and when I'd concluded, I saw stark worship replace the fear-haunted expression in her eyes.

"Randall"—her voice was vibrant with all the love a good woman feels in her soul and can not express with mere words—"you'd dare that awful being, risk your life, perhaps your very soul for—me?"

"Risk my life, perhaps my soul, for you, Rhoda? Mine would be but a pitifully weak love if I hesitated to do so. I most certainly am going to do that very thing, if need be. Your troubles henceforth are my troubles too, so that's that! Now let's drop all this cross-purpose talk and talk sense for a while. I've already asked you to marry me, and now I'm saying it differently—we two are going to get married right now, at once, immediately, today! Get me? You've got absolutely nothing to say about it. *I'm* Boss, with a big 'B'! And how do you like *that*?"

"Oh, I—I—give up," she faltered. "Only you will simply have to wait at least a week. We've simply got to conform somewhat to the standard conventions and tell a few people; otherwise tongues are sure to wag, unfavorably."

I was too well pleased to argue. After all, that day or a

week later, mattered but little. The monster had not slain her up till then, and had had plenty of time in which to have done so, had such been his purpose. So I let it go as she stipulated, with one amendment.

"If that 'What-you-may-call-it' reappears in your room, you tell him my name and address; try and make him comprehend *me*, then tell him to come and annoy *me* for a change and let you take a rest. I've an idea that I can cope with him. . . ."

That night things did happen!

Rhoda told me later what her experience was that night. Unpleasant, very, but fortunately brief; and in a way it was merely the preliminary to what I went through immediately afterward.

She had no sooner retired than the Thing appeared, seemingly more tangible than ever before. It made no attempt to actually molest her, but was obviously in a towering rage. It did everything but rave aloud. It stamped about the room, gnashing its teeth in a perfect frenzy; frowning and grimacing intimidatingly; shaking a huge fist in her face; pantomiming strangling her with its enormous hands; and plainly conveying through sheer force of wrath that she'd gone to the ultimate limit of its patience. Above all, it made her understand that it was *jealous*! Which gave her her cue. It speaks well for her brave spirit that she faced the ugly apparition with a smile of contempt, jeered at it, and demanded in a whisper:

"If you're jealous of Randall Crone, why don't you go and try to bully him, instead of acting like a coward by tormenting me all the time?"

To make a good job of it, she exerted all her will to picture me and my abode so clearly that he could catch her thought-images. And after a bit she succeeded; for a look of comprehension and hatred came over the savage features, and a second afterward the apparition vanished from her room.

I'd been reading and at the same time hoping that the Thing would pay me a visit that night. I had no idea as to how to cope with it. I do not claim to be a great hero, but had the Devil himself threatened Rhoda's peace of mind, though he came to me with horns, barbed tail, talons all sharpened, cloven hoofs, flaming eyes, breathing sulfur fumes, and with his white-hot pitchfork raised to strike, still I would have fought him to the best of my ability and trusted to luck to defeat him somehow. But I didn't intend to be caught asleep and off guard if I could help myself. Hence I sat and read.

And it came!

The same huge, savage warrior that Rhoda had so graphically described. And the instant it assumed visibility, I knew that I was in for a most unpleasant time. The utter malignity of its expression proclaimed that here was a being to whom the very ideas of mercy, reason, or even caution, were completely unknown.

It had the power of rendering itself visible, but could not make itself audible, although had it spoken, I'd been none the wiser, for I could not have understood whatever uncouth language might have been its native tribal tongue. But it certainly could and did make its thoughts register on my brain. He—for there's no need to longer call the Thing "it"—warned me very emphatically that *he* owned that red-headed woman; had owned her since the world was young, and always would own her till long after the world died of old age; and that if I wanted to remain all in one piece I'd best never go near her again. All this was punctuated by flourishing an enormous knotted—spectral—club which he wielded in one huge fist.

I never did like being bullied!

And the more that infernal savage phantom raved, the less I liked it. A slow anger began to burn within me. I had my own ideas about this asserted ownership of Rhoda. I wasn't conceited enough to think that I owned her, but I was quite sure that *he* didn't! While as to me staying away from her simply because he bade me do so——

I came to my feet, "seeing red" literally, and hurled myself at him with all my inhibitions inherited from my civilized ancestry wholly in abeyance. I was fully as much a savage as

ever he had been! My entire being was filled with but one
desire—to get my hands, aye, my teeth even, to working on
him; to batter, to rend, to tear, kick, bite, gouge, and strangle
until he was——

Something seemed to burst within my skull; a terrific blaze
of scarlet light which blinded me for a bit—in my ears was a
roaring like to the four winds of the world colliding simultaneously—a queer rushing sensation as if I were hurtling
through the boundless abyss of space——

I regained consciousness. . . .

I was in a village of some fifty-odd stone huts. Low round
buildings they were, wherefrom smoke rose lazily into the
air through holes in the high-pitched peak-roofs. It was late
in the day, for the long shadows stretched almost eastward.
Skin-clad men and women moved about the huts. White of
skin they were, the majority light-haired, with blue or gray
eyes. The women for the most part were short, broad, stocky
of build; none of them really bad-looking, yet none really
comely, let alone any of them having even a remote approach
to beauty. Their faces were too stolid, and their voices were
too harsh to render any of them attractive.

The men were proportionately taller, equally as broad, their
faces more savage in expression; and all, even in the com-
parative safety of their own village, were armed with various
weapons—a stone knife in a skin girdle, or a short stone-
headed spear carried in one brawny hand; or a stone ax; or
a knotted club; but I saw no missile weapons such as bows
and arrows or slings; nor did any of the warriors bear shields.

I saw myself as one of their number; knew myself as Ran
Kron, a savage youth, a mere stripling not as yet a warrior;
still untried, longing, yearning, looking eagerly forward to
that time when I might stand with these hard-faced warriors
in the whirl and tumult of a battle, that I might prove myself
a man.

Wherefore I exercised at all the warlike pastimes and prac-
tices and in my spare time haunted the abode of old Juhor
the Snake, the tribe's most highly skilled weapon-maker.

* * *

To return to this present time in which I now write—I realize how difficult it is to make plain just how I knew all this which I've just described. All that I can say is—I did know. The same difficulty is confronting me in regard to what now follows. I can only write it as I knew it to be occurring while I was living in that phase of my existence. I knew my own experiences. But I knew, too, the experiences of others, insofar as those were intertwined with my own. So from here on, for a while at least, I must write in the third person instead of the first person, singular. . . .

Juhor the Snake, old, bent, crippled, and incredibly wrinkled, looked up from his work of chipping and polishing at the head of a green-stone war-ax he was making. A crafty gleam shone, transient, in his one good eye, as he beheld the tribe's mightiest fighting-man passing some few yards from where he, Juhor, sat at the door of his stone hut.

"Ho, Athak, Great Warrior! Athak the Swift! Athak the Strong! Athak the Terrible! Come and see!"

The gigantic, frowning war-chief turned shortly and strode to where sat the tribal weapon-maker.

"Well?" he snarled.

Juhor the Snake indicated the well-nigh completed jade ax-head.

"What of that, O mighty one?" he asked with the pride of a master craftsman.

Athak inspected it critically, with the shrewd scrutiny of another master craftsman, which he was, albeit no weapon-maker but a user of them instead.

"Put a handle to it," he commanded.

"Not yet," Juhor objected. "It is too heavy for its size. No warrior could wield it for very long. In steady fighting it would soon tire the strongest arm."

"A lie," snarled the surly giant. "It could not tire *my* arm to use it through a whole day's steady fighting!"

"Not all men are as Athak," flattered the old man.

"That is true," nodded Athak. "Put a handle to it, and

we will see how heavy it is. Soon shall I return. Have it waiting.'' And with that he strode off.

Juhor the Snake smiled slyly to himself. Things were going well for him, very well indeed. So, carefully and skilfully and patiently too, he tugged and strained at the wet rawhide lashings which, drying, would shrink and bind helve and head till both were as rigid as if but one piece.

Some two hours later the shadow of Athak fell again athwart old Juhor's gnarled and twisted body. The old weapon-maker looked up in feigned surprise.

''The ax,'' Athak demanded, shortly.

Juhor indicated it where it leaned against his door-post. Athak closed his huge fist about the thick, tough oaken handle. A smile of ferocious pleasure came over his usually stolid features the instant he lifted the weapon, while into his eyes came a covetous light such as nothing in all his life had ever aroused before.

''Truly, a weapon worthy of even me,'' he rumbled. ''Its price, O Juhor?''

''Canst thou pay it, O Athak?''

''Whatever be the price, I will pay it. That ax shall be mine!''

''Thine after it be paid for,'' nodded the cripple. ''Neither thou, O Athak, nor any other in this tribe shall own that war-ax till it be paid for.''

''No?'' Athak sneered. ''Look now, Juhor the Snake. In my grasp is thy handiwork. Since the price be so great, what shall hinder me, Athak the Terrible, from testing it on that old skull of thine? So shalt thou lose ax, price, and life all together!''

Juhor gazed calmly up at him.

''What shall hinder, O Athak the Fool? Only this! With every stroke, as I worked I breathed a charm, a curse, on the head of him who should possess that ax unearned. Strike if thou wilt. Juhor is old and crippled, and can not prevent thee!''

Athak hurriedly stood the ax against the wall and squatted down by Juhor.

"Nay," he rumbled, "I did but jest, old man! Name me the price I must pay for that wonder-ax. It will go hard with me if I earn it not."

"It is a long tale, Athak the Chief," said Juhor. "I must tell it in mine own way. Hast time and patience to listen?"

"Aye," grunted Athak. "Time enow, patience too, so be it ends in my ownership of that ax."

"Harken, then!" Juhor settled himself more comfortably, relaxing perceptibly indeed, for up till that moment he had not been sure if Athak would prove to be the man he, Juhor, had hoped for; or if it would be necessary to tempt some other mighty warrior with the bait of that great jade-headed war-ax. For a long moment the gnarled old cripple sat silent; then:

"As a little boy, O Athak, dost recall that in those days Juhor was tall and straight and a warrior even as thou art now?"

"War-chief thyself, for a while," Athak nodded, "if I recall aright."

"True, O Athak! And now—Juhor the Snake, as thou seest! Broken, twisted, old and ugly. Maker of weapons and—dealer in magic, among other things. But in those days whereof I now speak, I was young, strong and restive. In war, Juhor was the foremost; in peace, unable to sit day by day while the women worked. Nay, I hunted big animals, and was a crafty hunter, too. Also I traveled much, visited other tribes, and strange sights did I see.

"One soft summer I journeyed far to the northward. Into a country of hills came I finally. Snow-crowned were those hills, robed in forests of pine and spruce and hemlock; and the lakes of water, which were many, were very beautiful to behold. So pure were the waters that they seemed black to one looking down into them from a height. Oh, a very fair country, Athak, but inhabited by a race of devils in the semblance of men.

"For as I slept one night on the banks of a small lake, all unaware that foes were nigh, the light of my fire was ob-

served by watchful eyes. And I awoke at the dawning with
two strong warriors atop of me! Of course I struggled, but to
what avail? Two had leapt on me, but a dozen more stood
ready to aid them, were there need. So they bound Juhor,
and bore him, trussed like a wild beast, to their tribal village.

"A hundred houses of stone were in that village. A high
stone wall enclosed them safely. Only one gateway pierced
that wall, and it was so narrow that two men with spears
might easily hold it against a strong war-party.

"Into the largest building they bore me and threw me into
a stone-floored room. Afterward I learned that the building
was their temple, where, with horrible rites, they worshipped
their devil-god.

"For a day and a night I lay there, bound hand and foot;
hungry, too, although I was filled full with rage; but to tell
truth, fearsome also, for I knew not what fate lay before me;
albeit I could guess, to some extent; and my guesses were
not of enjoyable matters—to me, at least.

"When on the second morning there entered one bearing
food and drink, I believed for a moment that I was dreaming,
or had gone mad and was seeing that which was not.

"But then *she* spoke. . . .

"And to my enchanted ears the sound of her voice was as
the song of birds in the golden springtime of the world. The
sight of her was like to the glory of the sun in the first bright
hour of the day. Tall she was—not squatty as are our women—
full-breasted, strong, yet shapely in body and limbs. Blue
were her eyes—blue as were the waters of the mountain lake
where I was captured. Pink were her cheeks as are the blooms
of the wild roses. Scarlet were her lips, even as the blood
from a fresh-dealt wound; no snow ashine in the light of the
full moon ever gleamed so brightly as did her strong white
teeth; and her head was crowned with a great mass of hair
red as the flames from a burning pitch-pine log—hair that fell
almost to her feet.

"Forgotten were food, drink, hunger, captivity, apprehension; and I knew but one desire. . . .

"Her I wanted, and her I would have; aye, though afterward I died ten deaths of torture before I were finally slain.

"With one powerful surge I burst the rawhide bonds against which I'd struggled in vain all through a day and a night! And she did not flinch, nor did she manifest aught of fear as I rose to my feet. Her blue eyes lit with a flame matching my own fire! Her scarlet lips smiled approval and she laid one finger, cautioningly, on her lip, in token of silence. Setting down the vessels of food and drink, she came, unfalteringly, straight into my opened arms.

" 'O Man of Might,' she whispered—for their language is very like to ours, and I could understand her fairly well— 'you have taken my heart in your keeping. Yet how shall it profit us? I am the Red Witch of Ugdarr, the 'God-Who-Eats-Human-Hearts!' I am sworn, virgin, to his service; and you, O Strong One, are destined to provide his next meal!'

"For a bit I stood afraid. To die in battle was one thing, but to die helpless, a sacrifice to some devil-god named 'Ugdarr', who ate human hearts. . . . Then I caught fast hold of my waning courage.

" 'When and how do I?'

" 'Three moons hence,' she said sadly. 'Four times in the year—and the last time was but a few days before you came. You will be fettered by one ankle atop of the great stone altar at the feet of the image of Ugdarr. You will be given any weapon you may select—ax, club, spear or knife. Three young warriors, desirous of proving themselves before the assembled tribe, will attack you, one at a time, armed with a similar weapon to your choice, but their ankles will not be bound! If you wound one so that he falls to the ground, his heart will be torn at once from his breast and given to the village dogs as something unfit for Ugdarr. But even should you slay all three, still you are doomed. You have but one advantage. They may wound you till you can not stand longer, but slay you outright they dare not. To be acceptable to Ugdarr, your heart must come from your yet living breast while you still breathe, however feebly. And—the tribe will eat your flesh!' "

" 'No hope of escape,' I whispered through dry lips.

" 'None,' she replied drearily.

"In my heart I swore that if I might not escape Ugdarr's hungry maw, at least I would make a mock of him. . . . And I did, Athak!

"Each day thereafter she came bringing food and drink, for part of her service to Ugdarr lay in feeding Ugdarr's victim. And the devil-god wanted his sacrifice well nourished, that his heart might be more of a dainty morsel.

"Not long dared she tarry at any one time during the daylight hours, but again and again in the dead of night when none suspected, she crept to my side and we lay in each other's arms till the first gray hint of dawn . . . and I knew, finally, that I had made a mockery of the devil-god Ugdarr. . . .

"Young was I in those days, Athak! I had no thought for the woman, whether or not her tribe would mete out vengeance upon her for daring to give herself to me—me, the captive destined for Ugdarr's gullet; her, the virgin priestess who had violated her office; but later I was to think—oh, many, many times!

"For one night we were discovered, despite all her imagined caution. An old, old man, servant also of the devil-god, whose office it was to cut out the hearts of the sacrifices, became suspicious. Nay, he came not alone, but with a dozen ugly-faced warriors at his back. . . .

"Surprised as we were, in store for me was another surprise when, before all the tribe at the following noon, that old man pronounced our dooms.

" 'The man-captive is no more fit for Ugdarr's sacrifice,' he said sternly. 'He shall be tortured thus—he shall be tied to a post and each member of the tribe, from the youngest child to the oldest man or woman, shall throw at him one stone each. If still he lives, maimed as he will be, let him be borne to that place where first he was found and there left with the curse of Ugdarr upon him. Should he die, there's an end. If he lives, then he is free to go whither he will, save to return to this village. But should he crawl back here, then he shall be burned, slowly, to ashes.

" 'For the woman who was a maid—this! Witch of Ugdarr she was, and Witch of Ugdarr she shall remain till the child reach adolescence. Then shall she rear it to serve the god. If a boy, he shall become a priest. If a girl, she shall take her mother's place as Witch; and then this evil-doer who preferred the caresses of a captive to the favor of the great Ugdarr shall be bound at Ugdarr's feet and there she shall be stoned to death by the tribe—and the village dogs shall devour her body. I have spoken.'

"So, O Athak, you behold Juhor the Broken One! 'Snake' they name me, partly because I have wisdom and magic of a sort. But at first they so called me because I *crawled* one day into this my native village—how I made that long, terrible journey, broken, shattered, maimed, warped and twisted as I am, I know not. It was all a horrible torment like a dreadful dream of the night. Yet I did it, my brain aflame with but one idea—vengeance!

"Now, O Athak, Great War-Chief, thou knowest the price of the ax—the beautiful green-stone war-ax! Not with that ugly wooden handle, either, but with this——" and Juhor held up a long, finely carved handle of pure ivory! Athak's eyes fairly blazed at the sight. He could hardly speak.

"Ax and handle, *mine*, if——"

"If thou wilt make war upon the tribe of Ugdarr, slaying man, woman, and child, save only the Red Witch and her—my—*our*—child: bringing her and the child, if both still live, here to me. . . ."

Athak nodded briefly.

"I am War-Chief," he said quietly. "The warriors and the young men will follow where I lead. I take the ax with me. Wielding that, not even this 'Eater-of-hearts' Ugdarr himself shall withstand the war-frenzy of Athak the Strong!"

"I said," old Juhor pointed out, "that the ax must be earned ere it be possessed. Otherwise a curse——"

"Athak has never lied yet! He does not begin now, even to gain that wonder-ax! It will be earned! Thy price will be paid as soon as I can rouse the warriors and reach that devil-god's village. But I use that ax in the fighting, or I stir not a single step on thine errand!''

For a long while Juhor stared at Athak. Then he nodded as if fully satisfied at what he read in the eyes of the great war-chief.

''The ivory handle from a mammoth's tusk shall be fitted ere morning,'' he promised. ''In Athak's grasp shall the magic war-ax earn its own purchase price. Juhor has said it!''

The exultant yell pealing from Athak's throat startled the entire village.

And Ran Kron, the untried stripling who aspired to the status of a warrior; sitting anigh and hanging breathless upon every word falling from the lips of Juhor the Snake, saw his opportunity and promptly grasped at it.

''Ho, Athak the Great Chief,'' he cried boldly. ''Here is one for thy war-party!''

Athak stared contemptuously at the slight figure.

''Girl with the semblance of a boy,'' he jeered. ''Thy mother made a mistake. . . .''

And a lightning-swift lunge with a slender white flint knife in the hands of the infuriated youth well-nigh despoiled old Juhor of his long-plotted vengeance, then and there.

''Thou fool ten times accursed,'' shrilled the old weapon-maker. But Athak laughed, a hearty, roaring bellow wherein was no trace of anger.

''Nay,'' he told Juhor. ''Let be! None are born full-grown and proven! The boy has the heart of a warrior. Even thus would I have replied to a like insult. He marches with the *other* fighting-men!''

The next night the old men sat in a circle, thumping on the snakeskin-headed war-drums, and the old women in a still larger outer circle banged and clattered cymbals of flat bone plates from the shoulder-blades of the larger animals.

The old men chanted and the old women shrilled at intervals, while every male of fighting size and age danced and leapt and pranced and shouted boastfully, waving and brandishing their weapons. Finally, as the fire in the center of the circles died down, each man tossed his weapon onto a pile in the dancing-space in token that even as the weapons were all together, so would each man be at one with all the others of the war-party. Athak, as leader, tossed his newly acquired jade-headed war-ax atop of all the rest, so that when the weapons were lifted, his would be first, even as he was first in command. As his wonder-weapon—the tale of which had already been bruited about the village—fell atop of the rest, the warriors broke into their deep-voiced battle-cry:

"A-Houk! A-Houk! A-Houk!"

Athak was a good leader. Never once did the war-party see anyone, nor were they seen by any wandering hunter from the morning they left their native village until they sighted the walls of Ugdarr's people. It called for craft and strategy to achieve this, but Athak's brain was equal to the task.

The first intimation in the gray dawning that the people of Ugdarr had of enemy proximity was the deep-toned:

"A-Houk! A-Houk! A-Houk!"

Into the undefended gate surged the men of Athak's band— for two skilled spear-throwers, at Athak's command, had crawled close an hour previously, while yet it was dark, and had made sure that the two men guarding the gateway slept the last long sleep.

Counter-yells arose of:

"Hah-Yah! Yah-Yah!"

And out from their huts like a swarm of angry hornets poured the men of Ugdarr. After all, it was not an all-day battle. At most, there were some hundred or a hundred and fifty savages locked together in one wild whirl of clubs, knives, spears and axes—a struggle in which quarter was neither asked nor proffered.

One savage fight is very much the same as another, the only thing which distinguished that one being that for the first time in his life Athak the Strong One was laid prostrate on his back. A fallen enemy had stabbed him in the calf of his leg at the same moment that another man of Ugdarr had hit him on the head with a club.

Ran Kron, fighting madly at the left side of his gigantic chief, promptly repaid the clubman by practically eviscerating him with the sixteen-inch stone knife which formed the young warrior's sole weapon, and then bestriding Athak's body, swinging in both hands the club he'd wrested from his victim as he fell. It was but a moment in which Athak lay dazed; then he was on his feet again, bellowing "A-Houk" as lustily as ever, and smiting even more furiously with the great jade ax. But he found breath between blows to shout to Ran Kron:

"No longer art thou an untried youth, but a warrior! Shalt be made Athak's blood-brother when this fighting ends!"

If the stripling had fought madly before, after that promise of Athak's he became like a youthful demon unleashed. And, in consequence, he was bleeding from a dozen minor wounds by the time the affray ended.

And its ending was complete. The huge war-chief had made a definite pledge to Juhor, and as he himself had declared, it was no habit of his to deal in lies. Wounded or whole, those of Ugdarr's people who survived the fighting were dragged before their own devil-god and knocked on the heads; all save a few strong-bodied women who were kept to act as beasts of burden and carry loot for their captors on their homeward journey; and even those would be slain as soon as the trip was ended.

From these women, questioned by Athak, it was learned that Juhor's Red Witch of Ugdarr had been slain a few years previously. But she had left a daughter, Red Dawn. . . .

"Where——"

Nobody knew. . . .

Athak picked up one woman and flung her, bodily, into a fire blazing near at hand. By the time the shrieking wretch crawled out, the other women recalled that in the Temple of Ugdarr there were a number of hidden rooms. . . .

It was Ran Kron who found her. What magical words he used, none knew, but she listened to him without fear, and came forth from the building hand in hand with the youth.

Nor did she relinquish her hold when he brought her before Athak.

"Which is the captive?" shouted the chief, in high good humor. Made bold by Athak's friendliness, Ran Kron grinned and replied:

"I am, O Athak!"

The chief stared a second, then grinned back.

"Had I the right, I'd say 'Take her, lad!' But she goes to old Juhor. It is for him to say what disposal shall be made of her."

Juhor the Snake heard the welcoming tumult heralding the returned war-party, and smiled his wry smile. When the gigantic form of Athak stood before him, the old weapon-maker looked up calmly, although deep within himself he was in a storm of emotion. Athak's right hand grasped the great war-ax, while his left he held fast-clamped on the shoulder of a slim, beautiful girl whose hair was a flaming red-golden glory.

"Ax and purchase-price, O Juhor the Snake. Athak keeps his word!"

"The ax is paid for, and is all thine, O Athak the Mighty! Upon the ax is no curse. Nay, so long as thou shalt hold it in battle, none may overcome thee. Dost want the maid, too, O Athak? None better could I give her to. As my son—with thy might, and my wisdom——"

"Not I, Juhor! The ax fills my one desire. Rather, I would that thou give her to my blood-brother, Ran Kron. He wants her, and I think he has her favor."

"Give *her*—to—that—*cub*! Athak, dost jest?"

"Cub?" roared the chief. "My blood-brother, I said! None braver than he ever went forth to war from this village. Swift of foot, great of heart, fearless, and a deadly killer with that long knife of his, I myself saw him account for five in the fighting at Ugdarr's village. Saved my life, too, *mine*, Athak the Chief! Young he is yet, it is true. Had he greater war-wisdom, and more years, I'd make him second in command under me. And *you* call him—cub!"

"Girl," said Juhor, hastily veering away from the subject

which had aroused Athak's wrath, "thou art my daughter.
Hath thy mother——"

"I heard him"—she indicated Athak—"name thee Juhor
the Snake. My mother, before they stoned her to death in
Ugdarr's village, told me a tale of a captive, Juhor the Strong
One, who was stoned by the tribe because of her, who was
borne into the wilderness, and there left to live or die even
as Ugdarr chose. Art thou in truth that same Juhor?"

The old cripple could only nod, for words failed him. The
girl looked too, too like another and elder Red Dawn. . . .
The girl flung herself impulsively on her knees beside him,
drew his old head to her young breast, smoothing his sparse
white locks with her slim soft hands, crooning over him. . . .
The warriors turned away at a grunt from Athak.

"This is no time to forward thy suit, my brother," the
chief told the young Ran Kron. And the youth nodded, un-
derstandingly. He could wait.

Red Dawn was the most beautiful woman the tribe had ever
beheld, and many were the young men who sought her from
old Juhor. But to one and all he gave the same reply:

"Her heart and her desire are all for Ran Kron. She is my
daughter and shall please herself."

So in due time the day came when before the whole people
Juhor tied Red Dawn and Ran Kron together with a strong
cord, calling down curses many and horrible upon the head
of whoso should attempt to sever that bond. And the tribe,
with feasting, and mirth, and jest, celebrated the wedding.
Yet some there were who reasoned that as the girl was the
most lovely, and Athak was the most mighty, she should have
been mated with the great chief rather than with the youthful
warrior.

But when some, made bold by drunkenness, ventured to
hint thus to Athak, he roared with laughter. Then, for he had
imbibed largely of strong drink himself, he became inspired
with a most wondrous idea.

"Juhor," he shouted, "in thy hands lies the power to bind
the cord of wedlock, where thine own offspring are con-

cerned. Thou hast wed Ran Kron to Red Dawn. Now, haste thee and wed me to thine other child!''

''My—other—child,'' Juhor stared in wonderment. ''Nay, O Athak! I have no child other than Red Dawn.''

Athak held up his jade war-ax.

''This,'' he shouted, so that all heard. ''The child that thou didst create. Wed me to her, for I love her more than I ever could love my woman of flesh and blood.''

The grim fancy caught the imaginations of the people, and they clamored for the ceremony. Juhor, knowing Athak's disposition, and seeing that he was at that pitch of drunkenness wherein good humor abruptly changes to fury when crossed, took a fresh cord and performed the rite with all the needful words and curses.

Again Athak tossed the weapon high in air above his head.

''Athak's wife!'' he bellowed. *''A-Houk! A-Houk! A-Houk!''*

Catching fire from his fire, the warriors responded in savage chorus: *''A-Houk! A-Houk! A-Houk!''*

Yet one old hag there was—own sister to Athak's mother who had died giving a man-child to the world—who dwelt in Athak's hut and cooked his food for him, who sat and glowered while all others made merry. She was getting old and lazy, and had long urged the giant chief to bring a younger woman into the hut as his wife. All through the feasting, the old woman said naught about what was in her mind, but next morning, well knowing that Athak's head was aching fit to burst, she queried with her tongue laden with venom:

''Was your stone bride kind to you in the night, O Athak, and were her caresses sweet?'' Then, with a cackle of derision, as he glared at her: ''She can never give you a son to boast that Athak the Mighty was his father. She can not cook for you. She can deal wounds, but she can not heal wounds with the poultices of soothing leaves . . . Better had you taken Juhor's *other* daughter——'' And with that, dodging a chunk of wood hurled at her by the exasperated chief, she fled the hut, still cackling evilly.

And thenceforward she lost no chance to prod Athak about

his folly in "choosing the wrong daughter of Juhor" until in
time her evil hints and slurs bore fruit. She was helped in
her work by the fact that since Ran Kron had had one taste
of war, he'd found it so greatly to his liking that twice afterward he'd gone out with small parties of young and ambitious
men; and in both cases had easily proved himself the foremost. And the hag hinted to Athak that his prestige as chief
was seriously threatened by this young upstart—as she termed
the youth.

Came a day when Athak harkened and took her gibing
seriously; so that thereafter he began casting meaning glances
at Red Dawn whenever they met. Worse still occurred when,
in one of his drunken spells, he sought to drag her into his
hut against her will.

His girl-wife's shrieks reached Ran Kron's ears where he
sat in converse with a group of other young warriors. With a
cat-like rush he hurled himself at the would-be ravisher. Twice
and thrice his long flint knife stabbed, lightning-quick, drawing
blood and eliciting a yell of pain each time he struck.

Completely lost to all thoughts of blood-brotherhood, and
driven by a two-fold lust—to have Ran Kron's wife and Ran
Kron's life, Athak let go his hold on the shrieking, struggling
Red Dawn and drew his great jade ax from his belt. Ran
Kron, seeing, leaped back, snatching a spear from the hand
of a bystander, and promptly lunged with it at the face of the
giant chief.

For a while it was either man's fight. Mighty as Athak was,
enraged, too, so that flecks of foam dripped from his lips,
still Ran Kron kept him busy; dodging, leaping, parrying, or
evading the sweep of the great green-flashing ax; from time
to time getting in a thrust with his spear that drew blood each
time, but never deep enough to reach a vital spot and end
matters.

Yet despite all his efforts, step by step the lighter man was
forced to retreat—suddenly a yell arose from the onlookers,
partly in triumph, partly in warning, according to their sym-
pathies. With a feeling that the end was nigh, Ran Kron realized that he'd reached the brink of the river, and that back

of him lay a fifty-foot drop to the swift, swollen, muddy waters below. In sheer desperation he hurled his spear straight at the face of his giant opponent.

Athak saw it coming, too swift for him to dodge it. He threw up both arms in front of his face. The stone spearhead drove deep into his right forearm, and a spurt of blood followed, staining the ivory helve of his battle-ax bright crimson.

In despair, Ran Kron whipped out his long stone knife, prepared to sell his life as dearly as possible. Athak bellowed his rage, and moved a step closer. The great ax swung up above his tousled head and swept down again on its death-dealing arc. Ran Kron, summoning up his fast-waning strength, dodged again, bending his torso far back. Athak's hands were too blood-smeared from the wound in his forearm. The ivory ax-handle slipped in his grasp. Flying through the air, it struck Ran Kron a glancing blow on the side of his head, stunning him. The young warrior, his balance overborne, went backward over the edge of the low bluff; and, with a sullen double splash, Ran Kron and the great jade ax that had overthrown him to his death disappeared together beneath the surface of the swollen stream. . . .

Now, how I, Randall Crone, know this latter part which ensued after Ran Kron fell into the river, I can not tell; for I do not understand. But know it I do, however.

Athak sank to the ground, gasping from his last terrific exertion. Red Dawn would have thrown herself into the river, there to join her man, Ran Kron, but was seized and held by certain ones who sought to curry favor with Athak.

Juhor the Snake hobbled up, stood in front of Athak, and shook his gnarled old fist in the giant's face. The old man was fairly a-quiver with the rage consuming him. Twice he opened his mouth and twice he closed it again before he could find words to express himself.

"Was it for this, thou fool, that I made for thee that magic ax? Did I not wed thee to the ax at thine express command, by thine own choice? Did I not lay curses many and deep upon the head of whoso should part ye twain who were one in wedlock? And now, it is thine own hands which have flung the magic ax into the deep, deep river!

"Now I, Juhor the Snake, prophesy to thee, O Athak the Fool! Thou shalt go accursed for all thy remaining days upon the earth. Evil shall befall thee ever, and when thou shalt die, in outer darkness shalt thou wander till once again the magic ax which thou thyself didst name 'Athak's Wife' shall return to thine embrace! Athak the Accursed, I, Juhor, have spoken thy doom!"

Athak staggered to his feet and clutched one great hand upon the old man's shoulder. "Aye," he snarled, "thou hast spoken—thine own doom, Juhor the Snake!" One shove he gave the old cripple, and Juhor, with a single quavering cry, vanished over the edge of the all-devouring river. . . .

One might say that I'd been dreaming; or that I'd been in a trance state and had left my body and gone into the astral plane—but neither hypothesis would account fully for the facts.

For I learned, upon my return to my Twentieth Century personality, that I'd been gone for a considerable time, *body and all*! My room had been found vacant and my bed unslept in, the morning after I'd been visited by the phantom of Athak.

Then as totally unproclaimed as my absence had been, I reappeared. And I had considerable difficulty in explaining matters to those most interested in my movements—business associates, and others. Of course I hastened to Rhoda as quickly as possible, and from her lips I had full confirmation of my strange experience. For she, too, had "vanished" insofar as her everyday environment was concerned, and she, too, had just reappeared. I did not have to make any explanations to her. She knew! She'd been through the same sort of adventures as had I. In other words, she had suddenly awakened from a sound sleep to find herself Red Dawn, the young Witch of Ugdarr! In fact, she was able to tell me the part I did not know, and describe the episode after Athak threw old Juhor over the bluff. Yet what she told was but little after all.

Athak had dragged her to his hut, where she naturally anticipated just about the worst fate that could happen. In a frenzy of fear, she had tried to stab herself, but Athak prevented that by hitting her with his fist the instant she caught up a knife.

But he had struck too hard, and thereby cheated himself of the woman he coveted so greatly that he'd slain his own chosen blood-brother in order to get her for himself. She recalled the terrific concussion of his fist against the side of her face. Ensued a brief period of unconsciousness, naturally, and when her consciousness returned, she was again Rhoda Day, in her own room, and her mother was bending over her, demanding a trifle crossly:

"Rhoda, where in the world have you been for the last few days, and why did you go away without saying anything about it to me, before you started?"

As to what happened to Athak, we neither of us knew; but could easily imagine, knowing him as well and unfavorably as we did. To use Rhoda's words:

"He probably went from bad to worse, just as Juhor predicted, until someone did the world a service by ridding it of his presence; and he has since, to use Juhor's very words, 'dwelt in outer darkness.' But in some manner he—or his spirit, rather—located my whereabouts, and he seems determined to assert his imagined ownership. Probably he doesn't even know that he is dead and hasn't a body in which to function any more."

Wherein she was wrong. Later again, we learned that Athak knew quite well that he was devoid of a body. All he was waiting for was a good chance to acquire one, in order to resume his age-old devilment just where he'd been compelled to leave off by reason of hitting Red Dawn too hard and thus cheating himself of her possession.

Apparently old Juhor's curse had taken effect, and Athak had, in truth, dwelt in outer darkness instead of coming back to earth via a rebirth, as we two had done. But the more we speculated, the more intricate and involved the problems became; so that finally we quit all speculating and preserved a policy of watchful waiting instead.

Meantime, at my urgency, Rhoda capitulated and we were married. For a brief while we managed to fool the savage phantom. Travelling on our honeymoon trip, we kept to the crowded cities, knowing that for us to isolate ourselves would best please the vindictive ghost who so hated us. In modern hotels and amongst throngs of people, he'd be out of his element.

But honeymoons end eventually, in this workaday world, and dollar-chasing is a very necessary pursuit if one would continue to enjoy life in its modern phase. So, regretfully, we returned home, not, of course, to Rhoda's parents, but to a little place of our own.

And Athak turned up the first night we were there!

His fury, when he grasped the situation, was something to tremble at. His futile attempts to wreak either or both of us bodily injury, had they not been so frightful, would have been ludicrous. For over half the night he carried on his antics. It was of no avail to turn off the light, so I left it burning. Rhoda was so unstrung that I feared a permanent shock to her nervous system would result.

I was angry, not with the ordinary type of wrath common to everyone at times, but that same savage ugliness I'd experienced once before. Much more of it, and I'd again become Ran Kron, the young savage warrior. . . . But Rhoda sensed the change taking place in me, and begged so earnestly that I control myself, that somehow, to please her, I succeeded in fighting back my rage. At that, I could not have done it, had she not whispered:

"Randall, my husband, for my sake be very careful! Can not you see that you are rapidly getting into a state such as will best please him, and render us accessible by translating us again to his plane, where he *can* function?"

It was a hard task, even then, but I did it. Then I had what I considered a happy thought, and carried it out; and it did win for us a modicum of rest from Athak's rage, if only for a short time. Deliberately I kissed Rhoda, then grinned triumphantly at the frenzied savage ghost; and for a second, I thought that Athak the Terrible would disintegrate from the hell-storm of wrath and jealous hate that simple act aroused on his part. But then he turned sulky, withdrew until he seemed to merge with the wall itself, and there remained, glowering. And finally we fell asleep and left him to sulk all he would.

But the next night he was back again, twice as ugly as before. And for many a night after that.

Then I thought up another bright idea, or deemed it one until——

It was summer, and the nights were warm, so we took to sleeping in a rose arbor in the garden. For the first night there was absolutely no sign of Athak. But on the second night, Rhoda wakened me from a sound slumber with the startled exclamation:

"Randall, what *is* that repulsive odor?"

One sniff told me instantly that it was the acrid, decayed-cucumber scent of a copperhead snake! Very cautiously, holding my breath in stark fear, I pressed the switch of a flashlight and swept the near-by ground with its bright rays. Luckily I managed to reach a stick with which I broke the reptile's back before it could—*ugh*! I shuddered at thought of what might have happened. And, somehow, in my mind, I associated that snake's arrival into our garden of peace with Athak's hatred. And instantly, although I heard no sound, I was aware of a burst of unholy glee that fully confirmed my conviction.

Next day I bought an automatic pistol equipped with a silencer, and a box of cartridges. Then I did that which would cause any alienist to suspect my mental condition; for I had every bullet extracted from the loaded shells and replaced by silver ones. I'd read somewhere that silver bullets are efficacious against such as Athak; and I was open to conviction. But when I laid in that equipment I unwittingly played into Athak's hands, completely.

Nightly thereafter I kept the loaded pistol within reach, and for several nights we were undisturbed. Yet always we had an uncomfortable sense of Athak's presence, albeit he kept himself invisible. Actually, I began to think that in some manner he'd sensed that I was organized for him with a potent weapon, and that he was correspondingly cautious about bringing matters to a definite showdown; which proves how little I know about the unseen world and still less about the abilities of those who dwell therein.

We had gotten so that we could fall asleep almost immediately after retiring in our rose arbor. It was around midnight one night that I awoke with the certitude that we had been outwitted and that even then we were exposed to some unutterably ghastly horror. Instinctively I grasped the pistol and threw off the safety catch. Rhoda had awakened at the same time, and we sat up simultaneously. She screamed, once, and I felt the cold sweat of fear break out all over me.

Not ten yards away was the phantom form of Athak. A leer of cruel, anticipatory triumph was on his ugly face, and he had reason for it, too; for although he himself was but a phantom, there was nothing intangible about the monstrous dog he had somehow introduced into our garden. It was just a dog; yes, but such a dog! It loomed as big as a calf! I learned, later, that the brute was a Tibetan mastiff belonging to a dog-fancier dwelling some twenty miles distant. And that breed of dog is one of the most ferocious of the entire canine species.

Its eyes were aflame with fury, and as they were fixed unwaveringly upon me, it was not difficult to imagine what was coming next. Its jaws dripped slaver, and its lips were drawn back in a soundless snarl. Its whole body was a-quiver with pent-up energy.

And even as I noted all this in one horrified glance, the phantom chief waved an arm in a gesture of command, and the huge beast launched itself straight at me! One bound brought it half-way, but then I brought the pistol into action. I'd had a gunsmith do a little juggling with the inner works of that automatic; so that in a way, it was more a miniature machine-gun than a pistol. Once the trigger was pulled, provided it was held back, the shots were continuous till the magazine was empty. I intended, when I had it fixed like that, to put sufficient of those silver bullets into, or through, Athak, to make a thorough job of it, or him. But as things turned out, it was the dog that got the entire load; and it needed them all, too, squarely in its big skull, to stop its ferocious rush.

Even at that, the brute didn't die instantly, but fell on the ground, almost at the entrance to the arbor, writhing and twitching in a fast-spreading pool of blood.

Athak's opportunity had arrived! That infernal savage had waited for just such a chance for ages! The blood furnished him with the medium for materialization, and he promptly utilized it. Before I could reload the pistol by inserting a fresh-charged magazine clip into the butt, the metamorphosis was achieved. It was, to all intents and purposes, a flesh and blood savage from out the distant Ice Age who hurled his huge bulk at us, whirling a heavy bludgeon in one knotted fist!

Rhoda gasped, moaned feebly, and slumped to the floor of the rose arbor in a limp heap. And I, feeling that this was the end for us, and the consummation of Athak's triumph, nevertheless flung myself off the bed in one wild leap, to meet him and have it over with.

I had naught save that empty pistol still in my hand wherewith to put up a battle, and that was but a poor and futile thing beside the club Athak flourished. Yet in some manner I dodged his first stroke, retaliating by throwing my empty pistol into his face as hard as I could slam it. Luckily for me, it landed just where eyebrows and nose meet. For a second it dazed him, and he paused, even in his frenzy, to shake his head to clear his sight, I suppose. And, in that one second of reprieve, a miracle and naught else came to my aid, or I should not be here now to tell this tale. . . .

Out of nowhere, apparently, appeared the gnarled, twisted,

crippled form of old Juhor the Snake! Into my hands he thrust the ivory handle of a green-stone war-ax!

"Heh-heh-heh!" laughed the incredible apparition. "Once he stole your wife! It is only fitting that now you should have his!"

What strange power lay in that ancient war-ax? I know not, even now. But this I do know: No sooner had my hands closed in a firm grip on the handle than a terrific surge of commingled hate and strength suffused my entire body! I felt that my muscles had doubled—nay! infinitely multiplied in power to smite. I heaved the heavy ax aloft and moved toward my enemy. He saw the weapon, and hell flamed in his face and eyes. In a low, dreadful tone he spoke:

"Now! Long have I waited for this day! Red Dawn, and the green ax! Once again are both within my reach! O Fool, who thinks to stand against Athak the Mighty with his own war-ax; now shall I slay thee, and take both weapon and woman! Then shall she and I together eat your heart, raw, torn from out your yet warm body. . . ."

He had no time for further boasting. With all the new strength that had flowed into me, I struck out at him. Skilled warrior that he was, he parried the ax-sweep with his club. Very craftily he struck just back of the stone head, turning the stroke aside thereby. The shock of his blow jarred my arms clear to my shoulder-sockets. And swiftly following came his counterstroke. He delivered it horizontally at my head, but I bent my knees quickly, and the club barely grazed my hair. The momentum of his blow turned him a trifle, and I swiped back again with the ax, and that time, despite his backward leap, the ax drew blood from his side; not a deep cut, but still enough to madden him.

With a snarl of pure fiendishness he drove in a blow I could not evade, so lightning-swift it came. Fairly on my left arm it landed, and my whole side went numb as if suddenly paralyzed. I had only my right arm then with which to wield that ponderous stone war-ax, while my eon-old enemy still had two arms with which to swing his no less ponderous club.

The derisive sneer on his hateful face drove me beyond all semblance of caution. As if it had been naught but a light throwing-hatchet, I whirled up that great stone-headed ax in one hand and hurled it! So quickly did I move that he had no chance to raise his club in order to ward off that hurtling weapon.

Edge first it struck him in his barrel-like chest, driving deep in through flesh and bone. With a bubbling grunt the breath went out of his lungs, followed by a gush of bloody froth. He threw both arms across his torso, hugging the ax-handle in his agony. . . .

The cracked voice of old Juhor rang out: "When Athak's wife returns to Athak's embrace, then shall the age-old curse lift; and Athak shall cease to dwell in outer darkness! *Athak the Mighty, get thee hence to the place appointed for all such as thou!*"

The giant stood swaying, his arms still clasping the handle of the ax. But as Juhor spoke his doom, he tottered and fell!

Unheeding aught else, I staggered wearily—for my strength left me even as Athak fell—over to where Rhoda lay, lifted her to the bed and turned—to see only a faint haze where a moment before had lain the gigantic materialized form of Athak the Terrible! As I looked, the haze vanished, too. Of old Juhor the Snake there was no sign. There remained only the carcass of an enormous, dead dog; an empty automatic pistol; and a great, ivory-handled war-ax lying where I had dropped it. Oh, yes! And a great bruise on my left arm. . . .

What is real, and what illusion, in this universe? Nobody knows, I least of all.

Juhor handed me that ax. I used it. Next day I hung it on the wall in my study. And that same evening I read in the newspaper that a jade-headed, ivory-handled battle-ax had been mysteriously abstracted some time in the night hours from a glass case in a scientific museum located over eight hundred miles from where I dwell, and had been missed the same morning I hung it on my wall! And the glass case had not been broken into, nor unlocked.

The news article went on to state that the weapon owed its

remarkable condition of preservation to the fact that it had been found fast-frozen in a huge fragment of ice that had "calved" from a glacier up under the Arctic Circle. . . .

Oh, my very soul faints when I try to make coherence of my jumbled data! Yet out of it all, dimly I get this for my comfort: Time, and Space, both are as naught to the self of man. Justice endures and Love is eternal; nor shall all the Powers of Darkness ever prevail against them!

THE SAPPHIRE GODDESS

By Nictzin Dyalhis

Suicide as a means of escaping trouble never appealed to me. I had studied the occult, and knew what consequences that course involved, afterward.

But I was fed up on life. I was destitute, and had no friends who might help, even were I to appeal to them. At forty-eight, one does not easily regain solvency. And, gradually, I'd lost all ambition. Not even hope remained.

If only there were some other road out—a door, for example, into the hypothetical region of four dimensions . . . it certainly couldn't be worse there than what I'd borne in the last three years. Well, I could try. . . .

I seated myself cross-legged on the floor. If I concentrated hard enough, perhaps the miracle might occur . . . at least I should have tried . . . a last resort. . . . Gradually a vague state ensued wherein I was not unconscious, for I still knew that I was *I*; yet a queer detachment was mine—there was a world, but of it I was no longer a part. . . .

Click!

Like a movable panel a section of the wall opened, revealing a most peculiar corridor—a strange Being stood smiling at me. It did not speak, yet I caught the challenge: "Dare you?"

With a single movement I rose and stepped into the opening. . . .

Oh, the agonizing, excruciating torment of that transition! Every nerve, tissue and fiber flamed and froze simultaneously. My brain seethed like a superheated cauldron. My blood turned to corrosive, searing acid. Tears suffused my aching eyes. I choked, unable to utter the groans my sufferings constrained me to emit. . . .

Had I landed in Hell? It certainly seemed so! . . . Then abruptly it was all over. I was still *I*, yet vastly different. I was *free*—and with senses above the dull senses of Earth, with power beyond Earth's muscular strength. I realized that I was in a different realm where the Laws were strange to me, and that I must be careful lest I be caught in some trap from whence escape might not be so easily achieved. But where, I wondered, was the Being who had dared me? . . .

"Here!"

"But—you seem not the same . . . there was a vague, misty, red haze—now you are distinct. . . ."

"Many high-speed light-waves formed a veil through which earthly eyes can not see clearly."

"Hence—the agony during transition?"

"Precisely! The vibrations altered your atomic structure. But you are still your true self."

"Perhaps," I assented. "But who are you, and why did you make it possible for me to come?"

"I am Zarf; and your subjects need you, to say naught of——"

We were interrupted by a most discordant howling, and abruptly some two dozen hideous dwarfs surrounded us. They bore long straight swords, were clad in iridescent scale armor, stood about five feet in height, and had the ugliest faces I ever saw.

"King Karan of Octolan—and the commander of his body-guard, Zarf!" Their voices were shrill with maniacal glee. Evidently they considered our capture a big event.

I did not like their looks. I did not approve of their air of insolent triumph. Back on Earth I had lost all material ambitions, but suddenly I regained one, and proceeded to realize it.

With all my new strength, I drove my clenched right fist into the face of a particularly burly dwarf standing about two feet away. His head snapped back, he went limp; I snatched his sword from him and set to work. Once and again I struck, caught the true balance of the weapon and saw a head leave its body—shouted:

"A sword for you, Zarf!"

Before the blade touched ground he caught it, then set his back against mine. . . . A wild delight filled me, yet through it I felt a vague wonder—where had *I* learned swordsmanship? For never on Earth had I held one in my hand!

Those dwarfs fought like fiends from Hell. More than once I felt the stinging kiss of dwarf steel. Once I heard Zarf gasp as a sword bit deep, and once he groaned in agony. It was a wild mêlée while it lasted; and never did I enjoy myself more. . . . Through a red haze of slaughter I saw that only two dwarfmen remained facing my blade. Lunge—slash—parry—slash and lunge again—but one left—I gathered myself—dimly saw another blade than mine pass through that last dwarf—heard Zarf as from a far distance crying exultantly:

"Lord King, you fight even better than in the other days! It is well—for you will have many a fight ere you sit once more on the Chrysolite Throne of your race."

Then I slid to a limp heap on the ground, exhausted from loss of blood—I could not speak—heard Zarf cursing furiously, virulently; then all consciousness flickered out. . . .

I regained my senses slowly. I lay on a pallet, a hand's breadth off a hard-packed earthen floor. A feeble lamp barely showed walls of stone chinked with moss and mud. Obviously a hut—but where? Then I saw Zarf. He sat on a low stool, chin on fist, elbow on knee, head bandaged, and his left arm in a sling. Looking at myself, I saw I was swathed worse than he in bandages.

"Zarf," I said weakly. "We look as if we'd been in a fight!"

"We have been," he nodded at cost of a twinge of pain. "But none of those Vulmins will ever take part in another— while we were just getting a little practice!"

"Zarf," I demanded, insistent. "Who are you, and why did you call me 'Master'? Surely there is some mistake. You know that I am but an Earthman upon whom you took pity and opened for him a door into this realm of Space. . . ."

Somberly he stared at me; then:

"King Karan, what pity was in the hearts of those Vulmin dwarf-devils when they strove to cut us into gobbets for their cook-pots? Yet they knew you and named you 'Karan of Oc- tolan, Zarf's royal Master.' Is it possible you have no mem- ory of the past—no knowledge of who and what you are? Do you not remember the rebel sorcerer, Djl Grm, who blasted your body and drove your self through a bent corridor down to the Earth, where you acquired a new body as an Earth- babe? Have you no recollection of your Imperial Consort? Shall that regal lady—so loved by all in your far-flung realm that she was deemed a goddess—be unavenged?

"What disposal that accursed sorcerer made of her, none knows. It is known that he sought to seduce her, and when she withstood him in that, she vanished! Yet sure I am he did not force her to the Earth, for then you twain might have found each other, and so defeated his major purpose. Nay, King Karan, she is *here*! In the nights her spirit whispers to mine:

" 'Zarf, I am still your Queen. Find my lord, wheresoever he be . . . watch over him . . . whenever possible, open for him a door. He will find me—free me—out of his love. . . .

"King Karan, must that regal lady's spirit wait in vain, believing Zarf a traitor, and you a recreant spouse?"

"I can not remember," I groaned. I was convinced—

believed Zarf fully; and oh! the anguish that was mine in that moment! Amnesia, it is called back on Earth, this inability to remember, with its concomitant of lost identity. . . . Then in the gloom of my mind, one insurmountable objection reared its ugly head, "If this sorcerer blasted my body, and drove my self down to the Earth, where through the medium of birth I regained a body and grew to my present stature—how shall any here recognize me as Karan the King of Octolan? Zarf, I still say you must be mistaken."

"My King," he replied pityingly, "you *are* sore bemazed! On Earth your body was shapen by parental influence; but *here*—when the agony shook you, the body reassembled about the self in its true semblance and substance. Nay! Karan of Octolan you are, and none who ever saw you during your reign would deny your identity, albeit there be many would gladly slay you to prevent you from regaining your throne.

"Lord, evil rules where once was good—and a fair, happy land has become a veritable antechamber of Hell. Vampyr and ghoul prey on the bodies of your people. Foes assail them from without, and devils plague them from within the borders. Your subjects, afraid, disheartened, hopeless, have fallen from their allegiance to the Karanate Dynasty. Scarce may we find a hundred loyal souls in all the eight provinces of Octolan. I myself am but a fugitive; and rich is the reward Djl Grm would pay for the head of Zarf the Proscribed! And as for our gracious Queen, Mehul-Ira——"

He groaned in heaviness of spirit; and I felt two scalding tears run adown my cheeks.

"I can not remember," I wailed. "Karan I may be, but I have not his memory! A great King would I be, and a wondrous leader—with Karan's body and an Earth-man's mind!" And I sank back on my bed all atremble from sheer, impotent fury at myself.

Zarf pondered for an interminable while; then:

"Lord, it would seem that Djl Grm, ere he drove your self to the Earth, laid an inhibition on your memory-coil. And if so, we may be sure he will never release it. But, Lord, it comes to my mind that afar from here dwells another magician—

Agnor Halit—fully as evil as Djl Grm, and also fully as powerful. It may well be that he can restore your memory—but it remains to be seen if he will. It is said that they hate each other as only two sorcerers can hate. And in that lies our hope. I think we would do well to start as soon as we are fit to travel, seek out this Agnor Halit, and try to enlist his aid."

"So be it," I assented. "Only, we start at dawn. Are we women, that we should lie at ease because of a few scratches?"

"But you are weak from your wounds," he objected.

"No more so than are you," I retorted. "As I say, we start at dawn. If I am indeed your King, it is for me to command—yours to obey! But for tonight, we sleep—if it be safe to sleep here."

"You will never be safe," he replied, "waking or sleeping, until you are once again on the Chrysolite Throne, surrounded by your own bodyguards. Still, we can take some small precautions to prevent a complete surprise."

He picked up a metal basin and two sticks, with which he rigged a device against the door, which would fall and make a noise were the door tampered with.

"There," he grunted. "Now we can sleep—and we need it!"

The clatter of the falling basin awoke me. I came erect, sword in hand, although I was wavering on my feet. Zarf looked at me in pity, but said naught. Slowly the door swung open, and a most grotesque visage peered in. Zarf audibly sighed his relief.

"Come in, good Koto," he invited soothingly, as one might speak to a timid child. "King Karan will do you no harm. Nor will I." And out of the corner of his mouth Zarf muttered—"Koto owns this hovel. He is a Hybrid, born of a lost woman of the Rodar race and an Elemental of the Red Wilderness. Yet Koto is very gentle and timid. Nor is he such a fool as he looks, for when I told him your identity, the poor creature wept because his hovel was no fit abode for royalty, even in distress. All his life long, Koto will be proud——"

"These 'Rodars'?" I asked, softly. "And this 'Red Wilderness'?"

"The Rodars? Gigantic savages, running naked. Gentle enough, and with child-like brains; and the Red Wilderness is a vast and dreary desert, all yours, but totally worthless."

"Enter, good Koto," I commanded. "I, Karan, King of Octolan, bid you enter and kneel before me."

With a snivelling howl the poor wretch of a Hybrid blundered in awkwardly and flopped asprawl before me. He grasped his head in both ape-like paws, looked at Zarf out of terror-filled eyes, opened his ugly gash of a mouth, and emitted a raucous howl. In a perfect paroxysm of fright he gabbled:

"I knew it! I knew it! This hut is unfit for King Karan the Splendid! And now he will cut off Koto's head with his sword—cut off Zarf's head, too, King Karan! He made me take you in——"

"But you are mistaken, good Koto," I assured the poor fellow. "I have no intent to cut off your head—nor Zarf's."

Then I tapped him on the shoulder with the flat of my blade.

"Rise, Baron Koto, Lord of the Red Wilderness and of all the Rodar-folk that therein dwell. Thus I, Karan, reward your service in giving us succor in our need!"

Zarf became angry at the audacity of my act. To him it was nigh to an insult to the entire order of knighthood. Then, abruptly, he laughed.

"Lord," he gasped, "had another than yourself wrought thus, I'd slay him with my own hand. But such pranks were ever your wont in the other days. Mad as is this one, still it may yet serve you well. You are too weak to travel, despite your bold heart, and we needs must wait in this castle of Baron Koto's until strength returns to us both. Perchance by then Koto may be able to secure for us riding-beasts on which we may travel faster than on our own legs."

At that last argument I capitulated. It was a good reason for waiting. But then I began to question Zarf about our intended journey.

"What manner of territory must we traverse, once we start? What sort of inhabitants dwell along our ways? Savage, or civilized? Wild, tame? Hostile or friendly? And will our swords be sufficient for our protection?"

"It will be a long and dangerous trip," he replied soberly. "Our way lies across this same Red Wilderness you just presented to Koto; thence across the Sea of the Dead, where evil ghosts arise from the foul waters; then over the Hills of Flint to the Mountains of Horror, where demons and vampyrs abound; and thence onward again to a city of devils who adore the lord of all devils. There, if we are fortunate, we may hope to find the sorcerer we seek."

"Cheerful prospect!" I commented acridly. "But are these assorted Hell-spawn sufficiently solid to be cut with good steel, or are they immune to injury?"

"Some are solid enough, while others are intangible, yet dangerous for all that. And there be various tribes of savages, none friendly to strangers. Oh, we may anticipate a most enjoyable trip!"

"Zarf," I demanded abruptly, thinking longingly of the guns and pistols of Earth—"Can you return me to Earth for a brief visit, and then bring me back here, together with certain heavy bundles? Also, can you provide me with gold or gems in quantity?"

"Lord," he mourned, "naught have I to give you saving my life and my love. Nor gold nor gems do I possess, or you should have all with no need of asking. Nor can I return you to Earth—but why do you so suddenly wish to go?"

I explained, and he understood, but reiterated his inability to do as I requested.

"Those 'ghunz,' " he marveled, enviously—"What a pity we have them not. Throwing-spears and knives are our nearest approach."

"Koto," I interrupted Zarf, a new idea arising in my mind. "Do you have a wood that will do like this, when seasoned?" I drew my sword, bent it in an arc, and let it spring swiftly back.

Koto nodded, then shambled from the hut. I heard sounds

of wood being split, and presently Koto was back with a long
strip of hard wood which he handed me deprecatingly. I was
overjoyed, for it was precisely what I needed.

"Bows and arrows," I exulted. "Now I feel better! Zarf,
we have reason to remain here for a while."

Rapidly I explained, using a pointed stick to make clear
my meaning, by drawing in the dirt of the floor. I had been
an archery enthusiast on Earth, and knew my subject, even
if I had never handled a sword.

Despite my earlier urgency, it was three weeks before wc
three men set forth from Koto's castle on the edge of the Red
Wilderness. Three men, because Koto had protested with lugubrious howls that he wasn't going to be left behind. I'd
made him a Baron, he claimed, and it was his right to ride
with me when I went forth to war! Zarf chuckled in grim
approval, and I, too, endorsed Koto's claim.

We rode the queerest steeds imaginable. Huge birds they
were, more like enormous game-cocks than aught else I can
compare them to; with longer, thicker spurs and bigger beaks.
Ugly-tempered, too. Zarf said they'd fight viciously whenever
it came to close quarters. And how those big birds could run!

I asked Koto where he got them, and he replied that he'd
gone out one dark night and taken them from a flock kept by
a petty lordling some distance away. When I laughed and
called him a thief, he said seriously he was no such thing:

"Was not Karan the King in need of them? And did not
the kingdom and all that therein was belong to the King?"

So we rode forth, all three mounted and armed with short,
thick, powerful bows and thick, heavy arrows. Zarf and I
had the swords we had taken from the Vulmins, and Koto
bore a ponderous war-club fashioned from a young tree having a natural bulge at the big end. Into this bulge he had
driven a dozen bronze spikes all greenish with verdigris—a
most efficient and terrible weapon, if he had the courage to
use it in hand-to-hand fighting. Zarf maintained that Koto
would be so anxious to please me that he'd fight like a maniacal fiend, should the opportunity present.

The crossing of that Red Wilderness was no pleasure jaunt. There were dust storms and blistering heat by day, and an icy wind o' nights that howled like all the devils of Hell let loose. But in time we came to the shore of the Sea of the Dead; and a most fitting name it was for that desolate body of putrescent water.

Dull grayish-greenish water, sullenly heaving and surging to and fro sluggishly and greasily; beaches of dull grayish-brownish sands; and huge dull grayish-blackish boulders and rocks—oh! a most nightmarish picture, taken all in all.

"Zarf," I shuddered, "may it not be possible to ride around this sea?"

"Perhaps," he returned, dubiously. "But we can cross it in one quarter of the time it would take to ride around."

"But," I queried skeptically, "how shall we cross? I see no boats, nor any way of making any."

"I have heard of a tribe hereabouts," he replied slowly, "and it may be that we can barter for, seize, or compel them to make for us a craft that will bear us over this pestilential sea. But now we had best think about making camp for the night."

We rode back from the beach until the sea was lost to view—and smell. A pleased cry from Koto finally caused us to halt. Where a mass of boulders had been piled up by some ancient cataclysm, there was a cave-like recess sufficiently large to afford safe refuge for all three of us and our mounts.

What had pleased Koto particularly was the presence of a lot of lumps resembling amber, but of a queer red color. After he had collected sufficient to satisfy his ideas, he laid a line of the stuff across the entrance, and set fire to them. They burned like coal or gum, and gave off a clear pale white flame, and a most pleasant odor, with no smoke.

"This region is infested with devils at night," Koto said seriously. "But no devil will ever dare pass that line of fire."

He was right. No devil did pass, but after darkness came, a lot of them tried. Failing in that laudable attempt, they drew anigh the opening, and stared in avidly at us. . . .

* * *

We divided the night into three watches. Zarf and I wrapped ourselves in our cloaks and slept, nor did aught disturb our rest. But Koto, when he wakened me, said he had seen plenty of devils moving about beyond the line of fire. Then he rolled himself up, and so became immovable. But I, hearing no snores, grew suspicious of such somnolence, considering that he had snored like a thunderstorm incarnate since we started from his castle. Finally I tricked him into betraying himself. With a jerk of my head I summoned him to my side.

"Koto, do you think your King unfit to keep guard, that you lie awake?"

"Lord," he replied, "there be many devils about, and some be very dangerous—tricky, too. I know their ways better than you do, and can better cope with them. Also, I await the greatest one of all, for I would talk with him on a certain matter."

"Your father, Koto?"

"Yes, my King. Koto sent him word by a lesser devil, and he will surely come."

"Koto," I demanded sternly, "would you betray your King?"

"Nay, I seek to serve my Master." He stared at me in hurt surprize. Ashamed of my suspicion, I made amends.

"I thank my Baron! Koto, have I your permission to see this father of yours?"

"So be it," he assented, after pondering the matter for a while. "But first I must tell him, or he will be angry."

A long interval passed. Out of the blackness beyond the fire two enormous crimson eyes glared balefully. Koto calmly arose, stepped across the glowing line of the Fire of Safety, and walked off in the darkness toward those glowing orbs. A thousand misgivings assailed me. I strained my eyes, but could see naught. Even the crimson eyes had vanished. Only one comfort did I have—if harm came to Koto, his howls would surely apprise me of his danger. So I strained my ears, but no faintest whisper came. Then, after an eon of suspense, Koto calmly returned, and muttered:

"Now if King Karan wishes to see Koto's father—come! He is very terrible to behold, but he has promised Koto that King Karan shall be unharmed. But do not awaken Zarf—yet!"

It took all the hardihood I could muster to step across the line of fire and walk out into that fiend-infested dark. Koto minded it far less than I. There was evil in the very air. Strange, terrible faces stared at me, half-heard voices moaned and gibbered in my ears, clammy hands grasped at my arms and clothing, yet could not hold. Once a pair of icy cold lips kissed me full on my mouth; and oh! the foul effluvium of that breath! . . . Abruptly, Koto halted. A huge mass of black seen against the murky blackness of the night barred further progress. We stood immovable, waiting—for what? After a bit I grew impatient, weary of standing like a rock, and reached for my sword.

"Well," I demanded of Koto. "What is this holding us here? And where is this mighty father of yours? I am minded to try my sword on this black barrier and find out if it be impassable."

Before he could reply—the black barrier was not! Only, two eyes that were crimson fires of hellishness were staring into mine from a distance of mere inches . . . no face, no form . . . just vacant air—and two eyes. With a snort of disgust, I turned my back to the phenomenon.

"Koto," I said severely, "I am Karan, rightful King of Octolan. I am not interested in child's play, nor am I to be frightened by any Elemental, devil, goblin, or fiend in all my realm. I am *their* King as well as yours! Let this father of yours show respect, or we return to our shelter. . . ."

A Being stood facing me! It was taller than Koto or I, albeit no giant. Yet I knew that an Elemental was capable of assuming, at will, any form it might choose. Its features were wholly non-human; at the same time its expression was in nowise repulsive, nor was it fear-inspiring. But there were unmistakable power and mastery stamped thereon and shining in its great, glowing eyes.

It was staring at me coldly, impersonally, with no sign of

hostility, friendliness, or even curiosity; and I stared back at it with precisely the same attitude. If it sought to overawe me, it was badly mistaken. Then I realized it was telepathically reading my soul. And strangely, I began to grasp some insight into its nature, likewise.

"Truly, you are King Karan of Octolan, returned to regain your own. And I, to whom past, present and future are one and the same, tell you that you will succeed in all you undertake. Aye! And more than you now dream. And because you have treated Koto as a man, and will eventually make of him one of whom I may yet be proud, I will transport you, Koto, that grim Zarf of yours, and your mounts as well, across the Sea of the Dead, and beyond the Hills of Flint. But across the Mountains of Horror you three must fight your own way. Certain powers of Nature I control, and naught do I fear; but there is an ancient pact between that magician whom you seek, and me. Therefore I will not anger him by taking you into his realms, uninvited.

"Yet this I tell you for your further guidance—he will demand of you a service. Give it, and all shall go well with your plans. Refuse it, and all the days of your life you will regret that refusal. At dawn, be in readiness, and I will carry out my promise. Fear not, whatever happens, for my ways are none that you can understand, even were I to explain them. And now, farewell till dawn!"

And with that—I stood, facing nothing! Koto's father had simply vanished.

Returning to the cave, we found a badly worried Zarf awake and cursing luridly. But he became considerably mollified when I explained, although he shook his head dubiously regarding Koto's father and his proffered assistance.

"His aid will more likely get us in trouble than help us out of it," he grumbled. "Still, as no better course presents, I suppose we will have to accept and run all chances."

At the first flush of dawn we were mounted and waiting. We noted that the air held a peculiar quality, indescribable, yet familiar, somewhat like the odor caused by a levin-bolt striking too close for comfort. Also, there came a strange, murky tinge in the air—a faint moan—icy winds—a howling, shrieking, roaring fury like all the tormented souls in Hell voicing their agonies—sand, dust and small pebbles tore past us—the world abruptly vanished, together with my companions, so far as I knew—naught remained—I was choked by dust and my eyes were blinded—I was dizzy and bemazed— I knew not for certain if I were alive or dead and buried— acute misery was the sole thing I was conscious of.

My mount stumbled and fell asprawl. I lurched to my feet, gasped, retched violently, and presently felt better. I stared about me, bewildered. Zarf and Koto were just scrambling to their feet, and facing us was Koto's father. And the great Elemental had a smile on his lips, and in his eyes a light of actual friendliness.

"Lord Karan, back of you are the Sea of the Dead and the Hills of Flint; and before you lie the Mountains of Horror. I have kept my promise to the King my son follows and honors. Farewell."

And before I could voice my gratitude, he was gone—as seemed a habit with him. One instant visible, then—vacancy!

"I know much about my father," Koto said slowly. "But I never knew he could do this."

A faint trail ran down into a wide valley, on the far side of which loomed the mighty ramparts of the Mountains of Horror. And they merited the appellation. They were evil, and evil dwelt in them.

Soon the dim trail became a wide road, albeit ancient and in dire need of repair. I do not believe it had been traveled for ages, until we came; the natural conclusion being that whatever race built it had passed into oblivion, leaving their handiwork to mark their passing.

As the day drew to its close, the road led us into the ruins of an ancient city. Not one stone stood atop of another. We decided to camp there for the night, and while Koto pitched camp and prepared a meal, I strolled about the ruins.

Everywhere I looked were slabs that were covered with

petroglyphs. Whatever the race, they had had a written language, and moreover, they had been prone to embellishment. They must have been, like the old Egyptians, dominated by a priesthood, to judge by the character of the many pictures illustrating the graven text. But if those same pictures were aught to go by, their gods must have been born from a union of a nightmare and a homicidal maniac's frenzy! It gave me the chill creeps just to look at those pictures, so foul and unholy were the rites and acts depicted.

It was during my watch. My companions snored in a most inharmonious concert; and while I was in nowise asleep, I had drifted into a sort of revery. Slowly I became aware of a pair of eyes gleaming with opalescent lights, staring across the fire at me. Thinking it might be Koto's father, I spoke low-voiced in greeting. But as no reply came, I grew angry and asked who it was and what it wanted. Again no reply, so I snatched up my short bow and drove an arrow beneath those glowing orbs.

A silvery laugh was my only reward. A hard-driven arrow is no laughing matter, but anything could happen in this accursed land, I decided.

"The little death-wand has no power to harm me," a voice asserted in those same silvery tones. "Nay, O Stranger; how may you slay one who died ages agone—but who still lives—and rules?"

"So that little 'death-wand' may not slay you," I snarled. "Well, we'll see what this will do!" And my sword leaped in a whistling cut across the tiny fire. Had there been a head and body there, they must have parted company! But the blade encountered—air!

Across the fire, smiling indulgently, as might one tolerantly amused by the tantrums of an otherwise interesting child, there sat a resplendently beautiful woman, a vivid, gorgeous brunette, with a slightly greenish tinge shimmering over her slender gold-bronze hued body. Her attire, a merest wisp of some pearly glimmering gossamer fabric, accentuated every personal charm of her exquisite form.

"Who are you?" I demanded.

"A Princess of Hell I am, yet having dominance here on this region, likewise. Ages agone I ruled in this city when it was in its height and glory. But there arose among the priests a mighty magician whose power became greater than mine. Quakes and fire and flood he loosed upon me and my people—and we became that which no more is—yet destroy us wholly he could not.

"So it is but a city of ruins you now behold, wherein, as ghosts, my people dwell; and I, a ghost, too, abide with them part of my time, and rule over a ghostly people and a wrecked city."

"If you are a ghost, you look like an extremely tangible one," I stated bluntly.

"Yes?" and she laughed in derision. "Was it an 'extremely tangible' ghost against which you tried two different death-wands? Still you are correct, in part. I am tangible enough now, as you may prove for yourself, should you care to do so. I build my body as I need it, or revert it to vapor when its use is over. Child's play, to my magic, O Stranger. . . . You disbelieve? See!"

She arose, a vision of alluring loveliness, passed deliberately through the fire, and seated herself at my side so closely that I could sense the magnetic radiations of her.

"You may touch me, take me in your arms if you will, kiss my lips till your blood is aflame, and cool your ardor in my embrace, nor shall you find me unresponsive!"

Her rounded arms stole about my neck like soft, satiny serpents.

"So," she murmured. "Am I not tangible? Desirable, too? Take me, and I will be to you as no other, woman, or spirit, or ghost, fiend, devil, or angel in all the universe can ever be! Power and wisdom and rulership will I place at your command . . . love and passion undreamed hitherto——"

I had sat immovable, silent up to that point—but suddenly I made up for lost time. A violent shove sent her asprawl, squarely into the fire; and from my lips came a word so descriptive that Earth's vilest would have blushed in outraged modesty had that epithet been applied.

But the seductively lovely Princess of Hell evidently took the word as a compliment. And if she were angry at being shoved into the fire, she showed no sign thereof. Out from the flames she glided, more alluring than ever; not a hair of her dusky tresses disturbed; with never a blemish on her gold-bronze skin; and with a provocative smile on her curving lips.

"What you have called me—I would be even that, for you," she sighed languorously. "You and I were meant for each other since ever Eternity began——"

But at that, I exploded! Meant for that she-devil? *I?* My hand shot out, seizing her slender throat in a vise-like grip, mercilessly.

"You——!" The word was even worse than the first epithet I had used. "Since arrow and sword fail, let's see what choking will do!"

I tightened my clutch, putting forth all my strength. For good measure, I drove my fist into her face—and nearly dislocated my arm! For the Princess of Hell, she-fiend—ghost—woman—or whatsoever she really was, or had been, simply wasn't there! In fact, I wondered if she'd ever been there, or had I dozed, and dreamed? . . .

"It was no dream, King Karan!"

The voice was full, sonorous, pleasant. Glancing up, I saw a tall, stately old man, bareheaded, smiling in amity.

"Zarf! Koto! *Up!*" I shouted, leaping to my feet, sword in hand. The old man raised his hand in protest.

"Nay, King Karan, they will sleep unless *I* release them from their slumber. That she-fiend put them into a trance from which only someone with power greater than hers can arouse them. Nor will I do so until after you and I confer on a matter of mutual benefit."

"Who are you?" I demanded. "And what devilment do you plan against me and my comrades?"

"Yon sleeper—Zarf—told you of a magician; and you set forth to seek that one, did you not? Well, I am he whom you seek, and your journey is at an end, King Karan. Knowing of your coming, I was prepared to greet you as soon as you entered my domains—and this ruined city marks my border-line. So, I am here!

"King Karan, you are naught to me, nor I to you. But we have a common enemy—Djl Grm! Between him and me there lies an ancient feud. You he has wronged. There is a ser-vice—I get that from your mind—which you hope I can and will render you.

"Karan, King afar from your crown, throne, and kingdom, you are a bold and resourceful man, and your two compan-ions are worth an army of ordinary folk. Render me one service, faithfully, without evasion or quibble, and I will re-lease your locked memory! Well?"

"Arouse Zarf and Koto," I commanded. "If you be the one I seek, they will identify you, nor will they harm you. I, Karan, give you protection!"

He actually laughed at that, although there was more of admiration than derision in his laugh.

"Bold as ever, King Karan," he complimented. "As you have said, so will I do." He made a slight gesture, murmur-ing something I could not catch. "Now, speak, in a whisper if you will, and see if they be asleep."

As I complied, they came abruptly to their feet, fully alert. . . . They took one look. . . . On Koto's ugly face came such an expression of ghastly fear that I hastened to assure him he was in no danger. Zarf bowed in respect, albeit he showed no fear. Our visitor spoke, in a courteous manner:

"You know me, Zarf? You, too, Baron Koto?"

"You are Agnor Halit, the mighty magician I persuaded my King to seek," Zarf responded gravely.

Koto nodded vehemently. "My father says you have more power than the devil himself, O Agnor Halit."

"Is King Karan satisfied?"

"I am," I confirmed. "But why do you meet me here, rather than making me journey all the way to your abode?"

"For this reason—the service I ask, if I am to release your inhibited memory, will take you back on your path, even to the near shore of the Sea of the Dead. And so, I save you many long, weary days of travel, hardship and danger.''

"And this service?"

"Give heed, then, and I will explain. There is a treasure I would fain possess. There be good reasons why I may not go after it myself, yet those reasons would not affect you. Truth to tell, it is hidden in the territory ruled by another magician who knows not it is there. The one who hid this treasure is another magician. . . . Long ago he hid the priceless thing for some dire reason of his own. It is the statue of a naked, beautiful female; yet it is an enormous jewel—a flawless sapphire, a trifle over half life-size——''

"No sapphire in all the worlds was ever that big," I objected. But Agnor Halit merely smiled as he assented:

"True! But magic works wonders, King Karan. Your throne is made of a huge chrysolite, albeit not in all the worlds was a chrysolite ever that big! Still are you 'King Karan of the Chrsyolite Throne.' Magic made your throne from certain substances, yet a trader in gems would tell you it is genuine chrysolite! . . .

"This sapphire statue was made from flesh and blood by enchantment. It is the actual body of a witch who dared withstand a great magician, long ago, until he conquered her by treachery. For punishment he transmuted her to sapphire, reducing her size to that of a half-grown child, and so left her a beautiful image in which her soul is still prisoned. But once I have that image in my possession, I will have a hold upon him. . . .

"He hated her so greatly that after turning her to crystal, he could in nowise abide to look upon her constantly; wherefore he hid her in a submerged cavern near this shore of the Sea of the Dead. But that cavern can be entered—at times.''

"And if I bring to you this statue——''

"Then will I release the bonds that hold your memory in abeyance. So be it that you release the Sapphire Image to me, without any reservation or quibble—your memories of all the past will be perfect. I, Agnor Halit, magician, do pledge you this, Karan of Octolan. And my pledges I do keep to the last atom. I have wrought every known sin, and many nameless evils—but of one thing is Agnor Halit thus far guiltless—a broken promise!"

"It is well," I answered. And not to be outdone by him, a dealer in all unholiness, I gave pledge in return: "I, Karan, will deliver to you that treasure if I succeed in carrying out my venture, nor will I claim part or parcel in it. For aught I care, you may shatter it to blue slivers the moment I deliver it to you."

A demoniacal light flickered momentarily in that dark sorcerer's eyes as he said vindictively:

"I may do an even stranger thing than that, once the thing is in my possession!"

"I am not concerned with your mysteries," I shrugged. "All I need to know about you is that you and I have an agreement which we both intend to keep. Now, tell me all you can, that I may surely find that place where the Sapphire Image is hidden."

So for the rest of the night we three sat listening while that gentle-seeming old man told us in detail all he knew about our course—while at the same time he warned us frankly that we were going direct into the worst antechamber of Hell when we reached the entrance to the cavern. And, as we later found out for ourselves, he understated. . . .

"Lord Karan," Koto said, pointing—"unless Agnor Halit lied, yon place is the entrance to the cavern we seek."

We dismounted after one glance, for the marks were unmistakable. Five huge boulders indicated the angles of a pentagon; in the center, a pool, evidently filled with water from the Sea of the Dead through some underground channel. To substantiate this supposition, the surface of the pool heaved with the heaving of the surges along the beach some few hundred yards distant.

Even as we watched, the surface became violently agitated; a vortex formed, became a miniature whirlpool, making queer sucking noises, strange gurglings and whistling moans. This lasted for upward of an hour. After that, the surface became level and still.

Then abruptly came a change. In the very center a huge bubble rose and burst, polluting the atmosphere with a most unholy stench. More bubbles rose and the stench grew worse. Bubbles came continually, and the pool boiled like a cauldron, filling the air with horrible odor. Then again the surface stilled.

Now my courage well-nigh forsook me, and without shame I admit it. For I knew I'd have to dive into that loathly pool while the vortex pulled downward; and come up—if ever I did come up—while the bubbles arose! And it was in nowise a pleasing prospect. After we'd been studying the pool for some time, Zarf evidently came to the same conclusion I had reached, for he said bluntly:

"My King, that old devil, Agnor Halit, laid a trap for you! It is well known that King Koran does not lightly break his word. But if I, Zarf, have aught to say about this matter, here is once Karan of Octolan breaks a pledge, nor gives it a second thought. To plunge into that pool is the act of a madman. If that damned sorcerer wants that image so badly, let him come and dive for it himself. He will only go to Hell a little sooner, through a most befitting gateway and this region of space will be that much improved because of his absence!"

"But my memory, Zarf?"

"Once you've gone into that filthy hole, you'll have no need for it, as you'll not come up to use it! Nay, let us rather go back to Koto's hut and plot to regain your kingdom. If successful, we can then force Djl Grm to undō his foul sorcery—"

"Not so fast, Zarf," Koto interrupted. "My father warned our King to comply with Agnor Halit's request, and said that if he did, all would go well with his plans. But my father said, too, that if our King refused, he'd regret it all his life long."

Now Zarf and I looked at each other blankly, for there was truth in what Koto had just said.

"I wonder if there is any other way to regain that statue,"
I suggested tentatively.

"I know a good way," Koto said simply. "It is just this:
Koto goes down, and comes up with the image, or stays down
there with it. And if aught goes wrong, Koto can well be
spared——"

"Nay, my Koto," I said huskily, for I was deeply moved
by the faithful fellow's loyal and courageous proffer—"I can
ill spare——"

A gurgling noise from the pool. Koto rose abruptly, said
no word and gave no sign, but dived like a frog, head first,
into the center of the rapidly forming whirlpool. Neither Zarf
nor I had been alert enough to prevent him, for he had moved
too quickly. We stared at each other, open-mouthed in
amazement.

"King Karan," Zarf's voice rang like a clarion—"when
you regain your kingdom remember that brave fool, Baron
Koto of the Red Wilderness, and sometimes think of—Zarf!"
Splash!

I stood alone, gaping stupidly at the spot where two splendid, loyal noblemen had disappeared. The vortex was growing weaker—it would cease ere long—then an eternity of
waiting, hoping—perhaps they would never come up—I'd be
alone—never see them again—I, a King minus crown, throne,
realm, memory, wife, subjects—why! the only *subjects* I
knew or cared about. . . .

I took a deep full breath, and dived.

That vile fluid that stank so abominably hurt worse than it
smelt. It was actually corrosive. It *bit!* Raw potash lye is its
nearest comparison. . . . I was still head down and going
deeper. I was spinning with the swirling until I grew dizzy.
My eyeballs felt as if burning out of their sockets from that
acrid solution—down, down, and down! A faint, dimly seen
blue light struck horizontally through the whirlpool—two
vague, shadowy figures barely seen as I whirled in that mad
headlong dance—a powerful grip clamped fast on one of my
ankles and I thought I was being rent apart—the vortex hated

to let go—but that mighty pull at my leg would not be denied—I looked up into Koto's ugly face—then Zarf's voice, heavy with reproach:

"King Karan, is this well? Go back, I pray you, as soon as the bubbles rise!"

But at that, I flatly refused, standing on my royal dignity; and I made them yield the point, maugre their stubborn insistence.

A tunnel stretched away into the dim distance, and up that tunnel we started—toward what? Steadily the blue light became stronger, and in my mind arose the certitude that it emanated from the Blue Image. Demon faces peered at us from cracks and crevices, but none of the devils of the place found hardihood to attack us.

The tunnel debouched into a great cavern. In the exact center, on a mound of bleached skulls stood the source of the blue radiance—the Sapphire Witch herself. I gasped in awed admiration at the flawless perfection of her beauty—and suddenly, how I did hate that sorcerer Agnor Halit, to whom I'd promised to deliver that exquisite Image of Incomparable Loveliness! Cheerfully would I have bartered the empires of the universe for its possession—did I but own those empires—nor would I have considered the price exorbitant. *I wanted it—I wanted it!* And I'd pledged—

Around that mound, in a ring on the floor of the cavern, lay many stones. Half the size of human heads they were, round as balls, and no two were of the same color. Every one was aglow, softly, with inward lights, as if each were afire deep inside—dark reds there were; dull orange; dusky blues, garish greens and sinister purples. We knew they were sentient, malignant, resenting our intrusion! Koto responded by kicking one stone that was apparently sneering at him and radiating contempt. At the impact of Koto's foot, the smoldering stone gave forth a metallic clang like a smitten gong, rose straight in the air to the level of Koto's face—then hurtled straight at him with a speed that would have cracked his skull, had not Zarf struck at the Flying Stone with his sword and deflected its course.

A dozen of them promptly left the floor and flew at Zarf—who as promptly turned and fled. But he was actuated by discretion rather than fear. I saw him race headlong into a crack in the tunnel wall—and shortly, the devil who dwelt therein came tumbling out, well-nigh sheared in two by Zarf's sword. Evidently Zarf preferred coping with devils, to the Flying Stones. Koto, having the same idea, hastily retreated to the tunnel mouth—and I went with Koto. In another moment Zarf rejoined us there, grinning sheepishly. The Flying Stones did not follow us that far from the Blue Statue. . . .

We stood disconsolate, wondering how we were to pass their formidable menace—and as if to show us how futile was our quest, of a sudden the entire ring of Flying Stones levitated to the height of a man's shoulders and head, and commenced to swirl about the Sapphire Witch who stood so serene on her altar of skulls. Truly a strange goddess, and guarded by even stranger acolytes!

Fast and faster swirled the Flying Stones, their colored lights glowing more and more brightly—faster yet, until we could no longer distinguish any single stone—they were merely a beautiful, gleaming blur of fire—gradually a humming sound became audible, swelling in volume till it became a roar like the diapason of a mighty organ—soon it became distinguishable as a chant of warning! . . .

And at that, a sort of madness came upon me. I had come for that image—to bear it away—not to stand and look at it from a distance. And that image I meant to take, forthwith! In my rage, all else faded—kingdom, wife, subjects, memory, Agnor Halit, Djl Grm, Zarf, Koto, even my own welfare mattered not. I ran forward, shouting:

"Fools! I am Karan of Octolan! I have come for that image! It shall be mine! Down and lie still, I say!"

Now who was I, after all, that those Flying Stones should obey me? Yet so it was! The fiery band settled down instantly. I walked confidently forward, picked up the image, and so, back to where Zarf and Koto stood staring in amazed incredulity.

"Somewhat of magic my King knows, it appears!" gasped

Koto shakily. I myself could hardly believe it. But the fact remained that I held the statue in my arms. And we three walked down that tunnel, nor did aught bother us all the way to the upper world!

Once at the surface, we wiped the foulness of the pool from the lovely image, and stood actually adoring the matchless treasure in the clear light . . . looked suddenly up, and saw Koto's father, and with him that utterly damned sorcerer, Djl Grm.

The sorcerer clutched swiftly for the image, but as swiftly Zarf spun his sword in a glittering wheel of defense in front of it—and the magician flinched back. Then he pointed a finger—and Zarf became temporarily paralyzed. Koto snatched up the image, and tucking it beneath his left arm, he waggled his formidable bludgeon under the sorcerer's nose with a meaning gesture.

"Try that trick on me!" he invited grimly. But the magician, for some reason, declined Koto's urgent invitation. Instead, I became aware of rapid interchange of telepathic speech between Koto's father and Djl Grm. The great Elemental turned to Koto.

"Are you my son?"

"That, you should know best," Koto responded with a grim smile. He seemed to know what was coming next.

"Then," his father commanded—"give the Blue Image to its proper owner!"

"No!" and Koto shook his head defiantly. "It is not seemly that my King should carry burdens while I, his follower, go empty-handed. I carry it for him. His it is by right of power— for he made the Flying Stones yield to him their trust, and he bore it away from the Altar of Skulls, unmolested!"

The Elemental grew black with rage. His eyes flamed crimson, and their awful glare frightened Zarf and me. Koto looked perturbed, but a faint reddish spark began flickering in his eyes, too.

"*Give that Image to Djl Grm, I said!*" The Elemental's voice held a note of awful finality.

Koto's arm flew back and swept forward again, and his bludgeon smashed full in his father's face.

"My father you are," Koto howled in fury—"but Karan is my King!"

Unharmed by the impact, the Elemental gravely handed Koto his great club. But it was to me he spoke:

"King Karan, I said I might yet be proud of Koto—*I am!*" Then to the sorcerer, sternly:

"Djl Grm, I know your power—and I know its limitations. And I know, likewise, what you have in mind. Summon your legions if you dare and I will summon mine. And what that will mean to us both ere all be ended, you know, as do I! To a certain extent, I aided you in this affair, for I wished to see how big my son had grown in the service of his King—and I am proud of his loyalty. So long as my son shall cleave to him, Karan of Octolan is my ally and friend. *Djl Grm, is it peace—or war?*"

The magician seemed like to explode with impotent fury. Suddenly he vanished with a scream of baffled, venomous rage. Then came a terrific sensation, comparable only to the emotion an arrow must feel as it leaves the string of a powerful bow.

Koto, still holding the Sapphire Image under his left arm and his great club clenched in his right fist—Zarf and I, still holding our drawn swords—and Koto's father, smiling as if pleased that he had broken openly with Djl Grm—stood looking at each other, hardly knowing what to say. But one thing we three realized—Koto's father had once again displayed his control of the forces of Nature, and we were in the city of ghosts, where I had promised to meet Agnor Halit. The Elemental said something to Koto that made him grin from ear to ear; then it vanished.

Night. And we three sat by a brightly burning campfire. Not one of us cared to sleep. We were taking no chances on some unexpected treachery assailing us at the last moment. Again and again I had tried to reach Agnor Halit mentally, bidding him come get his Blue Image and give me my price, that I might be done with a distasteful business; because *I* wanted that statue for myself, and also because I liked old Agnor Halit not one whit better than his fellow sorcerer, Djl Grm. And the sooner I was quit of further doings with either or both of those two, the more pleased I'd be. . . . But Agnor Halit came not. A hope dawned in my mind—perhaps he had met with some disaster. Then Koto caught my mind and spoiled that idea.

"Nay! He lives. He will come whenever it pleases him to come—till then—we—can—but—wait."

Koto sagged where he sat, slumped over on his side—and snored! Zarf, a second later, did likewise. Amazed, I shouted at them. As well shout at two solid rocks! I grew afraid at that, for I saw what was toward—they, of their own free wills, would never have acted thus! Some malign power had wrought a sleep-spell on them, and I was left to face whatever might happen.

And it started immediately!

The ruined city was materializing as it was before calamity fell upon it! Stone upon stone, tier upon tier, story upon story, tower and turret and pylon, pinnacle, spire and dome, it grew in might and beauty, albeit the mighty suggested cruelty and the beauty was wholly evil.

The streets filled with people—men, women, and little children; and on no face did I see aught written of good, but only all wickedness. Before I could decide what to do, of a sudden a detachment of soldiery bore down on me, surrounding me before I could rise to my feet. Again I shouted to Zarf and Koto; and deep as was the slumber-spell, Koto's brain must have caught, in part, my warning. For he moved uneasily, flinging out one arm restlessly. That arm fell across the image where it lay wrapped in my cloak.

Roughly I was yanked to my feet. The soldiers disregarded the two others, for some reason. Through the streets they led me, into a splendid edifice that proved to be a temple of the loathly devil-gods I had seen depicted on the various rock-faces among the ruins.

Seated on a resplendent throne was the seductively lovely

Princess of Hell, looking more alluring than when first I saw her. Languidly smiling, she addressed me as if naught but utmost amity had marked our former brief acquaintance.

"All this I have wrought for your sake, O Stranger for whom I yearn. I did it that you might have proof it is no weakling wraith who seeks your love, but one truly great, powerful, and—if you will have it so—kindly disposed toward you."

"What do you really want of me?" I demanded bluntly. "I'm not a total fool, to believe you're actually in love with me, a mere mortal nobody!"

"A mere mortal nobody?" The Princess smiled, highly amused. "Karan of Octolan, Lord of the Chrysolite Throne, is hardly a mere mortal nobody. You do yourself injustice, for you are very much a man. And not a maid in all my train but would be happy to be your mate—and myself most of all.

"Secretly, you regard me as a fiend. Well, I *am*! But I want you to know me fully. Between such as I, and your sort, exists an almost impassable barrier—unless one of your sort invites one of my order across the border. You have a different magnetism, highly beneficial to us, and we delight to bathe therein, returning in exchange a portion of our own powerful vibrations. Thus impregnated, new powers and capacities are yours for the wielding.

"We 'fiends' do not seek your souls! Most of your souls are not worth having, so weak, so embryonic are they. Not good enough to attain to celestial realms, nor wicked enough to be welcome in Hell, naught remains for most of your race but return, life after life, to some of the material planes. But within you, Karan, are great capacities for absolute Evil or absolute Good. Aye, a fit mate for even me——"

"You've said enough," I interrupted harshly. "Mate with *you*? Give you of my magnetic radiations—draw from *you* strength, power, and capacities? Why, you she-devil, sooner would I spend eternity adoring hopelessly——"

"That Blue Witch you stole," she hissed venomously. "O Fool ten thousand times accursed! You dare compare me to that icy cold crystal that can not move? I would have crowned you Lord of Hell itself in a century's time, had you accepted my offer; but since you dare to refuse me—you shall pay! . . ."

And pay I did!

In obedience to some unspoken command from the infuriated she-fiend, a particularly malignant-appearing priest stepped forward from amidst a group of his kind. I had never before seen a face so utterly unhuman. His body was more ape-like than man-like.

The priest laid one prehensile paw on my shoulder—and received a smashing blow full in the face from my fist. The priest did not even change expression, but my fist felt as if I had hit a solid rock. Holding me at arm's length, he jabbed me lightly with one finger. He knew anatomy and neurology, that devil-priest, for that light touch wrung a gasp of agony from me, and brought the cold sweat from every pore of my body, while it sent a terrific thrill like commingled ice and fire along every fiber of my nervous system.

That was merely a preliminary. . . .

A vise-like grip on my temples with thumb and finger—what sort of uncanny powers did that devil-priest control? And throb after throb of lance-like twinges tore through my brain, each one a solid impact, each impact worse than the preceding one; until at each twinge bright sparks burst within my skull, rending and searing the tissues of my brain, and I, all fortitude lost, howled, moaned, shrieked and yelled like any madman in Bedlam as those awful pulsations continued into an eternity of anguish.

But that became monotonous. My howls were too much alike, and wearied the Princess. The devil-priest tried a new one. Releasing my temples, he lightly slapped me on the chest with the flat of his hand, meantime blowing his breath on my forehead. . . .

A most delightful sense of surcease from torture after anguish unbearable swept all through me, and I sighed my relief; but that devil-priest ran his thumb along my spine, once, and the terrific agony of that caress made all I had suffered previously seem but exquisite delight!

Stepping back a pace, the devil-priest levelled his arm, his stiffly extended fingers pointing straight at me, and I commenced to gyrate, at first slowly, then with ever accelerating speed; fast and faster, and faster yet, until the surroundings became a blur—and faster still, until the surroundings and the blur, too, disappeared, and naught remained but myself aspin on my own axis!

Crash!

The motion was instantaneously reversed, and what ghastly effect that simple action had upon me can never be imagined or described. It had to be undergone to be understood, and what little sense I'd still managed to retain thus far left me entirely. . . .

I awoke! I was stretched out on a couch, suffused with untellable fatigue, acutely conscious of agonies endured beyond all endurance. . . .

"O my beloved! Such sufferings! But never again! In my arms, O loved man, shall you regain strength and know bliss beyond all thinking."

Hovering over me, holding me in her arms, shielding and protecting me from further harm, was a superbly beautiful woman. Azure was her hair, blue as the midsummer skies was her shimmering skin that shone with a clear luster surpassing any gem; yet in nowise was she a stone statue, but a living, breathing, loving, tender, soft-bodied woman of flesh and blood! I reached up feeble arms about her neck, drawing her down to me—almost had her lips touch mine—a lambent reddish light flickered momentarily in her wondrous blue eyes——

"You infernal hag!"

It was but a putrid corpse I held so lovingly within the circle of my arms—and in it the worms and maggots were acrawl! . . .

The Princess of Hell, on her gorgeous throne, gave utterance to a trill of merry laughter at the success of that final glamorous torment of the man who had dared refuse her proffered love. . . .

That laugh changed to a shriek of fury ere the last silvery

note of her mirth died out! Facing her where she sat surrounded by her guards and courtiers stood a tall, robed figure, grimly eyeing her in a silence more fraught with menace
than any words could have conveyed.

"Agnor Halit!" she screamed in a paroxysm of terror, as
she recognized the mighty sorcerer.

"Even so, O Princess of Hell, Queen over a ghostly race
and a ghost city that I shattered with my magic, ages agone.
And now! For that you have not felt the weight of my hand
in the last few centuries, you have grown overbold. You actually dared molest this man, knowing that he was at the time
engaged in serving my purpose!"

Agnor Halit drew from the breast of his robe a most peculiar reptile, more like a short, extremely thick centipede
than aught else. He held it up between thumb and finger. His
words came slow, heavy, laden with doom:

"Into this vileness shalt thou go, nor ever come forth from
it until I, Agnor Halit, am no more!"

He flung the small abhorrence on the dais, before the feet
of the Princess. It remained there, immovable, its full eyes
fixed on her face; and she stared back in awe-stricken, horrified fascination.

The sorcerer stretched out his arms, his quivering fingers
aimed at the beauteous, erotic fiend trembling in an ecstasy
of fear there on her sumptuous seat. Over guards and courtiers, priests and populace an icy terror fell; they stood staring
with incredulous eyes, immovable—I myself could scarce
breathe from the suspense of that tense waiting. . . .

The Princess of Hell began to shrink. Small and smaller
she became, dwindling visibly before our eyes—she became
as tiny as the reptile—every exquisite feature of her loveliness
remained intact, in miniature—a gray mist swirled between
reptile and Princess—*they became one!*

Agnor Halit snapped finger and thumb, deliberately, in-
sultingly contemptuous. At the *"tshuk"* he made, the entire
scene vanished!

I rubbed my eyes . . . I could not believe . . . a tiny reptile, most resembling a centipede, ran before my foot and

around the corner of a boulder . . . but facing me was the sorcerer I sought. . . .

"King Karan, you had a narrow escape," he assured me, earnestly. "But she is harmless now. Not even her devil-friends can enable her to work further mischief. She will be naught but a venomous worm so long as I shall continue to live—and as I may perish only by one method which none knows save me, she is like to endure for ages! Her bite might prove dangerous, but the fear I inspired in her will prevent her from trying that, even."

While talking, we had drawn to where lay Zarf and Koto. At our arrival they sat up as if waking from a natural nap. Zarf stared at the magician with undisguised hostility. Koto, most surprisingly, gave the magician a wide grin of welcome; more, he threw back my cloak and permitted Agnor Halit to see that we actually had the image he so desired. But Koto kept nigh, with a wary eye on the sorcerer's every move. Agnor Halit's eyes gleamed with a baleful light, his voice held a note of repressed, unholy exultation:

"King Karan, I am ready to fulfil my part of our pact. Once again, are you willing to renounce all claim to this Sapphire Image, yielding it to me to do with as may please my whim?"

"I am," I replied briefly. "Take the thing and give my price to me—the release of my memory. I grow weary of this magic and mystery-mongering, and would be about my own proper affairs."

"Not so fast," grinned Koto as the sorcerer turned eagerly to the statue. "King Karan has shown you his part of the bargain. Touch this image, ere you fulfil your part—which is not visible, but must be made evident to King Karan's satisfaction—and you have the father of Koto to reckon with—and, Agnor Halit, his power is greater than yours. If you doubt that—try conclusions with him! Shall I, his son, summon him?"

"King Karan," and Agnor Halit ignored Koto completely—"your word is inviolable, nor do I break promises.

Yet Baron Koto is right. I can see your part—and you shall receive mine ere I take my payment. Is that satisfactory?''

"Magician," I exclaimed, impatient, "do more, and talk less! And you, Koto, let him have the thing as suits him best. I have taken his word, even as he accepts mine. Shall we quibble endlessly?"

"Yet will I do even as Baron Koto wishes," the sorcerer smiled. He laid his left hand on the back of my neck. The forefinger of his other hand he pressed tightly against my forehead just between the eyebrows.

A slight tingling flowed from that fingertip, through my brain, to the center of the palm against my neck. A tiny spark like a distant star lit in the center of my brain. It grew and grew, filling my entire skull with a silvery-golden brilliance shot through with coruscations and sparkling, scintillant flashes. . . .

CRASH!

Insofar as I was aware of anything, my head had just exploded! . . . All the agonies I had ever experienced were as naught compared to that! I was so absolutely stunned I could not even fall down and die! Across immeasurable voids came a trumpet-like voice:

"King Karan, I have kept my promise!"

I blinked, and my dazed mind cleared. *Gods and Devils!* . . . In one terrific rush, I knew all! Not one trifling detail of all the long reign in Octolan as Karan of the Chrysolite Throne was lacking in my memory! And thereupon my soul descended into Hell even as I stood facing that damnable sorcerer who openly sneered in my very face, gloating over my mental anguish—for I knew one thing which wrecked all benefits I had hoped to gain by my memory's restoration. . . .

That Sapphire Image was the actual body of my wife and Queen, Mehul-Ira, transmuted by the hellish magic of that rebel sorcerer, Djl Grm, into a flawless jewel, with her pure soul imprisoned within the depths of the wondrous blue crystal—and *I* had renounced all claim to the image, thereby giving my royal spouse to another sorcerer quite as evil as the one I'd rescued her from! . . .

"Karan, becozened and bejaped King, I claim my price!"

"Take it—you—devil!" I managed to gasp finally, albeit my soul was dying within me, and my anguish was plainly visible to my followers. . . .

"Take the image, magician," Koto grinned.

Almost was I tempted to slay Koto for grinning like that when my very soul was suffering all the agonies of dissolution without the comfort of death's release.

Agnor Halit moved not from where he stood. Only he pointed his finger at the image. A pink mist enshrouded the statue, turned to a deep rose-red, then to scarlet, and finally became crimson like rich blood. Gradually it faded, and a living, breathing woman, radiantly lovely, arose from where she lay on the hard ground, stood erect, turned, smiling at me with an unmistakable light in her great softly shining eyes—she stretched out longing arms—Koto flung my cloak about her, concealing her exquisite perfection from the avid gaze of the sorcerer—she spoke, and the music of her voice tore my heart with its sweetness:

"Karan! *My* Karan! After all these dreary years! I am still all yours. . . ."

"Nay!" Agnor Halit interrupted harshly. "Karan has renounced all his claim to you! You are *mine*!"

That devilish magician, inspired by the malice common to all his ilk, had perpetrated upon me a treachery so utterly fiendish that even the demons in Hell must have shrieked and rocked in glee upon their white-hot brazen seats!

He opened his mouth to its fullest extent, and peals of gargantuan laughter bellowed forth. In a daze, I noted dimly that Koto had stopped and now held something in his hand—why! it looked like a short thick worm—or a centipede. . . .

"Agnor Halit!" Koto spoke with a sneer more bitter than aught the sorcerer knew how to use—"King Karan gave you the image, to do with as pleased your whim—but he gave not his wife! Upon her you have no claim! But I, Koto of the Red Wilderness, in her place give you—*this*!"

Flung with unerring accuracy, the tiny reptile, writhing and twisting, shot from Koto's hand, disappearing in the yawning cavity of the sorcerer's mouth.

Agnor Halit closed his mouth with a gulp of surprise. He staggered—his face turned to a ghastly greenish hue—the body that had so long defied the ravages of death dashed itself to the ground, rolling in hideous torture—convulsion after convulsion shook it—then slowly ceased—and a second later we were gazing, incredulous, at a carrion corpse that stank most outrageously and in which the worms and maggots were already at work.

"Somewhat of magic Koto knows," Koto grinned. "While my body lay still, my spirit went with my King and saw all; then, returning, I dreamed the secret Agnor Halit deemed that none knew save himself! The Princess of Hell crawled into my hand that I might use her, and so, she revenged herself! Agnor Halit is now in Hell, where she can deal with him according to her fancy!"

We mounted our great birds. My Queen sat before me, my arm steadying her. Before us, smiling pleasantly, was Koto's father. Koto grinned at him.

"Am I your son?"

"I myself could have wrought no better," responded the great Elemental, generously.

"Your son is sorry his father has lost his once mighty power." Koto's tone was lugubrious in the extreme.

"Lost my power?"

"Aye! My King would rest tonight within my castle on the far edge of the Red Wilderness, my Barony—yet here we sit on these ugly, slow birds. . . ."

Again the fury of the elements were loosed for my benefit. . . . We slept that night at Koto's castle!

THE SEA-WITCH
by Nictzin Dyalhis

Heldra Helstrom entered my life in a manner peculiarly her own. And while she was the most utterly damnable woman in all the world, at the same time, in my opinion, she was the sweetest and the most superbly lovely woman who ever lived.

A three-day northeast gale was hammering at the coast. It was late in the fall of the year, and cold as only our North Atlantic coast can very well be, but in the very midst of the tempest I became afflicted with a mild form of claustrophobia. So I donned sea-boots, oil-skins and sou'wester hat, and sallied forth for a walk along the shore.

My little cottage stood at the top of a high cliff. There was a broad, safe path running down to the beach, and down it I hurried. The short winter day was even then drawing to a close, and after I'd trudged a quarter of a mile along the shore, I decided I'd best return to my comfortable fireside. The walk had at least given me a good appetite.

There was none of the usual lingering twilight of a clear winter evening. Darkness fell so abruptly I was glad I'd brought along a powerful flashlight. I'd almost reached the foot of my path up the cliff when I halted, incredulous, yet desiring to make sure.

I turned the ray of the flashlight on the great comber just curling to break on the shore, and held the light steady, my breath gasping in my throat. Such a thing as I thought I'd seen couldn't be—yet it was!

I started to run to the rescue, and could not move a foot. A power stronger than my own will held me immovable. I could only watch, spellbound. And even as I stared, that gigantic comber gently subsided, depositing its precious living burden on the sands as softly as any nurse laying a babe into a cradle.

Waist-deep in a smother of foam she stood for a brief second, then calmly waded ashore and walked with free swinging stride straight up the beam of my flashlight to where I stood.

Regardless of the hellish din and turmoil of the tempest, I thrilled, old as I am, at the superb loveliness of this most amazing specimen of flotsam ever a raging sea cast ashore within memory of man.

Never a shred of clothing masked her matchless body, yet her flesh glowed rosy-white, when by all natural laws it should have been blue-white from the icy chill of wintry seas.

"Well!" I exclaimed. "Where did *you* come from? Are you real—or am I seeing that which is not?"

"I am real," replied a clear, silvery voice. "And I came from out there." An exquisitely molded arm flung a gesture toward the raging ocean. "The ship I was on was sinking, so I stripped off my garb, flung myself on Ran's bosom, and Ran's horses gave me a most magnificent ride! But well for you that you stood still as I bade you, while I walked ashore. Ran is an angry god, and seldom well-disposed toward mortals."

"*Ran?*" The sea-god of the old Norse Vikings! What strange woman was this, who talked of "Ran" and his "horses," the white-maned waves of old ocean? But then I bethought me of her naked state in that unholy tempest.

"Surely you must be Ran's daughter," I said. "That reef is ten miles off land! Come—I have a house near by, and comforts—you cannot stand here."

"Lead, and I will follow," she replied simply.

She went up that path with greater ease than I, and walked companionably beside me from path-top to house, although she made no talk. Oddly, I felt that she was reading me, and that what she read gave her comfort.

When I opened the door, it seemed as if she held back for a merest moment.

"Enter," I bade her, a bit testily. "I should think you'd had enough of this weather by now!"

She bowed her head with a natural stateliness which convinced me that she was no common person, and murmured something too low for me to catch, but the accents had a distinct Scandinavian trend.

"What did you say?" I queried, for I supposed she'd spoken to me.

"I invoked the favor of the old gods on the hospitable of heart, and on the sheltering rooftree," she replied. Then she crossed my threshold, but she reached out her arm and rested her shapely white hand lightly yet firmly on my left forearm as she stepped within.

She went direct to the big stove, which was glowing dull-red, and stood there, smiling slightly, calm, serene, wholly ignoring her nakedness, obviously enjoying the warmth, and not by a single shiver betraying that she had any chill as result of exposure.

"I think you need this," I said, proffering a glass of brandy. "There's time enough for exchanging names and giving explanations, later," I added. "But right now, I'll try and find something for you to put on. I have no women's things in the house, as I live alone, but will do the best I can."

I passed into my bedroom, laid out a suit of pajamas and a heavily quilted bathrobe, and returned to the living-room where she stood.

"You are a most disconcertingly beautiful young woman," I stated bluntly; "which you know quite well without being told. But doubtless you will feel more at ease if you go in there and don some things I've laid out for you. When you come out, I'll get some supper ready."

She was back instantly, still unclad. I stared, wonderingly.

"Those things did not fit," she shrugged. "And that heavy robe—in this warm house?"

"But——" I began.

"But—*this*," she smiled, catching up a crimson silk spread embroidered in gold, which covered a sandalwood table I'd brought from the orient many years before. A couple of swift motions and the gorgeous thing became a wondrous robe adorning her lovely figure, clinging, and in some subtle manner hinting at the flawless splendor of her incomparable body. A long narrow scarf of black silk whereon twisted a silver dragon was whipped from its place on a shelf and transposed into a sash from her swelling breasts to her sloping hips, bringing out more fully every exquisite curve of her slender waist and torso—and she smiled again.

"Now," she laughed softly, "am I still a picture for your eyes? I hope so, for you have befriended me this night—I who sorely need a friend; and it is such a little thing I can do—making myself pleasing in your sight.

"And because you have holpen me"—I started at the archaic form she used—"and will continue to aid and befriend (for so my spirit tells me), I will love you always, love you as Ragnar Wave-Flame loved Jarl Wulf Red-Brand . . . as a younger sister, or a dutiful niece."

"Yet of her it is told," I interrupted, deliberately speaking Swedish and watching keenly to see the effect, "that the love given by the foam-born Sea-Witch brought old Earl Wulf of the Red-Sword but little luck, and that not of a sort desired by most men!"

"That is ill said," she retorted. "His fate was from the Norns, as is the fate of all. Not hers the fault of his doom, and when his carles within the hour captured his three slayers, she took red vengeance. With her own foam-white hands

she flayed them alive, and covered their twitching bodies with
salt ere she placed the old Jarl in his long-ship and set it
afire. And she sailed with that old man on his last seafaring,
steering his blazing dragon-ship out of the stead, singing of
his great deeds in life, that the heroes in Valhalla might know
who honored them by his coming.''

She paused, her superb bosom heaving tumultuously. Then
with a visible effort she calmed herself.

"But you speak my tongue, and know the old tales of the
Skalds. Are you, then, a Swede?''

"I speak the tongue, and the old tales of the Skalds, the
ancient minstrels, I learned from my grandmother, who was
of your race.''

"Of my race?'' Her tone held a curious inflection. "Ah,
yes! All women are of one race . . . perhaps.''

"But I spoke of supper,'' I said, moving toward the
kitchen.

"But—no!'' She barred my progress with one of her lovely
hands laid flat against my chest. "It is not meet and fitting,
Jarl Wulf, that you should cook for me, like any common
house-carle! Rather, let your *niece*, Heldra, prepare for you
a repast.''

" 'Heldra'? That, then, is your name?''

"Heldra Helstrom, and your loving niece,'' she nodded.

"But why call me Jarl Wulf?'' I demanded, curious to
understand. She had bestowed the name seriously, rather than
in playful banter.

"Jarl Wulf you were, in a former life,'' she asserted flatly.
"I knew you on the shore, even before Ran's horse stood me
on my feet!''

"Surely, then, you must be Ragnar Wave-Flame born
again,'' I countered.

"How may that be?'' she retorted. "Ragnar Wave-Flame
never died; and surely I do not look that old! The sea-born
witch returned to the sea-caves whence she came, when the
dragon-ship burned out. . . . But ask me not of myself, now.

"Yet one thing more I will say: The warp and woof of this
strange pattern wherein we both are depicted was woven of

the Norns ere the world began. We have met before—we meet again, here and now—we shall meet yet again; but how, and when, and where, I may not say.''

"Of a truth, you are 'fey,' '' I muttered.

"At times—I am,'' she assented. Then her wondrous sapphire eyes gleamed softly into my own hard gray eyes, her smile was tender, wistful, womanly, and my doubts were dissipated like wisps of smoke. Yet I shook an admonitory forefinger at her:

"Witch at least I know you to be,'' I said in mock harshness. "Casting *glamyr* on an old man.''

"No need for witchery,'' she laughed. "All women possess that power!''

During the "repast'' she spread before me, I told her that regardless of who I might have been in a dim and remote past of which I had no memory, in this present life I was plain John Craig, retired professor of anthropology, ethnology and archeology, and living on a very modest income. I explained that while I personally admired her, and she was welcome to remain in my home for ever, yet in the village near by were curious minds, and gossiping tongues, and evil thoughts a-plenty, and if I were to tell the truth of her arrival——

"But I have nowhere to go, and none save you to befriend me; all I loved or owned is out there.'' Again she indicated the general direction of the reef. "And you say that I may remain here, indefinitely? I will be known as your niece, Heldra, no? Surely, considering the differences in our age and appearance, there can be no slander.''

Her eyes said a thousand things no words could convey. There was eagerness, sadness, and a strange tenderness. . . . I came to an abrupt decision. After all, whose business was it? . . .

"I am alone in the world, as you are,'' I said gravely. "As my niece, Heldra, you shall remain. If you will write out a list of a woman's total requirements in wearing-apparel, I will send away as soon as possible and have them shipped here

in haste. I am old, as all can see, and I do not think any
sensible persons will suspect aught untoward in your making
your home with me. And I will think up a plausible story
which will satisfy the minds of fools without telling, in reality, anything.''

Our repast ended, we arose from the table and returned to
the living-room. I filled and lighted a *nargilyeh*, a three-
stemmed water-pipe, and settled myself in my armchair. She
helped herself to a cigarette from a box on the table, then
stretched her long, slender body at full length on my divan,
in full relaxation of comfort.

I told her enough of myself and my forebears to ensure her
being able to carry out the fiction of being my niece. And in
return I learned mighty little about her. But what she did tell
me was sufficient. I never was unduly curious about other
people's business.

Unexpectedly, and most impolitely, I yawned. Yet it was
natural enough, and it struck me that she needed a rest, if
anyone ever did. But before I could speak, she forestalled
me.

With a single graceful movement she rose from her reclining
posture and came and stood before me within easy arm's-
reach. Two swift motions, and her superb body flashed rosy-
white, as nude as when she waded ashore.

The crimson silken spread she'd worn as regally as any
robe was laid at my feet with a single gesture, the black scarf
went across my knees, and the glorious creature was kneeling
before me in attitude of absolute humility. Before I could
remonstrate or bid her arise, her silvery voice rang softly,
solemnly, like a muted trumpet:

"Thus, naked and with empty hands, out of the wintry
seas in a twilight gray and cold, on a night of storm I came.
And you lighted a beacon for my tired eyes, that I might see
my way ashore. You led me up the cliff and to your hospitable
hearth, and in your kindly heart you had already given the
homeless a home.

"And now, kneeling naked before you, as I came, I place

my hands between your hands—thus—and all that I am, and such service as I can render, are yours, hand-fasted.''

I stared, well-nigh incredulous. In effect, in the old Norse manner, she was declaring herself to all intents and purposes my slave! But her silvery voice went on:

"And now, I rise and cover myself again with the mantle of your bounty, that you may know me, indeed your niece, as Jarl Wulf knew Ragnar Wave-Flame!''

"Truly,'' I gasped in amazement when I could catch my breath, "you are a strange mixture of the ancient days and this modern period. I have known you but for a few hours, yet I feel toward you as that old Jarl must have felt toward that other sea-witch, unless indeed you and she are one!''

"Almost,'' she replied a trifle somberly. "At least, she was my ancestress!'' Then she added swiftly: "Do not misunderstand. Leman to the old Jarl she never was. But later, after he went to Valhalla, in the sea-girt isle where she dwelt she mated with a young Viking whom Ran had cast ashore sorely wounded and insensible. She nursed him back to life for sake of his beauty, and he made love to her.

"But he soon tired of her and her witch ways; wherefore, in wrath she gave him back to Ran—and he was seen no more. Of that mating was born a daughter, also given to Ran, who pitied her and bore her to an old man and his wife whose steading was nigh to the mouth of a fjord; and they, being childless, called her Ranhild, and reared her as their daughter. In course of time, she wed, and bore three tall sons and a daughter. . . .

"That was long and long ago—yet I have dived into Ragnar's hidden sea-cave and talked with Ragnar Wave-Flame face to face. All one night I lay in her arms, and in the dawning she breathed her breath on my brow, lips, and bosom; and all that following day she talked and I listened, and much I learned of the wisdom that an elder world termed witchcraft.''

For a moment she lapsed into silence. Then she leaned forward, laid her shapely, cool hands on my temples and kissed me on my furrowed old forehead, very solemnly, yet with ineffable gentleness.

"And now," she murmured, "ask me never again aught concerning myself, I pray you; for I have told all I may, and further questioning will drive me back to the sea. And I would not have that happen—yet!"

Without another word she turned, flung herself at full length again on the divan, and, like any tired child, went instantly to sleep. Decidedly, I thought, this "niece" of mine was not as are other women; and later I found that she possessed certain abilities it is well for the world that few indeed can wield.

She gave me another proof of that belief, by demonstrating her unholy powers, on the night of the next full moon after her arrival.

It was her custom of an evening to array herself as she had done on her first night—in crimson robe and black sash and naught else, despite the fact that her wardrobe which I had ordered from the great city forty miles away contained all any woman's heart could wish for. But I admit I enjoyed seeing her in that semi-barbaric attire.

At times she would sit on the arm of my chair, often with her smooth cool cheek laid against my rough old face, and her exquisitely modeled arm curved about my leathery old neck. The first time she had done that, I had demanded ironically:

"Witch, are you making love to me?"

But her sighing, wistful reply had disarmed me, and likewise had brought a lump into my throat.

"Nay! Not that, O Jarl from of old! But—I never knew a father."

"Nor I a fair daughter," I choked. And thereafter, when that mood was upon her I indulged in no more ironies, and we'd sit for hours, neither speaking, engrossed in thoughts for which there are no words. But on the night whereof I write, she pressed her scarlet lips to my cheek, and I asked jestingly:

"Is there something you want, Heldra?"

"There is," she replied gravely. "Will you get a boat—one with oars and a sail, but no engine? Ran hates those."

"But surely you do not want it now, tonight, do you?"

"Yes, if you will be so kind to me."

"You must have a very good reason, or you'd not ask," I said. "I'll go and get a centerboard dory and bring it to the beach at the foot of the cliff path. It's clear weather, and the sea is calm, with but a moderate breeze blowing; yet it is colder on the water than you imagine, so you'd best bundle up warmly."

"You will hasten," she implored anxiously.

"Surely," I nodded.

I went out and down to the wharves in the village, where I kept the boat I said I'd get. But when I beached the dory at the foot of the path I stared, swearing softly under my breath. Not one stitch of apparel did that witch have on, save the crimson silk robe and black sash she'd worn when I left the cottage!

"Do you want to freeze?" I was provoked, I admit. "The very sight of you dressed like that gives me the shivers!"

"Neither you nor I will be cold this night," she laughed. "Isn't it glorious? And this is a good boat you brought. Please, let me sail it, and ask me no questions."

She took the tiller, hauled in on the sheet; the sail filled, and she began singing, with a queer, wild strain running through her song. That dory fairly flew—and I swear there was not enough wind to drive us at such speed.

Finally I saw something I didn't admire. No one does, who dwells on that part of the coast.

"Are you crazy, girl?" I demanded sharply. "That reef is dead ahead! Can't you see the breakers?"

"Why, so it is—the reef! And am *I* to be affrighted by a few puny breakers? Nay, it is in the heart of those breakers that I wish to be! But you—have *you* fear, O Jarl Wulf?"

I suspected from her tone that the witch was laughing at me; so I subsided, but fervently wished that I'd not been so indulgent of her whim for a moonlight sail on a cold winter's night.

Then we hit those breakers—or rather, we didn't! For they seemed to part as the racing dory sped into them, making a smooth clear lane of silvery glinting water over which we glided as easily as if on a calm inland mill-pond!

"Drop the sail and unstep the mast," she called suddenly.

I was beyond argument, and obeyed dumbly, like any boat-carle of the olden days.

"Now, take to the oars," she directed, "and hold the boat just hereabouts for a while," and even as I slid the oars into the oarlocks she made that swift movement of hers and stood nude, the loveliest sight that grim, ship-shattering, life-destroying reef had ever beheld.

Suddenly she flung up both shapely white arms with a shrill, piercing cry, thrice repeated. Then without a word she went overside in a long clean dive, with never a splash to show where she'd hit the water.

"Hold the boat about here for a while," she'd bidden me! All I'd ever loved in this world was somewhere down below, in the hellish cross-currents of that icy water! I'd hold that boat there, if need were, in the teeth of a worse tempest than raged the night she came to me. She'd find me waiting. And if she never came up, I'd hold that boat there till its planks rotted and I joined her in the frigid depths.

It seemed an eternity, and I know that it was an hour ere a glimmer of white appeared beneath the surface. Then her shapely arm emerged and her hand grasped the gunwale, her regal head broke water, she blew like a porpoise; then she laughed in clear ringing triumph.

"You old *dearling*!" she cried in her archaic Norse. "Did I seem long gone? The boat has not moved a foot from where I dove. Come, bear a hand and lift my burden; it is heavy, and I am near spent. There are handles by which to grasp it."

The burden proved to be a greenish metal coffer—bronze, I judged—which I estimated to measure some twenty inches long by twelve wide and nine inches deep. And how she rose to the surface weighted with that, passes my understanding.

But how she knew it was down there passes my comprehension, too. But then, Heldra Helstrom herself was an enigma.

She re-wrapped herself in her flimsy silken robe of crimson and smiled happily, when she should have been shivering almost to pieces.

"If you'll ship the mast and spread the sail again, Uncle John," she said, surprisingly matter-of-fact now that her errand was successfully accomplished, "we'll go home. I'd like a glass of brandy and a smoke myself; and I read in your mind that such is your chief desire, at present."

Back at the cottage again, and comfortable once more, Heldra requested me to bear the coffer into her room, which I did. For over an hour she remained in there, then returned to the living-room where I sat, and I stared at the picture she presented. If she had always been beautiful, now she was surpassingly glorious.

Instead of the usual crimson robe, her lovely body was sheathed in a sleeveless, sheer, tightly fitting silken slip, cut at the throat in a long sloping V reaching nearly to her waist. The garment was palest sea-green, so flimsy in texture that it might as well have been compounded of mingled moon-mist and cobwebs. Her rosy-pearl flesh gleamed through the fabric with an alluring shimmer which thrilled anew my jaded old senses at the artistic wonder of her.

A gold collar, gem-studded, unmistakably of ancient Egyptian workmanship, was resting on her superb shoulders—loot of some Viking foray into the far Southlands, doubtless. A broad girdle of gold plates, squared, and also gem-studded, was about her sloping hips, and was clasped in front by a broader plate with a sun-emblem in jeweled sets; from which plate or buckle it fell in two broad bands nearly to her white slender feet.

Broad torques of gold on upper arms and about her wrists, and an intricately wrought golden tiara with disks of engraved gold pendent by chains and hanging over her ears, set off her loveliness as never before. Even her red-gold hair, braided in two thick ropes, falling over her breasts to below her waist, was clasped by gem-set brooches of gold.

"Ragnar Wave-Flame's gift to me, O Jarl Wulf," she breathed softly. "Do you like your niece thus arrayed?"

Norse princess out of an elder day, or Norse witch from an even older and wickeder period of the world—whichever this Heldra Helstrom was, of one thing I was certain, no lovelier woman ever lived than this superb being who styled herself my "niece."

And so I told her, and was amply rewarded by the radiance of her smile, and the ecstatic kiss she implanted on my cheek.

Despite her splendid array, she perched on the arm of my chair, and began toying with my left hand. Presently she lifted it to the level of my eyes, laughing softly. I'd felt nothing, yet she'd slipped a broad tarnished silver ring of antique design on my third finger.

"It was yours in the ancient days, O Jarl Wulf," she whispered in her favorite tongue—the archaic form of the Norsk language. "Yours again is the ancient ring, now! Ragnar herself carved the mystic runes upon it. Shall I read them, O Jarl, or will you?"

"They are beyond my skill," I confessed. "The words are in the 'secret' language that only the 'Rime-Kanaars' understood. Nor was it well for others than witches and warlocks to seek to understand them."

"Ragnar took that ring from Jarl Wulf's finger ere she set fire to the dragon-ship," Heldra murmured. "Had those runes been on the ring when your foes set upon you—they, not you, would have perished in the sword-play, Jarl Red-Brand!

"But the sea-born witch knew that you would weary of Valhalla in a day to come, and would return to this world of strife and slaying, of loss and grief, of hate and the glutting of vengeance—and, knowing, she carved the runes, that in time the charmed ring would return to its proper owner.

"It is her express command that I read them to you, for knowing the runes, never shall water drown or fire burn; nor sword or spear or ax ever wound you, so be it that in time of danger you speak the weird words!

"And for my sake—you who are my 'Uncle John' to all the rest of the world, but to me are dearer than old Jarl Wulf was to Ragnar the sea-witch—I implore you to learn the runic charm, and use it if ever danger menaces. Promise me! Promise me, I say!"

Her silvery voice was vibrant with fierce intensity. She caught my right hand and pressed it against her palpitant body, just beneath her proudly swelling left breast.

"Promise!" she reiterated. "I beg your promise! With your right hand on my heart I adjure you to learn the rune."

"No fool like an old fool," I grumbled, adding a trifle maliciously, "particularly when in the hands of a lovely woman. But such a fuss you make over a few words of outlandish gibberish! Read me the rune, then, witch-maid! I'd learn words worse than those can be to please you and set your mind at rest."

With her scarlet lips close to my ear, with bated breath, and in a tone so low I could barely catch her carefully enunciated syllables, she whispered the words. And although her whisper was softer than the sighing of gentlest summer breeze, the tones rang on my inner hearing like strokes of a great war-hammer smiting on a shield of bronze. There was no need to repeat them—either on her part or mine. There was no likelihood of my ever forgetting that runic charm. I could not, even if I would.

"Surely," I muttered, "you are an adept in the ancient magic. Well for me that you love me, else your witcheries might——"

Most amazingly she laughed, a clear, ringing merriment with no trace of the mystic about it.

"Let me show you something—a game, a play; one that will amuse me and entertain you."

She fairly danced across the room and into her own room, emerging with an antique mirror of some burnished, silver-like metal. This she held out to me. I grasped it by its handle obediently enough, humoring this new whim.

"Look into it and say if it is a good mirror," she bade, her sapphire eyes a-dance with elfin mirth.

I looked. All I could see was my same old face, tanned and wrinkled, which I daily saw whenever I shaved or combed my hair, and I told her so. She perched again on the arm of my chair, laid her cheek against mine, and curved her cool arm about my neck.

"Now look again!"

Again the mirror told truth. I saw my face the same as ever, and hers as well, "Like a rose beside a granite border," as I assured her.

"You do but see yourself as you think of yourself," she murmured softly, "and me you behold as you believe me to be."

She brought her lips close to the mirror and breathed upon its surface with her warm breath. It clouded over, then cleared. Her voice came, more murmurous than before, but with a definite note of sadness:

"Once more, *look*! Behold yourself as I see you always; and behold me as I know myself to be! And when I am gone beyond your ken, remember the witch-maid, Heldra, as one woman who loved you so truly that she showed you herself as she actually was!"

The man's face was still my own, but mine as it was in the days of early manhood, ere life's thunders had graven their scars on brow and cheeks and lips, and before the snows of many winters had whitened my hair.

Her features were no less beautiful, but in her reflected eyes I saw ages and ages of life, and bitter experience, and terrible wisdom that was far more wicked than holy; and it came to me with conviction irrefutable that beside this young-appearing girl, maid, or woman, all my years were but as the span of a puling babe compared to the ageless age of an immortal.

"That, at least, is no *glamyr*," her voice sighed drearily, heavy with the burden of her own knowledge of herself.

I laid my thick, heavy old arm across her smooth satiny white shoulders, and I turned her head until her sapphire eyes met mine fairly. Very gently I kissed her on her brow.

"Heldra Helstrom," I said, and my voice sounded husky

with emotion, "you may be all you have just shown me, or worse! You may be Ragnar Wave-Flame herself, the sea-witch who never dies. You may be even what I sometimes suspect, the empress of Hell, come amongst mortals for no good purpose! But be you what you may, old or young, maid or woman, good or evil, witch, spirit, angel or she-devil, such as you are, you are you and I am I, and for some weird reason we seem to love each other in our own way; so let there be an end to what you are or have been, or who I was in other lives, and content ourselves with what *is*!"

Were those bright glitters in her sapphire eyes tear-drops ready to fall? If so, I was not sure, for with a cry like that of a lost soul who has found sanctuary, she buried her face on my shoulder. . . .

After a long silence, she slipped from the arm of my chair, and wordlessly, her face averted, she passed into her room. After an hour or so, I went to my own room—but I could not sleep. . . .

Time passed, and I dwelt in a "fool's paradise," dreaming that it would last forever.

The summer colony began to arrive. There were cottages all along the shore, but there were likewise big estates, whose owners were rated as "somebodies," to put it mildly.

A governor of a great and sovereign state; an ex-president of our nation; several foreign diplomats and some of their legation attachés—but why enumerate, when one man only concerns this narrative?

Michael Commnenus, tall, slight, dapper, inclined to swarthiness, with black eyes under crescent-curved black eyebrows; with supercilious smiling lips, a trifle too red for a man; with suave Old World manners, and a most amazingly conceited opinion of himself as a "Lady-charmer."

It was not his first summer in our midst; and although when he was in Washington at his legation I never gave him a thought, when I saw his too handsome face on the beach, I felt a trifle sick! I *knew*, positively, that the minute he set eyes on Heldra. . . . Of course I knew, too, that my witch-niece could take care of herself; but just the same, I sensed annoyance, and perhaps, tragedy.

Well, I was nowise mistaken.

Heldra and I were just about to shove off in my dory for a sail. It was her chief delight, and mine too, for that matter.

Casually, along strolled Michael Commnenus, twirling a slender stick, caressing a slender black thread he styled a mustache, smiling his approbation of himself. I'd seen that variety of casual approach before. As our flippant young moderns say: It was "old stuff."

Out of the corner of my eye I watched. The Don Juan smirk faded when his calculating, appraising eyes met her sapphire orbs, now shining like the never-melting polar ice. An expression of bewilderment spread over his features. His swarthy skin went a sickly greenish-bronze. Involuntarily he crossed himself and passed on. The man was *afraid*, actually fear-struck!

"Ever see him before, Heldra?" I queried. "He looked at you as if the devil would be a pleasanter sight. That's one man who failed to fall for your vivid beauty, you sea-witch!"

"Who is he?" she asked in a peculiar tone. "I liked his looks even less than he liked mine."

"Michael Commnenus," I informed her, and was about to give her his pedigree as we local people knew him, but was interrupted by her violently explosive:

"Who?"

"Michael Commnenus," I stated again, a trifle testily. "And you needn't shout! What's he done——" but again she interrupted, speaking her archaic Norsk:

"Ho! Varang Chiefs of the Guard Imperial! Thorfinn! Arvid! Sven! And ye who followed them—Gudrun! Randvar! Haakon! Smid! And all ye Varangs in Valhalla, give ear! And ye, O fiends, witches, warlocks, trolls, vampyrs, and all the dark gods who dwell in Hel's halls where the eternal frozen fires blaze without heat, give ear to my voice, and cherish my words, for I give ye all joyous tidings.

"He lives! After all these long centuries Michael Commnenus dwells again on the bosom of fair Earth! In a body of flesh and blood and bone, of nerve and tissue and muscle he lives! He lives, I say! And *I* have found him!

"Oh, now I know why the Norns who rule all fate sent me to this place. And I shall not fail ye, heroes! Content ye, one and all, *I shall not fail!*"

Was this the gorgeous beauty I'd learned to love for her gentleness? Hers was the face of a furious female demon for a moment; but then her normal expression returned and she sighed heavily.

"Heed me not, Uncle John," she said drearily. "I did but recall an ancient tale of foul treachery perpetrated on sundry Norsemen in the Varangian Guard of a Byzantine emperor ages agone.

"The *niddering*—worse than 'coward'—who wrought the bane of some thirty-odd Vikings, was a Commnenus, nephew to the Emperor Alexander Commnenus. . . . I live too much in memories of the past, I fear, and for the moment somewhat forgot myself in the hate all good Norse maids should hold toward any who bear the accursed name of the Commneni.

"Still, even as I *know* you to be old Jarl Wulf Red-Brand returned to this world through the gateway of birth—it would be nothing surprising if this spawn of the Commneni were in truth that same Michael Commnenus of whom the tale is told."

"The belief in reincarnation is age-old," I said reflectively. "And in several parts of the world it is a fundamental tenet of religion. If there be truth in the idea, there is, as you say, nothing surprising if anybody now living should have been anybody else in some former life. . . . And that sample of the Commneni appears quite capable of any treachery that might serve a purpose at the moment! But, Heldra," I implored her, struck by a sudden intuition, "I beg of you not to indulge in any of your devilries, witcheries, or Norse magic. If this Michael is that other Michael, yet that was long ago; and if he has not already atoned for his sin, you may be very sure that somewhere, sometime, somehow he will atone; so do not worry your regal head about him."

"Spoken like a right Saga-man," she smiled as I finished

my brief homily. "I thank you for your words of wisdom. And now, Jarl Wulf Red-Brand, I know you to be fey as well as I am. 'Surely he will atone for his sin' . . . oh! a most comforting thought! So let us think no more about the matter."

I glanced sharply at her. Her too instant acquiescence was suspicious. But her sapphire eyes met mine fairly, smilingly, sending as always a warm glow of contentment through me. So I accepted her assurance as it sounded, and gave myself up to the enjoyment of the sail and the sound of her silvery voice as she sang an old English love ballad I'd known as a young man. And under the spell of her magnetic personality gradually the episode of Michael Commenus faded into nothingness—for a while.

A couple of days later, just about dark, Heldra came down the stairs from the attic, where she'd been rummaging. In her hand she carried an old violin-case. I looked and grinned ruefully.

"You are a bad old Uncle John," she scolded. "Why did you not tell me you played the 'fidel,' even as Jarl Wulf played on in his time? Think of all the sweet music you might have made in the past winter nights, and think of the dances I might have danced for your delight while you played—even as Ragnar danced for her old Jarl."

"But I did not tell you that I played a fiddle—because I don't," I stated flatly. "That is a memento of an absurd ambition I once cherished, but which died a-borning. I tried to learn the thing, but the noises I extracted were so abominable that I quit before I'd fairly got started."

"You are teasing," she retorted, her eyes sparkling with mischief. "But I am not to be put off this easily. Tonight you will play, and I will dance—such a dance as you have never beheld even when you were Jarl Wulf."

"If I try to play that thing," I assured her seriously, "you'll have a time dancing to my discords, you gorgeous tease!"

"We'll see," she nodded. "But even as my magic revealed

to me the whereabouts of the *'fidel,'* so my spirit tells me that you play splendidly.''

"Your 'magic' may be all right, but your 'spirit' has certainly misinformed you,'' I growled.

"My spirit has never yet lied to me—nor has it done so this time." Her tone was grave, yet therein was a lurking mockery; and I became a trifle provoked.

"All right," I assented grouchily. "Whenever you feel like hearing me *'play,'* I'll do it. And you'll never want to listen to such noises again.''

She went into her room laughing sweetly, and took the fiddle with her.

After supper she said nothing about me playing that old fiddle, and I fatuously thought she'd let the matter drop. But about ten o'clock she went to her room without a word. She emerged after a bit, wearing naught but a sheer loose palest blue silk robe, held at the waist only by a tiny jeweled gold filigree clasp. Loose as the robe was, it clung lovingly to her every curve as if caressing the beauteous, statuesque body it could not and would not conceal.

She was totally devoid of all ornament save that tiny brooch, and her wondrous fiery-gold hair was wholly unconfined, falling below her waist in a cascade of shimmering sunset hues, against which her rose-pearl body gleamed through the filmy gossamer-like robe.

Again she sat and talked for a while. But along toward midnight she broke a short silence with:

"I'll be back in a minute. I wish to prepare for my dancing.''

From her room she brought four antique bronze lamps and a strangely shaped urn of oil. She filled the lamps and placed one at each corner of the living-room, on the floor.

Back into her room she went, and out again with an octagonal-shaped stone, flat on both sides, about an inch thick, and some four inches across. This she placed on the low taboret whereon I usually kept my *nargilyeh*. She propped up that slab of stone as if placing a mirror—which I decided it couldn't very well be, as it did not even reflect light but seemed as dull as a slab of slate.

As a final touch, she brought out that confounded old fiddle! And on her scarlet lips was a smile that a seraph might have envied, so innocent and devoid of guile it seemed.

"What's this?" I demanded—as if I didn't know!

"Your little *'fidel'* with which you will make for your Heldra such rapturous music," she smiled caressingly.

"Um-m-m-m!" I grunted. "And what are those lamps for—and that ugly slab of black rock?"

"That black slab is a 'Hel-stone,' having the property of reflecting whatever is directly before it, if illumined by those four lamps placed at certain angles; and later it will give off those same reflections—even as the stuff called luminous calcium sulfide absorbs light-rays until surcharged, and then emits them, when properly exposed. So, you see, we can preserve the picture of my dance."

"Heldra," I demanded sharply, "are you up to some devilishness? All this looks amazingly like the stage-setting for witch-working!"

"I have sung for you, on different nights," she replied in gentlest reproach, "and have told old tales, and have attired myself again and again for your pleasure in beholding me. Have all these things ever bewitched you, or harmed anyone? How, then, can the fact of my dancing for my own satisfaction, before the mystic Hel-stone, do any harm?"

As ever, she won. Her sapphire orbs did queer things to me whenever they looked into my own gray, faded old eyes—trusting me to understand and approve whatever she did, simply because she was she and I was I.

"All right," I said. "But you're making a fool of me—insisting that I play this old fiddle. Well—I'll teach you a lesson!" And I drew the bow over the strings with a most appalling wail.

And with the unexpected swiftness of a steel trap closing on its victim, icy fingers locked about my wrist, and I knew very definitely that another and alien personality was guiding my arm and fingers! But there came likewise a swift certitude that if I behaved, no harm would ensue—to me, at least. So I let the *thing* have its way—and listened to such music as I had not believed could be played on any instrument devised by a mortal.

I wish that I could describe that music, but I do not know the right words. I doubt if they have been invented. It was wild, barbaric, savage, but likewise it was alluring, seductive, stealing away all inhibitions—too much of it would have corrupted the angels in heaven. I was almost in a stupor, intoxicated, like a *hasheesh*-eater in a drugged dream, spellbound, unable to break from the thralldom holding my will, drowning in rapture well-nigh unbearable.

Heldra suddenly blew out the big kerosene lamp standing on the table, leaving as sole illumination the rays from those four bronze lights standing in the corners.

Her superb body moved gracefully, slowly at first, then faster, into the intricate figure and pattern of a dance that was old when the world was young. . . .

With inward horror I knew the why and wherefore of that entire ceremonial; knew I'd been be-cozened and be-japed; yet knew, likewise, that it was too late for interference. I could not even speak. I could but watch, while some personality alien to my body played maddeningly on my fiddle, and the "niece" I loved danced a dance deliberately planned to seduce a man who hated and feared the dancer—and for what devilish purpose I could well guess!

I saw the light-rays converge on her alluring, statuesque body, saw them apparently pass through her and impinge on the surface of that black, sullen, octagonal Hel-stone, and be greedily swallowed up, until the dull, black surface glowed like a rare black Australian opal; and ever the dancing of the witch-girl grew more alluring, more seductive, more abandoned. And I knew why Heldra was thus shamefully—shamelessly, rather—conducting! She had read Michael Commnenus his character very accurately; knew that his *soul* had recognized her hatred for him, and *feared* her—and that her one chance to get him in her clutches lay in inflaming his senses . . . and she'd even told me the properties of that most damnable Hel-stone!

Wilder and faster came the music, and swifter and still more alluring grew the rhythmic response as Heldra's lovely body swayed and spun and swooped and postured; until ultimately her waving arms brought her fluttering hands, in the briefest of touches, into contact with the tiny brooch at her waist and the filmy robe was swept away in a single gesture that was faithfully recorded on the sullen surface of the Hel-stone.

Instantly the dancer stopped as if petrified, her arms outstretched as in invitation, her regal head thrown back, showing the long smooth white column of her throat, her clear, half-closed, sapphire-blue eyes agleam with subtle challenge. . . .

The uncanny music died in a single sighing, sobbing whisper, poison-sweet . . . the clutching, icy fingers were gone from my wrist . . . my first coherent thought was: Had that spell been directed at me, the old adage anent "old fools" would have been swiftly justified!

And I knew that to all intents and purposes, Michael Commnenus was sunk!

Just the same, I was furious. Heldra had gone too far, and I told her so, flatly. I pointed out in terms unmistakable that what she planned was murder, or worse; and that this was modern America wherein witchcraft had neither place nor sanction, and that I'd be no accessory to any such devilishness as she was contriving. Oh, I made myself and my meaning plain.

And she stood and looked at me with a most injured expression. She made me feel as if I'd wantonly struck a child across the face in the midst of its innocent diversions!

"I don't actually care if the devil flies off with Michael Commnenus," I concluded wrathfully, "but I won't have him murdered by you while you're living here, posing as my niece! No doubt it's quite possible for you to evade any legal consequences by disappearing, but what of me? As accessory, I'd be liable to life imprisonment, at the least!"

Her face lightened as by magic, and her voice was genuinely regretful, and in her eyes was a light of sincere love. She came to me and wrapped her white arms about my neck, murmuring terms of affectionate consolation.

"Poor dear Uncle John! Heldra was thoughtless—wicked me! And I might have involved you in serious trouble? I am ashamed! But the fate laid upon me by the Norns is heavy, and I may not evade it, even for you, whom I love. Tell me," she demanded suddenly, "if I should destroy the vile earthworm without any suspicion attaching to you, or to me, would you love me as before, even knowing what I had done?"

"No!" I fairly snarled the denial. I wanted it to be emphatic.

She smiled serenely, and kissed me full on my lips.

"I never thought to thank a mortal for lying to me, but now I do! Deep in your heart I can read your true feeling, and I am glad! but now"—and her tone took on a sadness most desolate—"I regret to say that on the morrow I leave you. The lovely garments you gave me, and the trunks containing them, I take with me, as you would not wish that I go empty-handed. Nor will I insult you, O Jarl Wulf, by talk of payment.

"When I am gone, you will just casually mention that I have returned to my home, and the local gossips will not suspect aught untoward. And soon I shall be forgotten, and no one will suspect, or possibly connect you, or me, with what inevitably must happen to that spawn of the Commneni.

"But of this be very sure: Somewhere, sometime, you and I shall be together again. . . ." Her voice broke, she kissed me fiercely on the lips, then tenderly on both cheeks, then lastly, with a queer reverence, on my furrowed old brow. Then she turned, went straight to her room, shut the door, and I heard the click of the key as she locked herself in, for the first time during her stay in my house. . . .

Next morning, as she'd planned, she departed on the first train cityward. I'd given her money enough for all her requirements—more, indeed, than she was willing to take at first, declaring that she intended selling some few of her jewels.

And with her departure went all which made life worth living. . . .

Heavily I dragged my reluctant feet back to the empty shell of a cottage which until then had been an earthly paradise to an old man—and the very first thing I laid my eyes on was that accursed Hel-stone, lying on the living-room table.

I picked it up, half minded to shatter it to fragments, but an idea seized me. I bore it down-cellar, where semi-darkness prevailed, and the Hel-stone glowed softly with its witch-light, showing me the loveliness of her who had departed from me. And I pressed the cold octagon to my lips, thankful that she'd left me the thing as a feeble substitute for her presence. Then I turned and went back upstairs, found an old ivory box of Chinese workmanship, and placed the Hel-stone therein, very carefully, as a thing priceless.

I went to bed early that night. There was no reason to sit up. But I could not sleep. I lay there in my bed, cursing the entire line of Commneni, root, trunk and branch, from the first of that ilk whom history records to this latest scion, or "spawn," as Heldra had termed him.

Around midnight, being still wakeful, I arose, got the Hel-stone and sat in the darkness—and gradually became aware that I was not alone! Looking up, I saw her I'd lost standing in a witch-glow of phosphorescent light. I knew at once that it was not Heldra in person, but her *"scin-lœcca"* or "shining double," a "sending," and that it was another of her witcheries.

"But even this is welcome," I thought. Then I felt *her* thought expressed through that phantasmal semblance of her own gorgeous self—and promptly strove, angrily, to resist her command. Much good it did me!

Utterly helpless, yet fully cognizant of my actions, but oddly assured that about me was a cloak of invisibility—the *"glamyr"* of the ancient *Alrunas*—I dressed, took the Hel-stone, and passed out into the night.

Straight to the cottage of Commnenus I went, pawed about under the door-step, and planted there the Hel-stone; then, still secure in the mystic glamour, I returned to my own abode.

And no sooner had I seated myself in my chair for a smoke, than I realized fully the utter devilishness of that witch from out the wintry seas whom I had taken into my home and had sponsored as my "niece" in the eyes of the world.

Right then I decided to go back and get that Hel-stone, and smash it—and couldn't do it! I got sleepy so suddenly that I awoke to find that it was broad daylight, and nine-thirty A.M. And from then on, as regularly as twilight came, I could only stay awake so long as I kept my thoughts away from that accursed Hel-stone; wherefore I determined that the thing could stay where it was until it rotted, for all me!

Then Commnenus came along the beach late one afternoon. He raised his hat in his Old World, courtly fashion, and tried to make some small talk. I grunted churlishly and ignored him. But finally he came out bluntly with:

"Professor Craig, I know your opinion of me, and admit it is to some extent justifiable. I seem to have acquired the reputation of being a Don Juan. But I ask you to believe that I bitterly regret that—now! Yet, despite that reputation, I'd like to ask you a most natural question, if I may."

I nodded assent, unprepared for what was coming, yet somehow assured it would concern Heldra. Nor was I at all disappointed, for he fairly blurted out:

"When do you expect Miss Helstrom to return, if at all?"

I was flabbergasted! That is the only word adequate. I glared at him in a black fury. When I could catch my breath I demanded:

"How did even *you* summon up the infernal gall to ask *me* that?" His reply finished flattening me out.

"Because I love her! Wait"—he begged—"and hear me out, please! Even a criminal is allowed that courtesy." Then as I nodded grudgingly, he resumed:

"The first time I saw her, something deep within me shrank away from her with repulsion. Still, I admired her matchless beauty. But of late, since her departure, there is not a night I do not see her in my mind's eyes, and I know that I love her, and hope that she will return; hence my query.

"I will be frank—I even hope that she noticed me and read my admiration without dislike. Perhaps two minds can reach each other—sometimes. For invariably I see her with head thrown back, her eyes half closed, and her arms held out as if calling me to come to her. And if I knew her whereabouts I'd most certainly go, nor would I be 'trifling,' where she is concerned. I want to win her, if possible, as my wife; and an emperor should be proud to call *her* that—"

"Very romantic," I sneered. "But, Mr. Woman-Chaser, I cut my eye-teeth a long while before you were born, and I'm not so easily taken in. The whereabouts of my niece are no concern of yours. So get away from me before I lose my temper, or I'll not be answerable for my actions. *Get!*"

He went! The expression of my face and the rage in my eyes must have warned him that I was in a killing humor. Well, I was. But likewise, I was sick with fear. What he'd just told me was sufficient to sicken me—the Hel-stone had gotten in its damnable work. My very soul was aghast as it envisioned the inevitable consequences. . . .

An idea obsessed me, and I needed the shades of night to cloak my purpose.

Aimlessly I wandered from room to room in my cottage, and finally drifted into the room which had been Heldra's. Still aimlessly I pulled open drawer after drawer in the dresser, and in the lowest one I heard a faint metallic *clink*.

The four antique bronze lamps were there. I shrewdly suspected she had left them there as means of establishing contact with her, should need arise. I examined them, and found, as I'd hoped, that they were filled.

Around ten o'clock I placed those lamps in the four corners of the living-room, and lighted them, precisely as I'd seen Heldra do. Then I tried my talents at making an invocation.

"*Heldra! Heldra! Heldra!*" I called. "I, John Craig, who

gave you shelter at your need, call to you now, wheresoever you be, to come to me at my need!''

The four lights went out, yet not a breath of air stirred in the room. A faintly luminous glow, the witch-light, ensued; and there she stood, or rather, the *scin-lœcca*, her shining double! But I knew that anything I might say to it would be the same as if she were there in the flesh.

"Heldra," I beseeched that witch-lighted simulacrum, "by the love you gave me, as Ragnar loved Jarl Wulf Red-Sword, I ask that you again enshroud me with the mantle of invisibility, the *'glamyr,'* and allow me to lift that accursed Hel-stone from where you compelled me to conceal it. Let me return it to you, at any place you may appoint, so that it can do no more harm.

"Already that poor bewitched fool is madly in love with you, because the radiations of that enchanted stone have saturated him every time he put foot on the door-step beneath which I buried it!

"Heldra, grant me this one kindness, and I will condone all sins you ever did in all your witch-life."

The shining wraith nodded slowly, unmistakably assenting to my request. As from a far distance I heard a faint whisper:

"Since it is your desire, get the Hel-stone, and bear it yourself to the sea-cave at the foot of the great cliff guarding the north passage into the harbor. Once you have borne it there, its work, and yours, are done.

"And I thank you for saying that you will condone all I have ever done, for the burden of the past is heavy, and your words have made it easier to bear."

The shining wraith vanished, and I went forth into the darkness. Straight to the house where I'd hidden the Hel-stone I betook myself, felt under the step, found what I sought, took it with an inward prayer of gratitude that because of Heldra's *"glamyr"* I had not been caught at something questionable in appearance, and started up the beach.

The tide was nearly out; so I walked rapidly, as I had some distance to go, and the sea-cave Heldra had designated could not be entered at high tide, although once within, one was safe enough and could leave when the entrance was once more exposed.

I entered the cave believing that I'd promptly be rid of the entire mess, once and for all. But there was no one there, and the interior of the cave was as dark as Erebus. I lit a match, and saw nothing. The match burned out. I fumbled for another—a dazzling ray from a flashlight blinded me for a moment, then left my face and swept the cave. A hated voice, suave yet menacing, said:

"Well, Professor Craig, you may now hand me whatever it was that you purloined from under my door-step!"

An extremely business-like automatic pistol was aimed in the exact direction of my solar plexus—and the speaker was none other than Michael Commnenus!

Very evidently the mystic *"glamyr"* had failed to work that time. And I was in a rather nasty predicament.

Then, abruptly, Heldra came! She looked like an avenging fury, emerging out of nowhere, apparently, and the tables were turned. She wore a dark cloak or long mantle draped over her head and falling to her feet.

Her right hand was outstretched, and with her left hand she seized the Hel-stone from my grasp. She pointed one finger at Commnenus, and did not even touch him; yet had she smote with an ancient war-hammer the effect would have been the same.

"You dog, and son of a long line of dogs!" her icy voice rang with excoriating virulence. "Drop that silly pistol! *Drop it, I say!*"

A faint blue flicker snapped from her extended finger—the pistol fell from a flaccid hand. Commnenus seemed totally paralyzed. Heldra's magic held him completely in thralldom. . . . I snapped into activity and scooped up the gun.

"Followed me, did you?" I snarled. "I'll——"

"Wait, Jarl Wulf!" Heldra's tone was frankly amused. "No need for you to do aught! Mine is the blood-feud, mine the blood-right. And ere I finish with yon Michael Commnenus, an ancient hate will be surfeited, and an ancient vengeance, too long delayed, will be consummated."

"Heldra," I began, for dread seized me at the ominous quality of her words, "I will not stand for this affair going any farther! I——"

"Be silent! Seat yourself over there against the wall and watch and hear, but move not nor speak again, lest I silence you forever!"

A force irresistible hurled me across the cave and set me down, hard, on a flat rock. I realized fully that I was obeying her mandate—I couldn't speak, couldn't even move my eyelids, so thoroughly had she inhibited any further interference on my part.

Paying no further attention to Commnenus for the moment, she crossed over to me, bent and kissed me on my lips, her sapphire eyes laughing into my own blazing, wrathful eyes.

"Poor dear! It is too bad, but you made me do it. I wanted you to help me all the way through this tangled coil—but you have been *so* difficult to manage! Yet in some ways you have played into my hands splendidly. Yes, even to bringing the Hel-stone back to me—and I would not care to lose that for a king's ransom. And *I* put it into yon fool's head to be wakeful tonight, and see you regain the Hel-stone, and follow you—and thus walk into my nice little trap.

"And now!"

She whirled and faced Commnenus. And for all that he was spellbound, in his eyes I read fear and a ghastly foreknowledge of some dreadful fate about to be meted out to him at her hands.

She picked up the flashlight he had dropped and extinguished it with the dry comment:

"We need a different light here—the Hel-light from Hela's halls!" And at her word, a most peculiar light pervaded the cave, and there was that about its luminance that actually affrighted. Again she spoke:

"Michael Commnenus, you utterly vile worm of the earth! You know that your doom is upon you—but as yet you know not why. O beast lower than the swine! Harken and remember my words even after eternity is swallowed up in the Twilight of the Gods! You are a modern, and know not that the self, the soul, is eternal, undying, changing its body and name in every clime and period, yet ever the same soul, responsible for the deeds of its bodies. You have even prated of *your* soul—when in fact, *you* are the property of the soul!

"Watch, now!" She pointed to the cave entrance. "Behold there the wisps of sea-fog gathering; and gradually will come the rising tide. And on the curtain of that cold, swirling mist, behold the pictures of the past—a past centuries old; a past wherein your craven, treacherous soul sinned beyond all pardon!

"Look you, too Jarl Wulf Red-Brand, so that in all the days remaining to you upon Earth, you may know that his doom was just, and that Heldra is but executing a merited penalty!

"And while the shuttles of the *Norns* weave the tapestry of the sin of this Commnenus, I will tell all the tale of his crimes.

"In Byzantium reigned the emperor, Alexander Commnenus. Secure his throne, guarded by the ponderous axes and the long swords of the Varangians, the splendid sons of the Norse-lands, who had gone a-viking. Trusted and loved were the Varangs by the emperor, and oft he boasted of their fidelity, swearing on the cross of Constantine that to the last man would his Varangs perish ere one would flinch a step from overwhelming foes, citing in proof their battle-cry:

" '*Valhalla! Valhalla! Victory or Valhalla!*'

"Into the harbor of the Golden Horn sailed the viking longship, the *Grettir*. Three noble brothers owned her—Thorfinn, Arvid, Sven. With them sailed their sister . . . her fame as an *Alruna-maid*, prophetess and priestess, was sung throughout the Norse-lands. No man so low but bore her reverence. Sin it was to cast eyes of desire on any *Alruna*, and the sister of the three brothers was held especially holy.

"Between the hands of the Emperor Alexander Commnenus, the three brethren placed their hands, swearing fealty for a year and a day. Thirty fighting-men, their crew, followed wherever the three brothers led. And the great emperor, hearing of their war-fame from others of the Varangian guard, gave the brothers high place in his esteem, and held them nigh his own person.

"Their sister, the *Alruna-maid*, was treated as became her rank and holy repute. Aye! Even in Christian Byzantium respect and honor were shown her by the priests of an alien belief. But one man in Byzantium aspired more greatly than any other, Norseman or Byzantine, had ever dared.

"A Commnenus he, grand admiral of Byzantium's war fleet, nephew to the emperor, enjoying to the full the confidence and love of his imperial uncle. Notorious for his profligacy, he cast his libertine eyes on the Norse *Alruna-maid*, but with no thought of making her his wife. Nay! 'Twas only as his leman he desired her. . . . So, he plotted. . . .

"The three brothers, Thorfinn, Arvid, Sven, with their full crew, in the long-ship *Grettir* were ordered to sea to cruise against certain pirates harrying a portion of the emperor's coasts.

"Every man of the *Grettir*'s crew died the deaths of rats—poison in the water-casks! . . . They died as no Norseman should die, brutes' deaths, unfit for Valhalla and the company of heroes who had passed in battle! And their splendid bodies, warped and distorted by pangs of the poison, were cast overside as prey for sharks, by two creatures of this grand admiral, whom he had sent with the three brothers as pilots knowing the coast. They placed the drug in the casks, they flung over the dead and dying, they ran the *Grettir* aground and set fire to her—but *his* was the command—*and his the crime*!"

And as Heldra told the tale, in a voice whose dreary tones made the recital seem even worse—the watching Commnenus and I saw clearly depicted on the curtain of the mist, each separate incident. . . . Heldra turned to the wildly glaring Michael.

"There was but one person in all Byzantium who knew the truth," she screamed in sudden frenzy. "I give back for a moment your power of speech. *Say, O fool! Coward! Niddering! Who am I?*"

Abruptly she tore off the somber cloak and stood in all her loveliness, enhanced by every ornament she once had worn for my pleasure in beholding her thus arrayed.

A cry of unearthly terror broke from the staring Commnenus. His voice was a strangled croak as he gasped:

"The *Alruna-maid*, Heldra! The red-haired sea-witch—sister to the three brothers, Thorfinn, Arvid, Sven!"

"Aye, you foul dog! And me you took at night, after they sailed away, and me you shut up where my cries for aid could not be heard; and me you would have despoiled—me, the *Alruna-maid*, sworn to chastity! Me you jeered at and reviled, boasting of your recent crimes against all that the Norse-folk hold most sacred!

"Yet I escaped from that last dreadful dungeon wherein you immured me—*how*?

"By that magic known to such as I, I called upon the empress of the Underworld, Hela herself, and pledged her my service in return for indefinitely continued life, until I could repay you and avenge the heroes denied the joys of Valhalla—by you!

"And now—comes swiftly the doom I have planned for you . . . you who now *remember*!"

Heldra spoke truly. Swiftly it came! Sitting where I was, I saw it plainly, a great dragon-ship with round shields displayed along her gunwales, with a big square sail of crimson embroidered in gold, with long oars dipping and lifting in unison—in faint ghostly tones I could hear the deep-sea rowers chanting, *"Juch! Hey! Sa-sa-sa! Hey-sa, Hey-sa, Hey-sa, Hey-sa!"* and knew it for the time-beat rowing-song of the ancient vikings!

The whole picture was limned in the cold sea-fires from whence that terrible viking ghost-ship had risen with its crew of long-dead Norsemen who were not dead—the men too good for *Hel*, and denied Valhalla. . . .

Straight to the mouth of the cave came the ghost-ship, and its crew disembarked and entered. Heldra cried out in joyous welcome:

"Even from out of the deeps, ye heroes, one and all, have

ye heard my silent summons, and obeyed the voice of your Alruna from old time! Now your waiting is at an end!

"Yonder stands the Commnenus. That other concerns ye not—but mark him well, for in a former life he was Jarl Wulf Red-Brand! See, on his left hand is still the old silver ring with its runes of Ragnar Wave-Flame!"

The ghost-vikings turned their dead eyes on me with a curious fixity. One and all, they saluted. Evidently, Jarl Wulf must have been somebody, in his time. Then ignoring me, they turned to Heldra, awaiting her further commands. Commnenus they looked at, fiercely, avidly.

Heldra's voice came, heavily, solemnly, with a curious bell-like tone sounding the knell of doom incarnate:

"Michael Commnenus! This your present body has never wrought me harm, nor has it harmed any of these. It is not with your body that we hold our feud. Wherefore, your body shall go forth from this cave as it entered—as handsome as ever, bearing no mark of scathe.

"But your niddering soul, O most accursed, shall be drawn from out its earthly tenement this night and given over to these souls you wronged, who now await their vengeance! And I tell you, Michael Commnenus, that what they have in store for you will make the Hades of your religion seem as a devoutly-to-be-desired paradise!"

Heldra stepped directly before Commnenus. Her shapely white arms were outstretched, palms down, fingers stiffly extended. A queer, violet-tinged radiance streamed from her fingers, gradually enveloping Commnenus—he began to *glow*, as if he had been immersed and had absorbed all his body could take up. . . .

Heldra's voice took on the tone of finality:

"Michael Commnenus! Thou accursed soul, by the power I hold, given me by Hela's self, I call you forth from your hiding-place of flesh—*come ye out!*"

The living body never moved, but from out its mouth emerged a faint silvery-tinted vapor flowing toward the *Alruna-maid*, and as it came, the violet glow diminished. The accumulating silvery mist swirled and writhed, perceptibly taking on the semblance of the body from whence it was being extracted. There remained finally but a merest thread of silvery shimmer connecting soul and body Heldra spoke beneath her breath:

"One of you hew that cord asunder!"

A double-bladed Norse battle-ax whirled and a ghostly voice croaked: *"Thor Hulf!"*

Thor, the old Norse war-god, must have helped, for the great ghost-ax evidently encountered a solid cable well-nigh as strong as tempered steel. Thrice the ax rose and fell, driven by the swelling thews of the towering giant wielding it, ere the silver cord was broken by the blade.

A tittering giggle burst from the lips of the present-day Michael Commnenus.

I realized with a sudden sickness at the pit of my stomach that an utterly mindless imbecile stood there, grinning vacuously!

"That *Thing*," Heldra said, coldly scornful as she pointed to the silvery shining soul, "is yours, heroes! Do with it as ye will!"

Two of the gigantic wraiths clamped their great hands on its shoulders. It turned a dull leaden-gray, the color of abject fear. Cringing and squirming, it was hustled aboard the ghostly dragon-ship. The other ghost-vikings went aboard, taking their places at the oars . . . yet they waited. Heldra turned to me.

"Be free of the spell I laid upon you!" Her tone was as gentle as it had been in her sweetest moments while she dwelt in my home as my niece.

I gasped, rose and stretched. I wanted to be angry—and dared not. I'd seen too much of her hellish powers to risk incurring her displeasure. And reading my mind, she laughed merrily.

Then her cool, soft, white arms went about my neck, her wondrous sapphire eyes looked long and tenderly into mine—and I will not write the message I read in those softly shining orbs. Once again her silvery voice spoke:

"Jarl Wulf Red-Brand! John Craig! I am the grand-daughter

of Ragnar Wave-Flame! And once I went a-viking with my three brothers, to far Byzantium. You know that tale. Now, once I said that Ragnar Wave-Flame never died. Also, I said that I had dived into her sea-cave and lain in her arms—and now I tell you the rest of that mystery: With her breath she entered this my body where ever since we have dwelt as one soul. I needed aid in seeking vengeance, for it was after I'd escaped the clutches of the Commnenus, and had passed through adventures incredible while making my way back to the Norse-lands—and my spirit was very bitter. And when I sought her council, Ragnar helped me. . . .

"This now do I ask of you: Do you, as I have sometimes thought, love me as a man loves a maid? Reflect well, ere you answer, and recall what I once showed you in a mirror—I am older than you! So, knowing that, despite my witcheries of the long, bitter past, and those of tonight, would you take me, were you and I young once more?"

"By all the gods in Valhalla, and by all the devils in Hela's halls: *yes!*" My reply was given without need of reflecting, or counting cost.

"Then, in a day to come, you shall take me—I swear it!"

Full upon my mouth she pressed her scarlet lips, and a surging flame suffused my entire body. Yet it was life—not death. Against my chest I felt the pressure of her swelling breasts, and fire undreamable streamed from her heart to mine. Time itself stood still. After an eon or so she unwound her clinging arms from about my neck and turned away, and with never a backward glance she entered that waiting, ghostly dragon-ship. The oars dipped. . . .

"Juch! Hey! Sa-sa-sa! Hey-sa! Hey-sa! Hey-sa! Hey-sa!" and repeated . . . and again . . . until the faint, ghostly chant was swallowed by distance. . . .

I left the cave.

The driveling idiot who had been Michael Commnenus was already gone. Later, the gossip ran that he'd "lost his mind," and that his embassy had returned him to his own land. None ever suspected, or coupled me or my "niece" with his affliction. And he himself had absolutely no memory—had lost even his own name when his soul departed!

But within a month, I sold my cottage, packed and stored all my belongings until I could find a new location, where I'd be totally unknown; and then I went away from where I had dwelt for years—and with urgent reason.

The fire with which Heldra had imbued me from her breath and breast was renewing my youth! My hair was shades darker, my wrinkles almost gone; my step was brisker, I looked to be nearer forty than almost sixty. So marked was the change that the villagers stared openly at what seemed at least a miracle . . . tongues were wagging . . . old superstitions were being revived and dark hints were being bandied about. . . . So I finally decided to leave, and go where my altered appearance would cause no comment.

I wonder if——